Forgotten Families

of Suffolk and Essex

by

Evelyn Wright

The Book Castle

Also by Evelyn Wright:

Six Weeks is Forever
A Hertfordshire Family 1555 - 1923
St Michael's Woburn Sands - The Church, the Parish and the People
A Scottish Country Doctor 1818 - 1873
Forgotten Families of Hertfordshire and Bedfordshire

First Published October 2008 by
The Book Castle
12 Church Street
Dunstable
Bedfordshire LU5 4RU

ISBN 978-1-903747-96-4

Typeset by Heath Publications Bedfordshire
Cover Design by Moren Associates Limited, www.morenassociates.co.uk
Printed in Great Britain by Antony Rowe Ltd., Chippenham, Wiltshire

Cover Picture : Gipping Hall, ... drawing by H. Davy

Contents

Illustrations

The picture of Dorothy Wadham on page 12 is reproduced by permission of the Warden and Fellows of Wadham College and photographs of the College on pages 23 and 24 are reproduced by courtesy of Cornelia Carson, who retains the copyright.

The picture of the 10th Lord Cobham and his family on page 27 is reproduced by permission of the Marquess of Bath.

The Three Browne Brothers on page 39 is reproduced by permission from the Burghley House Collection from a miniature by Isaac Oliver.

Pictures on pages 12, 13, 15 and 20 are reproduced by permission of Lord Petre of Ingatestone.

Photographs of Aspall Hall; Clopton Hall; Giffords Hall, Wickhambrook; Giffords Hall, Stoke-by-Nayland (including the Mannock portraits), and Moat Hall, Parham are reproduced by permission of the owners.

Photographs of Wingfield on pages 4, 5, 8, 10, and 134 were taken in 1924 by J E Groom, Esq., of Wingfield College.

The photograph on page 32 is reproduced by permission of the Chevallier-Guild family.

The photograph of St Mary's Church, Bures is reproduced by courtesy of the Churchwardens.

Pictures on pages 11, 49, 72, 79; 100, 103, 111, 114, 116, 119 and 139 are reproduced by permission of the Suffolk Record Office.

Pictures on pages 19, 34, 58, 89 and 147 are reproduced by courtesy of the Essex Record Office.

The pictures on pages 60 and 143 are reproduced by permission of the Bedfordshire and Luton Archives and Records Service.

The Cover picture of Gipping Hall, from a drawing by H Davy, is reproduced by courtesy of the Suffolk Record Office (Ref: K681/1/181/1).

Sources and Acknowledgements

The main sources of information have been: Copinger's Manors of Suffolk; the Victoria County Histories and the Heralds' Visitations. Other books and papers consulted include: *Wingfield, its Church, College and Castle* by the Rev'd S.W.H. Aldwell; *Tudor Food and Pastimes* by F.G.Emmison; *The Paston Letters* ed. John Warrington; *Bess of Hardwick* by Mary S. Lovell; *A History of Suffolk* by David Dymond and Peter Northeast; *The Suffolk Guide* by Norman Scarfe; *Ruth Rendell's Suffolk*; *Timpson's English Eccentrics*; *Timpson's Travels in East Anglia*; *Suffolk Houses* by Eric Sandon; *The Kings England* by Arthur Mee; *The Most Haunted House in England* by Harry Price; *Stars of Fortune* by Cynthia Harnett; *The Biography of John Daye* by Elizabeth Evenden; *Little Bradley, The People and their Church* by Wendy Barnes; *The Autobiography and Correspondence of Sir Simonds D'Ewes*; *The History and Antiquities of Hengrave* by John Gage.

I am extremely grateful to all who have allowed us to visit and photograph their beautiful homes: to Sir David Rowland; Chris Hollingsworth; John and Jenny Chevallier-Guild; James Brocklebank; and the Weller-Poley family.

Sincere thanks to all who have allowed us to use pictures from their collections, including Lord Petre of Ingatestone Hall and Lord Bath of Longleat, with thanks to Dr. Kate Harris for organising the Lord Cobham picture. Our thanks to Cliff Davies at Wadham College for his help and interest, and to Cornelia Carson for her lovely photographs of the College, some of them taken specially for the book.

I acknowledge with thanks the help and co-operation of the Archivists and staff at the Suffolk and Essex Records Offices at Ipswich, Bury St Edmunds, and Chelmsford. Thanks also to Nigel Lutt at the Bedfordshire and Luton Archives and Records Service for his help in obtaining the picture of Ickwell Bury.

Finally, my special thanks to my husband John, for his help and encouragement, and for his technical skill with regard to the photography, the formatting of the book and the adapting of the pedigrees, which were first produced for our earlier book *A Hertfordshire Family with links in Bedfordshire, Suffolk and Essex*.

Evelyn Wright
October 2008

For James, Katie, William, Viola and Oliver
whose ancestors were part of the story

Introduction

When I started researching my family history about 20 years ago, I never expected to get very far with my father's ancestors - the Harmers of Hertfordshire. My mother's family was easy. The Galbraiths were Shipping Agents in the City of London, well documented in all the Trade and Court Directories. We followed her line back to Scotland, finding links with the medical profession, including David Galbraith who qualified in London in 1789, and died in Jamaica a few years later, having been employed as a Ship's Doctor on one of the slave ships.

The Harmers, who were country Squires and yeoman farmers, surely could not compete with this! But we soon managed to trace a direct line back to 1555, followed by links which led back to Bedfordshire in the 13th century. This resulted in the discovery of a network of families in Hertfordshire, Bedfordshire, Suffolk and Essex who had been marrying into each other for hundreds of years. How they kept in touch we cannot imagine. There were occasionally links with more distant families - in Devon, Cornwall, and even Kendal. Just think of travelling from the Lake District to Suffolk or Essex on horseback!

The title of this book is perhaps rather misleading. Historical details may have been forgotten, but some of the families are still living in their ancestral homes, where they continue to play an important part in the life of the local and wider community, just as their ancestors did many years ago.

We may wonder why so many of the families were 'recusants', holding firmly to their Roman Catholic principles in the face of possible imprisonment and death. Perhaps it was because of strong traditions going back hundreds of years. There was also the dilemma of loyalty to the reigning monarch which often conflicted with the requirements of their faith.

There were those who, like the Vicar of Bray, didn't really care, and changed direction according to the fashion of the day. But most of the families in our book had the courage to stick to their beliefs.

Many people living in Suffolk and Essex today will be descendants of these ancient families, and in any case we all have ancestors who lived through this period of history. To find out how they lived, and to get to know them as real people, is to ensure that they will live on, not just in our genes but also in our imaginations. They are our past, and we are their future, and it is right that we should acknowledge them and honour their memory.

A present-day view of Wingfield

Chapter 1

The de la Pole Family of Wingfield

If by chance you happened to find yourself in the village of Wingfield, it would probably mean you had lost your way. Perhaps you were travelling from Stradbroke to Hoxne or Diss and took a wrong turning. The road to Wingfield doesn't really lead to anywhere except Wingfield - you simply take a round trip and end up on the road you started from, about 100 yards further on.

But having reached the village you would find your detour well worthwhile. As you round the bend at the bottom of a gentle hill you come upon one of the most beautiful churches in the area. Close by you would see the imposing building which is Wingfield College, and further on you would even find a castle.

Wingfield, now a quiet and unassuming village with about 300 inhabitants, no village shop or Post Office and just one pub, was once the home of the de la Pole family, one of the most powerful families in the country, closely linked to royalty and at one time coming very close to the throne itself.

Inside the church you would find further reminders of this now mainly forgotten family. Here they lie, peaceful and dignified - Michael de la Pole and his wife Katharine Stafford; John de la Pole and Elizabeth Plantagenet; and oldest of all, Sir John Wingfield who died in 1361.

Six centuries have passed, seasons have come and gone. Succeeding generations have worshipped here - baptisms, marriages, burials. Times of joy and times of sadness.

Yet the memory of these ancient families lives on. They remain here in this church, silent witnesses to all the changes and turmoils of the passing years. But the more we look into the past the more we realise that although the world has changed, human nature remains the same.

The Wingfields

The family from which the village took its name was possibly here before the Norman Conquest. There is an old rhyme which goes:

> Wynkefeld the Saxon held Honour and Fee
> Ere William the Norman came over the sea.

Whether or not this is true we do not know, but they definitely came into prominence at the time of Edward I when Sir Robert Wingfield was Lord of the Manor. The Manor House would probably have been near the church, on the site where the College now stands, and there was another important house about half a mile further on which later became the Castle.

The Wingfields were linked to many of the leading families in Norfolk and Suffolk including the Fastolfs who are reputed to have built The Ancient House in Ipswich, and the Peche family, whose ancestry can be traced back to King Alfred the Great and beyond.

A Friend of the Black Prince

The most famous member of the family was Sir John Wingfield who was married to Alianore, the daughter of Sir Gilbert Glanville. Sir John fought at the Battle of Poitiers and was a close friend of the Black Prince.

Although he spent much of his life fighting in France, both he and Alianore had a great love and concern for Wingfield. Together they planned to found and endow a Collegiate Church and a Chantry College which would include a school for boys and a training college for priests, as well as providing choristers, and clergy to pray six times a day for their souls, and for the souls of the Black Prince and King Edward III.

Sadly John died from the Black Death in 1361 before the building was started, so there were no priests to pray for his soul!

But Alianore, his devoted wife, would no doubt have offered a little prayer from time to time - though probably not six times a day. The Lady of the Manor at this time led a very busy life, working alongside the servants and organising the large household.

Sir John had left directions in his Will for the foundation of the church and college, and Alianore herself had already dedicated a great deal of money for the purpose, including land and rents in Wingfield, Earsham, Fressingfield and Weybread, and the advowson of the Churches of Wingfield, Stradbroke and Syleham. The statutes of the College were drawn up by Thomas, Bishop of Norwich, and his seal was affixed to them on June 6th 1362.

Under the supervision of Alianore and John's brother Thomas the building went ahead. It was a great undertaking but the final result was the church we see today, with possibly just the tower remaining from an earlier church.

The College buildings on the site of the old manor house nearby were also completed, and the school with its priests and pupils installed according to John's wishes.

The present college building bears little resemblance to the original, having been re-built in the 18th century, but during restoration in the 1970s parts of the mediaeval building have been revealed and brought into use.

Sir John and Alianore were the last of the Wingfields of Wingfield. But their only daughter Katherine married Michael de la Pole, a wealthy merchant, and they went on to found the dynasty which for the next 150 years was to play an important part in the history of the country.

The de la Poles of Hull

The founder of the family was William atte Poole, a merchant of Hull at the time of Edward I. His son William was knighted by Edward III in return for his financial support (many thousands of pounds in gold) at the beginning of the Hundred Years War.

Not only did William help the King when he desperately needed money, he was also a great benefactor of the church and made provision for the foundation of a religious house for nuns and sisters, and a hospital for the needy people of Hull.

He died in 1367 and his tomb, with elaborate effigies of himself and his wife Catherine of Norwich, is in the Church of the Holy Trinity at Hull. It was his eldest son Michael who married Katherine Wingfield, and they settled in the family home which was soon to become Wingfield Castle. It was in 1384 that Michael obtained the King's leave to crenellate the house and enclose the woods and lands belonging to the estate. Only a small part of the original castle now remains, and a farmhouse was built within its walls during the Tudor period, but some of the ancient features can still be seen.

The castle was a large and handsome structure. It had a moat 50ft wide and was approached by a stone bridge with a drawbridge and portcullis. To the north lay the deer park which extended from the castle almost to Syleham Hall. Wingfield Castle remained the home of the de la Poles for 150 years, and it was here that many dramatic and heart-rending events were to take place.

Michael de la Pole, 1st Earl of Suffolk

Wingfield Castle showing the Tudor House on the west side.

Michael was a great favourite of Richard II and soon after his marriage he was made Earl of Suffolk and Chancellor of England. Michael and Katherine had eight children - five sons and three daughters. Although Michael was away in London and elsewhere for much of the time, he supported and took a great interest in the church and the newly founded college.

We read that in 1402 Michael granted land and rents in Stradbroke, Wingfield and Earsham Street to the Master and Chaplains of the Church of Wingfield, and four years later he granted messuages, woodlands, pastures, and meadows in Saxmundham, Farnham, Sternfield, Rendham, Snape, Swefling, Cransford and Great Glemham to maintain a priest to perform divine service at the Altar of the Holy Trinity for the soul of Richard de la Pole, his brother.

There are also records of the school which was educating the young boys, most but not all of whom would go into the priesthood. They would be taught to read and write, to speak and read Latin, to copy and illuminate manuscripts, and to read and sing music. Mathematics is not mentioned!

A School Visit from the Bishop of Norwich

The Bishop of Norwich would visit the school from time to time. On one occasion he reported that the Master was too slack on organisation and discipline, also that he ought to appoint someone to teach grammar to the boys. Some things never change!

Although his life at Wingfield appears to have been happy and fulfilled, it seems that things were not going so well in the political field.

As Earl of Suffolk and Chancellor of England Michael became unpopular with his fellow peers, possibly through jealousy, because in those days it was unusual for the son of a merchant to be raised to such high office. Although he is quoted by a contemporary historian to have been "an able and apparently honest administrator, who upheld the King's prerogative against the encroachment of Parliament", he was accused of misgovernment and corruption, stripped of rank and property and exiled to France where he died in 1389.

His body was brought back to Hull and buried in the Carthusian Monastery, but there are now no remains of his tomb, as the Monastery was destroyed by Henry VIII at the time of the Dissolution.

Meanwhile Katherine and the family lived on at Wingfield and their eldest son Michael was restored to the Earldom and the family estates.

Michael, 2nd Earl of Suffolk

Michael, now the 2nd Earl of Suffolk, married Katharine, daughter of the Earl of Stafford. Michael was a courageous soldier who accompanied Henry V to France but died of a fever at Harfleur in 1415 just before the battle of Agincourt. Michael and Katharine are both buried in Wingfield Church where their effigies, beautifully carved in wood, can still be seen.

Michael de la Pole and Katharine Stafford

Soon after his father's death, his eldest son Michael was killed at Agincourt. Michael, who was married to Elizabeth the daughter of Thomas Mowbray Duke of Norfolk, had three daughters but no sons, and it was his younger brother William who succeeded to the titles and estates.

William the Most Famous of the de la Poles

William was to become the most famous of all the de la Poles. His whole life was dedicated to the service of his country. He spent his early years fighting in France and the remaining years were devoted to political affairs at home.

William was married to Alice Chaucer, the daughter of Thomas Chaucer of Ewelme in Oxfordshire, and granddaughter of the famous poet. Alice was a widow, having been previously married to the Earl of Salisbury, who was killed when leading the English army in France.

William was only about 15 years old when he went to France, just after his brother Michael was killed at Agincourt. The Hundred Years War was nearing its end. Joan of Arc had inspired the French with fresh courage and now disaster after disaster faced the English troops.

The Siege of Orleans

After the death of the Earl of Salisbury, William de la Pole took command of the army. But after the siege of Orleans he was taken prisoner, and two of his brothers, Miles and Alexander, were killed.

It must have been a tragic time for Katharine at Wingfield Castle, with all her men-folk away in France fighting distant wars. To have lost her husband at Harfleur, her son Michael at Agincourt, and then her younger sons, Miles and Alexander, at Orleans, must have been almost unbearable. Fortunately William was finally released on payment of £20,000 (probably about £1,400,000 in today's currency!).

The fighting dragged on for several years until William, seeing that further resistance was hopeless, began negotiations for peace. It is said that he refused to surrender to anyone except Joan of Arc, whose courage he admired, even though she was the enemy.

Although William almost certainly acted wisely, this decision made him unpopular at home. He became even more unpopular when, in order to promote more friendly relations with the French, he arranged the marriage between Henry VI and Margaret of Anjou, a cousin of the French king.

William, 1st Duke of Suffolk

King Henry had always thought a great deal of William and rewarded him for his services by making him Duke of Suffolk and a Knight of the Garter. But his enemies were determined to bring about his downfall.

The House of Commons accused him of High Treason and demanded a trial. The King could possibly have helped him, but he was too weak to stand up to Parliament. However, he decided to save him from the trial by banishing him from the country.

In the archives of the Paston family is one of the most moving letters to have survived from those far off days. It was written by William at Wingfield Castle on April 30th 1450, the day before he left England for ever.

> My dear and only well-beloved son, I beseech Our Lord in heaven, the maker of all the world, to bless you, and to send you ever grace to love Him and to dread Him ... And that also, wittingly, ye do

> nothing for love nor dread of any earthly creature that should
> displease Him ...
> Secondly, next Him above all earthly things, to be true liegeman in
> heart, in will, in thought, in deed, unto the King our aldermost high
> and dread sovereign lord, to whom both ye and I be so much bound
> to; charging you, as father can and may, rather to die than to be the
> contrary ...
> Thirdly, in the same wise, I charge you, my dear son, alway ... to
> love, to worship, your lady and mother; and also that ye obey alway
> her commandments, and to believe her counsels and advices in all
> your works.
> Furthermore, as father may and can, I charge you in any wise to flee
> the company and counsel of proud men, of covetous men, and of
> flattering men ... and to draw to you and to your company good and
> virtuous men, and such as be of good conversation, and of truth...
> And I will be to you as good lord and father as my heart can think.
> Written of mine hand, the day of my departing fro this land. Your
> true and loving father, Suffolk.

That night William de la Pole set out from Wingfield Castle for Ipswich (Yepeswych) where he embarked for France. He obviously had a large retinue because it is recorded that John Houghton, the King's Sergeant-at-Arms, was ordered to gather as many ships as possible from the ports of "Lyme, Crowimere, Yernemouth and Yepeswych".

But the Navy was under the command of the Duke of York, one of William's bitterest enemies, and as soon as William's fleet set out from Ipswich they were pursued and intercepted just off Dover.

Half a Dozen Strokes of a Rusty Sword

William was taken aboard one of the Naval ships 'Nicholas of the Towr' and condemned to death. The next day he was taken into a boat and beheaded with half a dozen strokes of a rusty sword.

There is no record of where William was buried - some say he was brought home and buried at Wingfield, but there is no real evidence for this.

In his "Historic Sites of Suffolk" John Wodderspoon tells the story of bringing his body at the dead of night to Wingfield Castle but the Rev'd Aldwell thinks this may be pure imagination. It certainly conjures up a very dramatic picture:

> Torches gleam upon the night, and a crowd of men, weary of foot,
> and cast down in spirit, approach the Castle through avenues of
> stately oaks, beeches, and elms. Mark how the red lights glance

amid the trees, and disclose even in far depths the lairs of the awakened deer. The black charger that once carried the chief now follows a bier. The head of the noble animal droops to the earth and his saddle is empty. As the cortege moves onward, a wail of women's voices rises on the wind. The drawbridge is let down. The hoofs of the horses clatter, for an instant, upon the wooden platform as they pass into the courtyard of the building, and the torches glare in the archway. The bier is uncovered and on it lies the body of the proud Suffolk - headless - bloody - and soiled - a victim to the outraged feelings of an injured nation.

Some say that William was buried in the Church of the Carthusians at Hull, and others think he may have been buried at Ewelme Church, but although as we know, there is a beautiful memorial there in memory of his wife Alice, there is no reference to William. It is possible he may have been dropped overboard with no Christian burial. We shall never know.

Wingfield Castle - Courtyard and Tudor House

The Ewelme Connection

After William's tragic death his widow Alice lived on for a while at Wingfield Castle before moving back to her old family home at Ewelme in Oxfordshire where she had inherited vast estates. She had often visited Ewelme with William, and they both had a great affection for the village.

In the 1430s they rebuilt the church (except for the tower) which is said to be a copy of Wingfield Church. They built a school for the village children which is still in use today, and they also built almshouses for 13 poor old men, who had a duty to pray in church several times a day for the souls of the de la Poles and for the King.

When she moved from Wingfield Alice took with her all her personal belongings, and there still exists an inventory, which shows the kind of things a great lady would have cherished. Some are household items and others would have been from the private chapel at Wingfield Castle. There are communion vessels in silver and gold, rich hangings and tapestries, books bound in leather with silver clasps and "cusshons of cloth of gold of damask". Also mentioned is a "materes of blu bukeskin for a cradell". This would have been a sentimental object, probably having been the cradle for her ba-

St Mary's Church, Ewelme

by son John or his little brother William, who did not survive. Alice died at Ewelme in 1475 at the age of 71 and is buried in the church which she and William had built 40 years earlier.

A beautiful effigy in alabaster remains as a memorial to this gentle lady. Close by is a brass to her father Thomas, famous in his own right as Speaker of the House of Commons and son of the poet Geoffrey Chaucer.

John de la Pole - 2nd Duke of Suffolk

The de la Poles were now to become even more closely connected with the Royal Family when John, the 2nd Duke of Suffolk, married Elizabeth Plantagenet, daughter of the Duke of York and sister of Edward IV and Richard III.

This seemed at first to be a good thing, but later led to the family's downfall. John, as brother-in-law to the King, was given certain honours and privileges. He was made a Knight of the Garter and his eldest son was created Earl of Lincoln.

The Duke was also made Constable of Wallingford Castle in Berkshire, and Commissioner for the Peace for Berkshire, Suffolk, Norfolk and Essex. In spite of all these honourable titles, he seems to have taken little part in political affairs and lived most of his life at Wingfield Castle.

According to the Paston Letters he had a keen eye to his own interests, and at one stage he attempted with the assistance of armed men to take Hellesden Manor in Norfolk from the Pastons. In view of the fact that he had inherited all the estates in Ewelme and in Suffolk, this would seem rather greedy!

John de la Pole, Heir-Presumptive to the Crown

When Richard III ascended the throne the fortunes of the de la Poles rose still higher. After the murder of the Princes in the Tower the King declared his nephew (John de la Pole, Earl of Lincoln) heir-presumptive to the Crown!

But soon afterwards came the Battle of Bosworth in which Lincoln fought on the side of the King. Richard was killed and Henry VII came to the throne. Lincoln escaped and fled abroad. Two years later he returned to England. He took part in an insurrection and was killed at the battle of Stoke on June 16th 1487.

For the moment however, the family still managed to stay in favour. John de la Pole, Lincoln's father, managed to make peace with the new King, and even bore the sceptre at his Coronation in 1485. History tells us that in the Royal Procession from the Tower of London to Westminster, just behind the King were to come "my lords the Duke of Bedford and Suffolk, the one by hynd the King on the right hand of the furst folver and on the left hand the Duke of Suffolk".

Death of John, Duke of Suffolk

Six years later John de la Pole, Duke of Suffolk, died at Wingfield Castle and was buried in the church. His wife Elizabeth Plantagenet was later buried by his

John, Duke of Suffolk and Elizabeth Plantagenet

side. Their monument, the figures of a knight and his lady, carved in alabaster, is probably the most beautiful of them all.

Edmund, their second son succeeded to the title and estates but only as Earl of Suffolk. He was always under suspicion, being too close to the royalty, and considered a hazard, following the conduct of his elder brother.

He went to live abroad, but returned to England when Henry VIII came to the throne. Soon afterwards however, he was executed by the King as being "a man of turbulent spirit and too nearly attached to the throne".

Their youngest son, Richard, wisely decided to remain abroad, but he was killed at the battle of Pavia in 1525.

With Richard the noble dynasty of de la Pole of Wingfield comes to an end. The castle, estates, church and college came into the possession of Henry VIII and most of the castle, except for the south front, was pulled down.

Fortunately for us and for future generations the church remained intact, and the college building also seems to have escaped, though its educational and priestly activities came to an end.

Wingfield today, quiet and unassuming perhaps to the outside world, is still not without its notable characters. In the 1920s the Rev'd Samuel Aldwell produced a book which has been a rich source of information for anyone researching local or political history. "Wingfield: its Church, College and Castle", published in 1925 is now out of print, but copies can sometimes be found in various bookshops. Details of the book and of the Harmer family who were involved in its production, can be found with the de la Pole pedigree at the end of this book.

In the 1970s the Chance family set up an Arts Centre at the College, and carried out a great deal of restoration work, revealing some of its long lost mediaeval features.

Wingfield is also the home of the world-famous coachman - John Parker, who with his Royal Mail coach and team of magnificent grey horses has appeared frequently in film and television over the past 30 years.

Finally, and perhaps most important of all, there is an enthusiastic group of people who in recent years have given up time and money to preserve Wingfield's rich heritage. Since 1985 more than half a million pounds has been spent on refurbishment of the church, thanks to the support of various charitable trusts and the generosity of local residents. All these people have helped to keep Wingfield a lively and vibrant community, looking not only to the past but to the future.

And if we visit Wingfield Church perhaps some of us might even offer a little prayer for the soul of John Wingfield who 600 years ago built the church for this very purpose. As Tennyson once reminded us "More things are wrought by prayer than this world dreams of".

Wingfield Castle

The daughter and daughter-in-law of Sir William Petre

Dorothy Wadham

Mary Petre

Dorothy was the eldest daughter of Sir William Petre. She was married to Nicholas Wadham, and together they founded Wadham College, Oxford. Mary Waldegrave, the daughter of Sir Edward Waldegrave of Borley, married Sir William's only son and heir (Master John). Sir John later became Lord Writtle and they lived at Thorndon Place, a beautiful mansion near Ingatestone Hall in Essex.

Chapter 2

The Petres of Ingatestone Hall

Although his name is not particularly well known, Sir William Petre was possibly one of the most influential 'behind the scenes' characters during the turbulent years of the mid 16th century. He was a gifted lawyer and statesman and it says a great deal for his wisdom and sense of judgement that he managed to keep his head when all around him were losing theirs - under the most tragic circumstances.

William Petre was born around 1505, the son of a country landowner, who held the manor of Tor Newton in Devon. As was the custom for the sons of the gentry at this time, he went to Oxford at the age of 15 and six years later graduated as a Bachelor of Civil and Canon Law.

William Petre, Secretary to George Boleyn

His first appointment was as Secretary to George Boleyn, the brother of Anne Boleyn. Mary, their sister, was married to William Cary, Lord Hunsdon, but her children, Henry and Catherine, were almost certainly the children of Henry VIII.

George Boleyn was the King's ambassador to Italy, France and Germany, and William travelled with him all over Europe before returning in 1583 to Oxford where he was made a Doctor of Civil Law.

Here he came to the notice of Thomas Cromwell, King Henry's Secretary and Vicar General, and the next year he was commissioned by the King to act as Cromwell's deputy.

Sir William Petre

The Surrender of Barking Abbey

During the following years Dr. Petre went all over the country, obtaining the surrender of numerous abbeys and priories, but unlike some royal agents, he was always fair and honest. We are told that the nuns at Barking Abbey were very happy with the terms he offered them.

The Abbess and thirty nuns assembled on 14th November 1539 to hand over the deed of surrender. Among them were ladies from many of the leading families of Suffolk and Essex, including the Tyrells, the Mordaunts, Wentworths, Drurys,

Sulyards and Kempes. "All were very contented with their annuities, Abbess Barley's being £133 13s. 4d."

All this throws a rather different light on the idea that there was nothing but distress and destruction at the time of the Dissolution. Obviously there was sometimes corruption and unfair dealing, but this was not always the case. With their annuities the displaced nuns would have been able to live modestly but comfortably in the community.

Many of the young ladies would have been delighted to be released from their vows, having been sent to the nunnery by their rich fathers, who would have paid a substantial sum to the Abbey to get their unmarried daughters off their hands!

The Purchase of Gynge Abbess

Petre was able to buy one of the most important properties from Barking Abbey, the manor of Gynge Abbess, or Abbess Hall, afterwards known as Ingatestone Hall. (This is not to be confused with Abbess Hall which was the alternative name for Abbess Roding, the home of the Browne family.) It is emphasised that Petre paid the full market price for the property - £849 12s 6d, to be paid over four years.

Now, after nearly 20 years of studying and travelling at home and abroad, William Petre was at last able to give a little more time to his own life on his new estates at Ingatestone.

Around 1534 he married Gertrude, who had previously been married to John Tyrell of Warley, a distant cousin of the Tyrells of Heron Hall and Gipping. Gertrude died in 1541, leaving William with two young daughters, Dorothy and Elizabeth. Little did he know that Dorothy would one day become famous as the co-founder of Wadham College at Oxford.

A year after the death of his wife Gertrude, William married Anne Tyrell, also a widow, the daughter of William Browne of Abbess Roding. The Brownes were a distinguished family, William having been lord Mayor of London in 1507 and again in 1513. Anne had previously been married to John Tyrell of Heron Hall, East Horndon, by whom she had two daughters, Anne and Catherine.

William obviously thought a lot of his step-daughter Catherine, and later provided her with a wonderful wedding feast which is described in detail in the Ingatestone archives. William and Anne had a little daughter, Thomasine, followed a year later by another daughter, Catherine, named, perhaps, after her step-sister. William clearly loved his daughters and step-daughters, but must have been disappointed that as yet there was no son to carry on the family name.

The Building of Ingatestone Hall

When he bought the manor of Gynge Abbess, William found the existing dwelling to be "an old house scant meet for a farmer to live upon", so he pulled down all the existing buildings and proceeded to build "new houses, very fair, large and stately, made of brick and embattled". The result is the very imposing building which still remains today.

Ingatestone Hall

The great hall was 40 feet long and 20 feet wide - and could seat 100 people. Beyond the buttery and beer cellar lay the kitchen, larder and scullery. There was a gallery for the musicians and also a 'Long Gallery'. These came into fashion with Hampton Court about 1530. The Long Gallery was for family music-making, entertainment and indoor exercise in bad weather, and also for displaying portraits. It was 94 feet long by 18 feet wide - which was short compared with Audley End (226 feet) or Hatfield (163 feet).

A Special Room for Mother-in-Law

There were numerous bedchambers and nurseries and a special room for William's mother-in-law. The house was built round a courtyard and there were various buildings to house the outdoor servants such as falconers, gardeners, brewers, laundry-maids, and dairy workers. There was also a hawks' mews, and east and west cheese store rooms.

Soon after taking over the Manor of Gynge Abbess, William was facing a crisis in his political life. His master, Thomas Cromwell, suddenly fell from favour and was sent to the block. It must have been an anxious time for William, but fortunately he remained in office and three months later was made a member of the King's Council. He became a Member of Parliament and in 1542 was made a Knight of the Shire. Then in January 1544 he was appointed King's Principal Secretary and a Privy Councillor.

From then on Sir William continued to hold high office until just a year before his death in 1567. When young Edward VI succeeded his father, Henry VIII, Petre was re-appointed Secretary and he continued to be a respected and trusted adviser throughout the reign of Mary and into the Elizabethan age.

But in spite of all his commitments and responsibilities to the Crown and the Country, Sir William was still at heart a family man. He delighted in entertaining not only his influential political colleagues such as the Cecils and the Dudleys but also his personal friends and family and their neighbours in Essex.

Christmas at Ingatestone Hall

Christmas at Ingatestone Hall was a great time for feasting and celebration, appreciated all the more perhaps because of all the 'fast days' which were observed during the year. The house would be full of visiting family and friends, and the servants too would share in the festivities. They would be working hard to produce the food and look after the needs of the guests, but would also enjoy the festive atmosphere and afterwards have a wonderful party of their own.

The day of the Nativity, Christmas Day, would have been very much a religious festival, though in every sense a Feast Day, but New Year was the great time for family and friends to get together.

William was not usually at home for Christmas Day, as he could rarely leave Court until the New Year. In 1548 for example, we read that he left Hampton Court on 3rd January. The roads were icy, so the Court blacksmith put 'frostnails' in the horse's shoes. Riding up Kingston Hill we are told he gave a groat in alms to two beggars, then accompanied by his steward and several servants, he reached London, crossing from the South Bank at Paris Garden to Paul's Wharf in time for supper. He probably stayed at his London house overnight. "After breakfast the next day", wrote his steward, "my master rode to Essex to join his wife and children".

We are very fortunate that William Petre and many of his descendants left detailed estate and household records, which give us a fascinating picture of life in Tudor England.

Entertaining the Guests

On Christmas Day 1551 many Ingatestone folk were invited to dinner and supper, and at Sunday dinner there were more than twenty Ingatestone men, mostly with their womenfolk, seven couple from Mountnessing and "eight poor folks, beside two mess that came unbid". (A mess was a serving for four people). The next day came villagers from Buttsbury and Margaretting, and tenants from other manors and estates.

Later in the week the festivities intensified, with family guests arriving. They included Lady Petre's kinsmen, the Tyrells, and also Richard Baker, the son and heir of Sir John Baker, Speaker of the House of Commons. Richard came from Kent with six servants and stayed for nearly a week. He was betrothed to Catherine Tyrell, Lady Petre's daughter by her first marriage.

On Twelfth Night, the final and chief feast day, there was "an animated crowd of humbler guests in the great hall below, fifty for dinner and many more for supper".

My Lady Norwich and Mr Secretary Cycill

During 1548 there were frequent visits from the Browne family of Abbess Roding, also from "my Lady Norwich and four servants, Mr Secretary Cycill and his wife". They also entertained Lady Darcy, wife of the Privy Councillor and owner of St Osyth's Priory, Lady Coates, wife of another Councillor and owner of Pleshy Castle, and Sir Arthur and Lady Cooke of Gidea Hall, Romford.

The guests usually brought presents of fruit, game, and sweet-meats including marchpaine - a kind of marzipan with real gold leaf on top. Probably the term 'gilding the gingerbread' arose from this custom. Sometimes the gift would be meat - either dead or alive. At Catherine Tyrell's wedding we hear that 3 oxen were given - by Sir John Mordaunt, Sir Harry Tyrell and Mr Anthony Browne.

Poultry, Fish and Ingatestone Cheese

The family archives give us a great deal of information about the food produced and consumed at Ingatestone Hall.

They had a large variety of poultry - including swan and geese, and almost every kind of wildfowl. Many kinds of fish were on the menu, coming mainly from their own fishponds, with small purchases of 'sea fish' from a fish market on Thames Creek. They also ate a great many oysters which were not considered a luxury in Tudor times. Fruit, vegetables and herbs came from the orchard or the 'cook's garden', and a large quantity of cheese was made in the dairy, much of it from sheep's milk. The poet John Skelton gave a rather horrific description of the Ingatestone cheese:

> A cantle of Essex cheese
> Was well a foot thick
> Full of maggots quick:
> It was huge and great
> And mighty strong meat
> For the devil to eat,
> It was tart and punicate.

A great deal of meat was recorded, mainly home produced. In 1548 the family (which included nearly 20 servants) and the guests consumed 55 oxen and calves, 2 cows, 133 sheep and lambs, and 11 swine. These are the calculated totals for 46 weeks (no meat in Lent). Other records mention deer, most of which came from Crondon Park, the rest were gifts. There were apparently few deer in Ingatestone Park.

Gallons of milk and cream, hundreds of eggs and vast quantities of pies and pastries are recorded.

A Very Special Christmas

Christmas would always have been a joyful time for William Petre, but in 1549 it would have been particularly special. In the past when he came home from his duties at Court he would be returning to a family of girls. But this year, on 20th December, a great event took place - the birth of a son, who was to become the first Baron Petre. There would have been great excitement and rejoicing. The baby was to be called John, and he would carry the family name down through many generations.

Lady Petre did not nurse her son. As was the custom, a foster nurse was hired, the wife of Robert Humfrey of Crondon, Petre's 'acater' (the buyer of provisions for the household). The choice of a nurse to breast-feed the baby was very important. She not only had to be healthy but also of good character, because her moral qualities were thought to be absorbed with the milk. The nurse's own new-born baby would be cared for by another wet-nurse. We find the following entry in the expenses for that year:

> Humfrey's wife for nursing Mr. John 13 weeks, after
> 10d the week, now due 25 March, 10s. 10d
> Blakborn's wife of Stock for nursing Humfrey's child
> 12 weeks, 9s.

The Baptism of Master John

Master John's baptism took place at the New Year, so there was a double celebration. He had two distinguished Godfathers - the Earl of Warwick and the Spanish Ambassador, Van der Delft. His Godmother, Lady Paget, was equally distinguished.

A vast number of presents are recorded. Lady Mordaunt from Thorndon sent a guinea-fowl, a mallard, a woodcock, two teals and a basket of wafers, while the neighbours' good wishes were accompanied by curlews, plovers, oxbirds, mallards and many small birds such as six dozen larks. Thomas Mildmay from Moulsham Hall sent seven partridges and ten snipes.

As Master John grew up it was considered necessary to provide him with male company, and several boys from noble families joined the household. They shared a tutor during the early years, and later went on to Oxford or Cambridge, each with his own tutor.

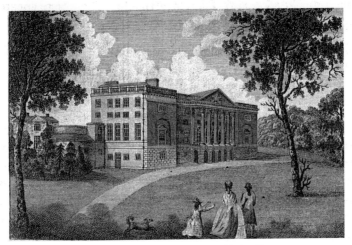

**Thorndon Place - The Home of John Petre
and his wife, Mary Waldegrave**

John later went on to become a very wealthy and highly respected member of the community. In 1603 he was created Lord Writtle by James I. He was married to Mary, the daughter of Sir Edward Waldegrave of Borley, and they lived at Thorndon Place, a grand mansion not far from Ingatestone Hall. They had a male heir, and members of the family continued to live at Thorndon and Ingatestone for many generations to come.

Young John Petre, a Gifted Musician

Music had always been very important to Sir William, and later his son John seems to have been quite a gifted musician. We read that he was able to sing madrigals and accompany them on the lute. There are records of the purchase of many musical instruments at various times, including virginals, lutes, violas and gitterns. The latter had a long neck, rounded back and oval-shaped body - an early version of the guitar - usually strung with four gut strings and played with a plectrum.

Thomas Tallis and William Byrd

There was an organ at Ingatestone Hall and also one in William's London house, which probably came from Waltham Abbey, the last local monastery to be dissolved by Petre. This would almost certainly have been the instrument used by Thomas Tallis, who was later a tutor of William Byrd. There is evidence that

Sir William Petre was a patron of the young William Byrd, and one of his Pavanes was dedicated to him. Later Byrd was to become a friend of John Petre, and was a frequent visitor to his houses at Ingatestone and Thorndon Place.

A page from Sir John Petre's Song Book about 1580

Sir William himself did not play an instrument, but certainly loved music. We read that Choristers from St Pauls came to his town house to sing for him while he was convalescing from one of his illnesses.

For much of his life William's health had not been good, and it was sad that when he was honoured by a visit from the Queen in 1561 he was really not well enough to enjoy it to the full. This is probably the reason why so few facts are recorded.

A Royal Visit to Ingatestone

The Queen arrived with a vast retinue, but the only name mentioned is that of Secretary Cecil, with whom she had supped the previous night at Theobalds, his grand house in Hertfordshire. Later James I greatly admired Theobalds and persuaded Cecil to exchange it for the old brick palace of Hatfield.

Though the records of the visit are few we do have a detailed account of all the food consumed during the four days of the Queen's visit. The Queen herself is reported to have been a very frugal and abstemious monarch, but it was a mark of respect to provide large quantities and varieties of food. Her retinue was large, and most of their appetites were enormous, so the food would not have been wasted. The day on which the Queen arrived was a fast day, so the menu was mainly fish including sturgeon - the royal fish. Apparently Cecil was a great believer in maintaining the number of fast days in order to help the fishing trade, whose seamen helped to man the Navy in times of need.

The whole visit cost the Petre family about £2,500 in food and drink. But apparently they got away with it quite lightly. The journey of 1561 was the first of the Queen's royal progresses, and as time went on, and as each noble family tried to out-do the last, they became more and more extravagant. Her visit to the Cecil household at Theobalds on the Hertfordshire-Essex borders in 1564 is said to have cost him considerably more.

Horrible Herbal Concoctions

William had been in poor health for many years. At one stage his Steward applied for an invalid's licence to eat flesh during Lent: "a bill to suffer my master's Lenten stuff to pass". The accounts of the medications and treatments he had to undergo make us very thankful to have been born in the 20th century. He suffered from a stone, which must have caused agonising pain, and the poor man was made to swallow dozens of different herbal concoctions to "crack the stone" or pulverise it.

Various remedies were suggested by his friends and we hear that Lord Cobham, son of the former Deputy of Calais, sent a box filled with dried samphire, and Mr Justice Browne sent "medicine for the stone in a bottle".

William also had varicose ulcers on his legs, and finally became very deaf, which was particularly sad because of his love of music. When he was no longer able to ride his horse a special litter was made for him - a seat of wood and leather which was slung between two horses. We can imagine the discomfort of this method of travel for a sick man.

But still William struggled on with his work as a lawyer and adviser to the Royal Household. He continued to pursue his various interests in art and music, sponsoring young poets and musicians, and encouraging them by inviting them to visit and perform at his London house and at Ingatestone Hall.

The Next Generation

We hear a great deal about Sir William's political life and about the domestic life at Ingatestone Hall. He obviously insisted that his Stewards and Estate Managers kept detailed accounts of all that went on in every part of the manor, and as a lawyer and business man he probably kept his own personal records and diaries. These records have proved a most valuable source of information for students and historians.

We hear less, however, about William's own family and his descendants. We know that he had four daughters, two step-daughters and finally a son John, who later married Mary Waldegrave, the daughter of Sir Edward Waldegrave of Borley Manor.

John and Mary lived at Thorndon Place, a beautiful mansion not far from Ingatestone Hall, where they brought up their three sons, William, John and Thomas. William later became the 2nd Lord Petre and had a son, Robert, the 3rd Lord Petre, who was married to Mary, the daughter of Anthony-Maria Browne (one of the Three Brothers in the Browne chapter).

John, the second son of John and Mary, was married to Catherine, the daughter of Lord Monteagle and Morley, the recipient of the famous Monteagle Letter which foiled the Gunpowder Plot. The third son, Thomas, married one of the Baskervilles of Wiltshire.

We know very little about Sir William Petre's younger daughters, except that Catherine had a daughter Gertrude who was married to Robert Wintour. He was one of the main conspirators in the Gunpowder Plot, and was finally hung drawn and quartered.

But it was William's eldest daughter Dorothy who was the most famous of all his children.

The Founding of Wadham College

Dorothy was married to Nicholas Wadham, a member of an old Somerset family. Nicholas died in 1609 leaving his vast fortune to endow a college at Oxford. After his death his widow Dorothy, 75 years old, but obviously a lady of character and determination, took on the responsibility of making sure that her husband's wishes were carried out. We are told that she "fought all the claims of Nicholas's relations, lobbied at court, negotiated the purchase of a site and drew up the college statutes".

She also added some of her own money to the endowment and kept a strict control on the organisation of the college. It was, of course, for male students only, and under the original statutes no women were even to be employed, except for the laundress, who was to be of "such age, condition, and reputation as to be above suspicion".

It was not until 1974 that the statutes were altered to allow the admission of women as full members of the college at all levels. The college was one of the first in Oxford to make the change.

William Petre did not live to see the founding of the College, but he would certainly have been very proud of his daughter. She was only six years old when her mother died, so she would have been brought up by William and his second wife, Anne (Browne). They would no doubt have recognised her outstanding intellect and strength of character and would have encouraged her to make the most of her talents.

A Loving Father and a Kind and Generous Master

William's family obviously meant a great deal to him. All his daughters and step-daughters were given wonderful wedding feasts, and later he enjoyed the company of his grandchildren, some of whom were brought up at Ingatestone Hall.

He was specially proud to have had a son and later grandsons, who would carry on the family name right up to this present day. We know too that William was a kind and generous master to his servants and tenants, and we are grateful to him and to his successors for the wonderful record of household and family details which have been preserved for future generations.

We can feel a real affection for Sir William Petre - honest and fair in all his dealings, courageous in facing years of pain and ill health, loving and caring to his fellow men. He died in 1572 at the age of 67 and was buried in Ingatestone Parish Church. In his Will he gave his son John a fatherly blessing, and asked that he would execute his bequests justly and fairly. He writes:

> So doing, God Almighty, by whose only goodness I
> have obtained all that I have had or shall have, shall
> and will bless, direct and assist him to pass the course
> of this vain and uncertain life to His pleasure.

The motto which William chose for the family seems to reflect the high ideals of a good and God-fearing man - "Sans Dieu Rien".

Nicholas and Dorothy - Founders of Wadham College

Wadham College, Oxford

Chapter 3

The Brookes and Chevalliers of Aspall

The history of the manor of Aspall goes back to Saxon times. It took its name from the aspen trees which grew prolifically in the area, and the Saxon word "halh" meaning land in the bend of a river - in this case the River Deben. In the very early days it was owned by the de Clares and the Peverell family. Ranulf Peverell held the manor before 1066, and at the time of the Domesday Survey (1086) the Lord of the Manor was Ralph Peverell, who would have been Ranulf's son or grandson.

Several generations later came Sir Payne Peverell, whom we meet in the Little Bradley pedigrees. His daughter married Hammond Lord Peche, and their great-granddaughter, Catherine Peche, later became the wife of Sir John Aspall. Exactly who this John Aspall was we do not know, but he presumably owned part of the manor. It is probable that at some stage Aspall was divided into two or even three manors, which all descended through different members of the same family, and that they were brought together again by this Peche and Aspall marriage.

Sir Thomas Brooke, 5th Lord Cobham

Sir John and Catherine Aspall had a daughter Mirabell whose marriage to William Gedding introduced many other closely related families, including the Poleys, the Hunts, and the de la Poles. Joan, the wife of John de la Pole, was the daughter of John, 3rd Lord Cobham, and she inherited the title as Baroness Cobham. When she married Sir Reginald Braybrooke he took the title as 4th Lord Cobham, but again there was no male heir and their daughter (also Joan) became the next Baroness Cobham. She married Sir Thomas Brooke, who now became 5th Lord Cobham. From this time the Brooke name was carried down through many generations until the early 18th century.

Joan and Thomas had two sons, and the elder son, Edward Brooke, became 6th Lord Cobham. He was married to Elizabeth, the daughter of Lord Audley. The Brookes were a zealous Yorkist family, and Edward took part in the battle of St Albans, where the Yorkists gained a famous victory.

From this point it was the younger branch of the family who inherited Aspall, while the older branch inherited the Cobham title. They had estates in Hertford-shire and Essex, but lived mainly in London, where they became closely linked with the Court and with the political intrigues of the time. This eventually resulted in one member of the family losing his head!

Edward's son, John Brooke, married into the Nevill family (the Abergavennys) and he was succeeded by his son Thomas, the 8th Lord Cobham, who was with the King at The Field of the Cloth of Gold in 1520.

George Brooke, 9th Lord Cobham

His son George Brooke, 9th Lord Cobham, had two daughters, Elizabeth, married to William Parr, Marquess of Northampton, and Catherine, who married George Kympton, the son of a City merchant who was living in Hertfordshire. Their daughter Jane was the wife of Thomas Harmer of Weston. Elizabeth, described as "My Lady Marquess of Northampton", was Godmother to the 4th child of Lady Cavendish, better known as Bess of Hardwick.

First Lady of Chatsworth

A great deal has been written about Bess of Hardwick, the "First Lady of Chatsworth", and any historical account of this remarkable lady would almost certainly include references to the Brooke family. Frances Brooke, the second wife of William the 10th Lord Cobham, was Bess's closest friend. Both were Ladies of the Bedchamber to Queen Elizabeth, and both shared a great love of needlework.

In her biography of Bess of Hardwick, Mary Lovell quotes from a letter written by Frances when she was pregnant with her second child. She was obviously very anxious about the confinement and asks Bess to pray for her. "I know I shall speed better for a good woman's prayers".

A New Year's Gift for the Queen

In the same letter Frances also discusses a gown which they were making as a New Year's gift for the Queen. Frances was making the sleeves "of a wideness that would best suit the Queen". Bess was evidently making the ruffs for the neck and wrists, and Frances tells her that 10 yards of caulle will be enough, "as the fashion is much altered since you were here". (This last comment suggests that Frances was somewhat concerned because Bess was spending most of her time at Chatsworth rather than in London where she was supposed to be attending the Queen).

A few weeks after this letter was written (in October 1564) Frances was safely delivered of a son, Henry, who was to become the 11th Lord Cobham.

There is a delightful picture of William and Frances with their family, which now hangs in the gallery at Longleat. We cannot be sure which one is Henry, but we know he was the second child, and presumably the eldest son. It is likely therefore that Henry is the little boy who is seated in front of his father.

The 10th Lord Cobham and his wife Frances (standing), with their children

Henry Brooke was a Knight of the Garter and Warden of the Cinque Ports, but was possibly rather too closely involved in the politics of the day. The Brookes were one of the leading recusant families in the 17th century, and they were related to the Mordaunts, Brownes, Wisemans and Throckmortons.

In 1603, two years before the Gunpowder Plot, Henry and his younger brother George were accused of complicity in the 'Raleigh Conspiracy'. This was a plot led by Lord Grey de Wilton and Sir Walter Raleigh to eliminate King James and his 'cubs' and put Arabella Stuart on the throne.

Both Henry and George were imprisoned in the Tower and George was executed. Henry escaped execution but some accounts say that he remained a prisoner for the rest of his life. Other historians have told us that he was released on payment of huge fines, but all his lands and titles were taken away.

Shortly before his imprisonment he had been married to Frances, daughter of Charles Howard, 1st Earl of Nottingham, but they had no children (which is not surprising if he spent the rest of his life in the Tower).

His brother George however did already have one son, William, and he became the next heir. He succeeded to the title as 12th Lord Cobham, and his lands and properties were restored.

It is interesting to note that Elizabeth, the sister of Henry and George Brooke, was married to Robert Cecil, Lord Salisbury, who was responsible for ordering their imprisonment and execution.

The friendship between the Brookes and Sir William and Lady Cavendish continued. When they were in London the Cavendishes frequently dined with Lord Cobham and also with Harry Skipwith, Henry Cary (Lord Hunsdon) and Lady Throckmorton, who all belonged to the same network of families.

Reginald Brooke of Aspall

While the senior branch of the Brooke family were making their mark in London, the younger branch were looking after the estates at Aspall. As country squires we hear less about their history, but they too played an important part in their own spheres.

In 1464 Reginald Brooke inherited Aspall from his brother Edward. Reginald married Anne Everton and their son Edward inherited the manor on his father's death in 1482. It was this Edward who built Aspall Hall, and although it has had additions and alterations, this is the same building we see today. It would have been built around 1500, so there must have been an earlier manor house in Aspall - but whether or not it was on the same site we do not know.

The Petre and Tyrell Connections

Edward also held Abbess Roding in Essex and Barkway in Hertfordshire jointly with Sir John Petre of Ingatestone Hall. Edward was married to Florence, the daughter of Robert Ashfield of Stowlangtoft.

The manor then passed down to their son George and their grandson - also George - who married Alice, the daughter of Sir John Tyrell of Gipping Hall. Their monument is in Stowmarket Church. Their son, another George, was married first to Mary Jobson, granddaughter of Sir Francis Jobson of Doniland in Essex, and secondly to Katherine, daughter of George Jernigan, Member of

Parliament for Orford. Their son Edward married Agnes, daughter of Thomas Fastolf of Pettaugh, and as we know, several members of this family served as Members of Parliament for Ipswich. Edward, the next heir, was married to Rebecca Wiseman. Edward died in 1679 and was buried at Aspall, while Rebecca lived on for another 20 years and was buried at St Margaret's in Ipswich.

The Brookes of Worlingworth

While the main branches of the family were at Aspall or in Hertfordshire other branches of the Brooke family evolved in various parts of Suffolk. There was a branch at Worlingworth, and another at Nacton. The Worlingworth Brookes were descended from John de Vere, Earl of Oxford. A member of this family, Philip Bowes Vere Brooke of Brook (or Broke) Hall, was famous for his gallantry as a naval officer in the American Civil War.

Sir Richard Brooke of Crows Hall

Sir Richard Brooke of Nacton, who died in 1529, was Recorder of London and Chief Baron of the Exchequer, and he represented the City of London in several parliaments. He built Crows Hall in 1526, but it was rebuilt and enlarged by Philip Bowes Brooke in 1767. Richard's son, Robert Brooke, owned lands in Nacton, Foxholes, Bucklesham and Levington, and his grandson, also Robert, was High Sheriff of Suffolk in 1623. Two generations later their descendant, another Sir Robert Brooke, married Ann the daughter of Sir Lionel Tollemache.

Bridget Brooke, the daughter of Sir Richard of Nacton, was married to George Fastolf, creating yet another link between the Brooke and the Fastolf families. Thomas Fastolf of Pettaugh, whose daughter Agnes had married Edward Brooke of Aspall, was almost certainly the son of this Bridget and George. Later the Brookes married into the Middleton family of Shrubland Hall.

There is an interesting note in the Ipswich Journal of 1740 which refers to Philip Broke of Nacton. It states that anyone who goes near Bixley Decoy without the permission of Philip Broke will be "sued as the law directs". Apparently some "malicious persons" had been disturbing the wild fowl, thereby upsetting the members of the local shoot.

This Philip Broke would have been the Philip Bowes Brooke mentioned earlier, or perhaps his father, Philip Brooke, who was married to Anne Bowes of Bury St Edmunds and died in 1762.

The Chevallier Family

After 700 years of family connections at Aspall, dating from the time when it was held by the Brooke ancestors - the Peches and the Peverells, the manor was finally sold in 1702 to Temple Chevallier. The Chevalliers were cider makers from Jersey, and ever since this time Aspall Hall has been famous for its cider. The Brookes were distantly connected to the Chevalliers through the Temple family of Stowe. Temple Chevallier's father, Clement Chevallier, married Susanna Temple, a descendant of John Temple of Stowe in Buckinghamshire. There were apparently links with the Brooke family in the 16th century, but the exact relationship is not clear.

Even though the Chevalliers were not strictly part of the family network they did in a sense 'inherit' the manor. They have loved and cared for it for over three hundred years, and the history of Aspall Hall would not be complete without them.

The Spirit of Cyder Making

When Temple Chevallier died childless in 1722 the manor went to his cousin, Clement Chevallier, who at first tried to grow vines, but when this proved unsuccessful he decided to revert to cider making, which had been a family tradition in Jersey for many years.

According to an old manuscript "The Chevalier family came from Jersey and brought hither with them the Spirit of Cyder-making". Not only did they bring the spirit of cider making, they also brought the equipment and the expertise. They even imported the apple trees from Jersey - a quarter of the island was devoted to apple growing at this time. They also brought the granite crushing wheel and trough, which remained in use until 1951.

The cider making was to continue at Aspall Hall and is still a flourishing industry at the present day. The original spelling was adopted and the product is always known as Aspall Cyder.

When the Chevalliers bought Aspall Hall it is not certain whether the house had already been restored, but it was around this time that the front of the house was rebuilt in the classical style, using bricks which were almost certainly made locally. Clement Chevallier is known to have made bricks nearby and a field bearing the name Brick Meadow still exists, so it seems likely that it was Clement who built the house that we see today.

The Rev'd Professor Temple Chevallier

Clement Chevallier's descendants included several distinguished scholars, among them the Rev'd Temple Chevallier, Professor of Mathematics and Astronomy at Durham University, who discovered a mountain on the moon. Then there was also the famous Rev'd John 'Barley' Chevallier, born in 1774, who was the ancestor of the Chevalliers who are still living at Aspall Hall.

The Reverend John 'Barley' Chevallier

The Rev'd John Chevallier MD was not only an ordained priest, but also a very enlightened medical doctor. His views on mental illness were far ahead of their time, when the 'insane' were looked upon as a social disgrace. Chevallier thought that these unfortunate people needed a domestic environment, and went on to make radical alterations to Aspall Hall so that his patients could live in safety and comfort. He built corridors between the wings and raised the entire roof to provide bedrooms for the children and staff. The first floor was kept for the patients, some of whom had their own bedrooms and sitting rooms.

John Chevallier qualified first as a doctor of medicine before taking Holy Orders in 1837, after which he became the Rector of Badingham. He must have been a very busy man, looking after the physical and mental health of his patients at Aspall Hall and caring for the spiritual needs of his parishioners at Badingham. In addition to being remembered as a compassionate doctor, he is also remembered for having introduced a new cereal variety - the once celebrated Chevallier Barley.

The Famous Lord Kitchener

John Chevallier's daughter Anne was baptised by her father in Aspall Church and spent her early years in the village. Her marriage also took place at Aspall. Her husband, Henry Kitchener, was a member of a Suffolk family with Hampshire origins. After their marriage they went to live in Ireland where their son Henry was born.

It was this Henry who was later to become the famous Lord Kitchener. Sadly John died a year after his daughter's marriage, so he never lived to see his famous grandson. Anne later returned to Aspall, and she was buried there in 1864. Her son, Lord Kitchener, had no known burial place. He was drowned in the North Sea when his ship, HMS Hampshire, was sunk by a German mine in 1916. There is a memorial to him in Aspall Church.

Perronelle Chevallier - A Remarkable Lady

One of the most remarkable 20th century descendants of the family which took over the Manor from the Brookes in 1702 must surely have been Perronelle Mary Chevallier. She was born at Aspall Hall in 1902 and lived to be 101 years old. She was the great-great-great granddaughter of Clement Chevallier who started the cyder business in 1728.

When Perronelle was a child there was no electricity or mains water at the Hall. The household was self sufficient, and had a dairy, laundry, carpenter's shop, bread oven and fish ponds.

During the First World War, when the men were away on active service, she would drive herself 15 miles into Ipswich in a pony and trap for French lessons. She was always a keen rider, and used to go hunting side-saddle, an extremely hazardous activity.

After the war she went to Reading University to study agriculture, but had to leave before taking her degree because her father ran out of money. Soon after this she met her future husband, Cyril Guild, at a fruit farming conference in Norfolk.

The First Lady Cyder Maker

In due course Perronelle and her husband took over the fruit farming and the cyder business. The cyder was transported all over the country, beginning its journey at Aspall Station on the Mid-Suffolk Light Railway (which also took the local schoolchildren from the remote villages of East Suffolk to the Grammar School at Stowmarket).

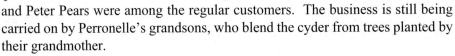

Perronelle was a founder member of The Soil Associ-ation, and from 1946 all the Aspall Cyder was made from certified organic apples. In 2002, at the age of 99, Perronelle was a 'poster girl' for Sainsbury's Organics, as one of the Soil Association's last origi-nal surviving members. Perronelle died at Aspall Hall on 15th February 2004.

As well as being marketed all over the British Isles, the cyder was sold to the public at The Cyder House - just across the moat from the Hall. Benjamin Britten and Peter Pears were among the regular customers. The business is still being carried on by Perronelle's grandsons, who blend the cyder from trees planted by their grandmother.

And so we leave the Brookes and the Chevalliers, Lords and custodians of this ancient manor. There are probably many Brooke families still living in Suffolk, and it is very likely that some of them may have had their roots in the manor of Aspall, and that their ancestral line would take them back to the days of the de Clares and the Peverells, who lived here more than 1000 years ago.

Chapter 4

The Brownes of Essex and Sussex

In researching the history of the Browne families of Essex and Sussex we have a problem. They were obviously linked in some way, but we have not yet been able to find a common ancestor.

Several historians have assumed that there was no connection at all, and even the College of Arms would not commit itself to a definite answer, using words such as "We find no link". As we know, Nelson is reported to have said "I see no ships" when he put the telescope to his blind eye!

But the evidence seems to indicate that there is a connection somewhere. The arms bear certain similarities, both displaying three lions. Then there is the name Anthony, which is significant. In most families there were endless Johns and Williams and Henrys, but Anthony was not a particularly common name.

The Sussex pedigree tells us that Sir Anthony Browne was knighted in 1377 at the coronation of Richard II. In the Essex pedigree we do not come across an Anthony until 1510, and when the name does occur it seems to cause some confusion. In at least one history book we find that the title "Lord Montague" has been wrongly attributed to Anthony Browne of Essex, when in fact it was Anthony Browne of Sussex who bore the title.

Who Presented the Ox?

Sir Anthony Browne is mentioned several times in connection with the Petre family of Ingatestone Hall. At the wedding of Catherine Tyrell, William Petre's step-daughter, various friends and neighbours contributed items of food for the banquet, and we are told that Sir Anthony Browne supplied an ox.

This of course would be Sir Anthony Browne of Abbess Roding, which was just a few miles away from Ingatestone. Or was it? Perhaps not.

We discover that a later Lord Petre was married to the daughter of Anthony Browne of Sussex. So the Sussex Brownes obviously knew the Petre family, and it may have been an earlier Sir Anthony Browne of Sussex who presented the ox. But if so he must have been living in Essex - it would hardly have been practical to bring an ox, either dead or alive, all the way from Sussex.

Another ambiguous Browne reference occurs in the history of the Petre family, when Sir William was suffering from a painful kidney condition, and various concerned friends were sending their favourite remedies. We read that Mr

Justice Browne sent "a medicine for the stone in a bottle". Since there were Justices and legal men in both families, Mr Justice Browne could have belonged to either.

The links between the two families continue. The Capells of Hertfordshire were related to both families, and the Ropers of Kent were also connected with both the Sussex and the Essex Brownes.

The Brownes of Abbess Roding

The Essex Brownes are said to have come originally from the west of England, and Thomas, who was married to Joanne Kyrkham of Devonshire, inherited Abbess Roding from his brother John in 1467.

The manor of Abbess Roding or Abbess Hall belonged originally to Barking Abbey, but was taken over at the time of the Conquest by Geoffrey de Mandeville, one of the Norman barons. Later Barking Abbey regained part of the manor and held it until the Dissolution, when it was granted by Henry VIII to Thomas Cromwell.

Abbess Roding Church

When Cromwell was disgraced and executed, Henry VIII gave the manor to Anne of Cleves. Richard Lord Rich (later Lord Chancellor) was her Steward. Later that year (1540), probably when Anne was divorced, the manor seems to have been in the possession of Richard Lord Rich and Oliver St John of Bletsoe.

In 1541 it was acquired by Edward Brooke of Aspall Hall in Suffolk, a cousin of Lord Cobham. Edward Brooke also had estates at Barkway and St Pauls Walden in Hertfordshire which he held jointly with Sir John Petre, son of Sir William Petre of Ingatestone Hall.

The Manors of Rookwood or Brownes

The other part of the Abbess Roding estate, which was not regained by Barking Abbey, passed in 1086 to Aubrey de Vere, ancestor of the Earls of Oxford and also of the Browne family who later inherited it. It was known as Rookwood or Brownes. There is some confusion about the names of the various manors at Abbess Roding. The main manor was known as Abbess Roding or Abbess Hall. But there was also Rookwood or Brownes, which was sometimes referred to as Clovills. Then there was Welde Hall and Ridley Hall.

Over the years some of the manors were acquired by other related families, including the Waldegraves, Brookes and Tyrells, and there were links by marriage with the Dacres, the Knightons, and the Underhills of Little Bradley.

The Mordaunts of Turvey

Thomas Browne and Joanne Kyrkham had a son - also Thomas (or Robert), and it was this Thomas who was the father of Weston Browne, the next Lord of the Manor. He was knighted by the King of Aragon at the time of Henry VII.

Sir Weston Browne was married to Maud or Elizabeth Mordaunt of Turvey, forming yet another link between these related families. The Mordaunts were one of the very strong recusant families during the reign of Henry VIII and Queen Elizabeth, so it is likely that the Brownes of Essex were also a Roman Catholic family - though we do not hear much about their religious beliefs. There seems to be no history of sequestration or imprisonment in the Tower.

Sir Weston and his wife Maud (or Elizabeth) had two sons and two daughters. Their eldest son John was to carry on the inheritance, but before we return to this branch of the family we move to Sir Weston's brothers, William and Humphrey, who both have interesting histories of their own.

William Browne, Lord Mayor of London

Weston Browne's brother William was a London merchant and was Lord Mayor of London in 1507 and again in 1513/14, when he died during his term of office. He had a daughter Ann, born in 1504, who was married first to John Tyrell of Heron Hall, and secondly to Sir William Petre of Ingatestone.

Ann had two daughters from each marriage, and also two step-daughters, the children of Sir William's first marriage. One of the step-daughters was Dorothy Petre, who later married Nicholas Wadham, and together they endowed and founded Wadham College at Oxford.

Sir Humphrey Browne of Ridley Hall

Weston Browne's other brother, Sir Humphrey Browne, lived at Ridley Hall, and he was Justice of the Common Pleas at the time of Henry VIII. Sir Humphrey was twice married - first to Ann, daughter of Henry de Vere of Hedingham Castle, and secondly to another Ann, the daughter of John, Lord Hussey. John

Hussey's sister Bridget was the wife of Francis Russell, 4th Earl of Bedford. By this second marriage Humphrey had a daughter Catherine, who was married to Sir William Roper. Sir William was the grandson of the earlier Sir William Roper who was married to Margaret the daughter of Sir Thomas More.

Now we come to an event which closely links the Essex and the Sussex Brownes. We find that this William, who married Catherine the daughter of Humphrey Browne of Essex, was the son of Thomas Roper and Lucy Browne, who was the daughter of Sir Anthony Browne of Cowdray House in Sussex. So Catherine Browne of Essex had a mother-in-law who was Lucy Browne of Sussex.

Sir Humphrey had no sons, just three daughters, so the inheritance of the Essex manors came down through his brother Sir Weston Browne. As we know, Sir Humphrey's first wife was Ann, the daughter of Henry de Vere, and now Weston Browne's son John (Humphrey's nephew) was marrying Audrey de Vere, Ann's sister.

Sir Weston Browne also had a daughter Katherine, who was married to Francis Knighton (the son of Thomas Knighton of Little Bradley) and another son who was the Sir Anthony Browne whom we met earlier. Sir Anthony is also mentioned in another chapter, when he was a guest at Catherine Tyrell's wedding (Catherine was his cousin). Sir Anthony Browne inherited Welde Hall, while John and his wife Audrey de Vere, inherited Abbess Roding.

George Browne of Clovills Hall

John and Audrey had a son George, who lived at Clovills Hall, which may have been another name for Abbess Hall. George was married to Elizabeth Leventhorpe. She was the daughter of Sir John Leventhorpe of Shingle Hall at Albury in Hertfordshire, whose wife was Joan Brograve of Hammonds Manor at Braughing. Sir John was Sheriff of Hertfordshire in 1510.

George and Elizabeth's eldest son and heir was another Weston Browne, named after his great-grandfather. He is said to be Weston Browne of Rookwood or Clovills. He was married to Mary, the daughter of Sir Edward Capell of Little Hadham Hall in Hertfordshire.

We meet the Capells of Hertfordshire in other chapters, particularly in connection with their role as Muster Captains at the time of the threat from the Spanish Armada.

From this time the family seems to have become very closely connected with the manors at Abbess Roding, which they eventually inherited. In this generation, however, the Capell line was not carried on, as Mary had no children. She possibly died in childbirth because we read that Weston Browne had a second marriage - to Elizabeth Pawlett. Meanwhile Sir Henry Capell, Mary's brother, was marrying Mary Browne of Sussex. It's no wonder we are confused!

Weston Browne and Elizabeth Pawlett had only one son who died without issue in 1583, just three years after his father, so he was probably quite a young man and not yet married.

But Weston Browne had two daughters - Catherine, who was married to Nicholas Waldegrave of Borley, and Jayne, whose second marriage was to Sir Gamaliel Capell of Little Hadham. Sir Gamaliel Capell now became Lord of the Manor of Abbess Roding.

The Capells of Hertfordshire, Suffolk and Essex

The Capells were a very well-known family in Hertfordshire, and they were now to become equally well known in Suffolk, giving their name to the villages of Capel St Andrews near Woodbridge, and to Capel St Mary on the Suffolk-Essex borders. Mrs Sarah Capell, who was buried at Abbess Roding in 1698, was probably the last member of the family to live there.

About 1700, Sir Gamaliel Capell, the great-grandson of the first Gamaliel, sold or mortgaged the manor to John Howland of Streatham, whose daughter and heir married Wriothesley Russell, 2nd Duke of Bedford. His son John, 4th Duke of Bedford, sold Abbess Roding in 1739 to the Skinner family.

In the 19th century the Rev'd Capel Cure, a descendant of the Capell family, bought the advowson of the Rectory. He did a great deal for the parish at his own expense, providing a village school and restoring the church.

The Capells were already related to many of the leading families of Hertfordshire and Essex, including the Littons of Knebworth, the de Veres, and the Darcys of Tolleshunt d'Arcy, and as we discovered earlier they were also related to the Brownes of Sussex.

The Brownes of Sussex

The Brownes of Sussex were one of the most influential recusant families in the country. About 15 years before the Gunpowder Plot, Anthony-Maria Browne, later 2nd Viscount Montague, had briefly employed Guy Fawkes as a footman. This situation became embarrassing in 1605 when Fawkes was arrested. It was also known that Sir Anthony had planned to be absent from Parliament on 5th November, and it was thought that he had probably been warned by Catesby.

All this was enough to implicate him in the Plot. He was questioned by his father-in-law, Thomas Sackville, Earl of Dorset, but denied all knowledge of the conspiracy. He escaped trial, but paid a fine and served a term in prison.

William Byrd

His grandmother, Magdalen Viscountess Montague, a courageous old lady and loyal Catholic, held to her faith through all the searches and persecutions. She remembered happier days, when as a young Maid of Honour she had walked in the bridal procession at the marriage of Mary Tudor and Philip of Spain in Winchester Cathedral. She died in 1608 at her home near Battle, where there were five priests in the house to say Mass. William Byrd, a good friend of the family, wrote an elegy to mark her death. It is interesting to note that William Byrd was also a good friend of the Brownes of Essex.

Sir Anthony Browne of Cowdray

Anthony Browne was born about 1528 and was created 1st Viscount Montague in 1554. He was the only temporal peer to vote against the Act of Supremacy in 1559, and his houses at Cowdray and Battle Abbey, and also Montague House in London were resorts for deposed clergy and seminary priests. Midhurst and Battle became Catholic communities with their own priests, schoolmasters and doctors. Yet at the same time Anthony was a trusted and well-respected public servant. As a mark of her high regard for him the Queen paid a week-long visit to Cowdray in 1591, where she knighted his son, Anthony.

This Sir Anthony was never to become Lord Montague, as he died five months before his father, in 1591. He was married to Mary, the daughter of Sir William Dormer of Wing in Buckinghamshire, and had a son - Anthony Maria. On the death of his grandfather he became the 2nd Viscount Montague, who as we heard earlier was involved in the Gunpowder Plot.

In Burghley House at Stamford, once the home of William Cecil, Lord Burghley, there is a miniature by Isaac Oliver showing the three Browne brothers and their servant. The significance and identity of the servant is unknown, but it could possibly be Guy Fawkes, during the time when he was their footman. The picture shows Anthony-Maria standing between his two brothers, John and William.

After all his hair-raising adventures during his youth, Anthony-Maria, as far as we know, settled down to lead a fairly uneventful life and died in 1629. He had six children including Francis, who later became 3rd Lord Montague. One of his daughters married into the St John family of Bletsoe, and another daughter, Mary, was married to Robert, 3rd Lord Petre of Essex. Mary and Robert were both buried at Ingatestone.

A later link in the family network was created when Anastasia, the great-great granddaughter of Anthony-Maria, married Sir Thomas Mannock of Stoke-by-Nayland.

With all these family connections - the Ropers, Capells, Petres, and Mannocks - there surely must be a blood relationship between the early Brownes of Sussex and Essex. Perhaps Sir Anthony, who was knighted in 1377 at the Coronation of Richard II, was the ancestor not only of the Sussex family but also of the Brownes of Essex. One day, maybe, we shall solve the mystery.

The Browne brothers and their servant

Poley Monuments in Boxted Church

The alabaster statues are in memory of Sir John Poley,
who died in 1638, and his wife, Abigail, who died in 1652

Chapter 5

The Poleys of Boxted, Badley and Columbine Hall

Boxted, a quiet Suffolk village a few miles to the south of Bury St Edmunds, is set in a wooded valley with the church on the hillside above. For more than five centuries this was the home of the Poley family, and their memory is kept alive by the many monuments which can still be seen in the 15th century parish church. Their descendants, the Weller-Poleys, are still living in the village today.

But the Poleys were not only to be found here at Boxted. Another branch of the family settled in Badley, and for a time there were Poleys at Columbine Hall, a beautiful moated manor house on the outskirts of Stowmarket. Columbine Hall is best remembered (by the older generation) as the place where the Land Army girls were billeted during the war. The Poleys also appear in many of the other related families in Hertfordshire, Bedfordshire and Essex, who were all closely linked during the 16th and 17th centuries.

A Hertfordshire Family

The family did in fact originate in Hertfordshire, in the village of Codreth, now known as Cottered. The antiquarian Simonds D'Ewes, writing around 1630, suggests that they took their name from "Polheye, a town in that County", but there is no evidence that such a town ever existed. There was certainly a Humphrey de Poley living in Hertfordshire in the reign of Henry I, and we can assume that this was an ancestor of the Thomas Poley who came to Suffolk in the early 14th century.

Boxted had previously been owned by a member of the Hervey family, and Thomas presumably acquired it through his second marriage to Ann Badwell, a great-granddaughter of William Hervey. In the 13th century the Herveys held both Boxted and Ickworth, but the male line died out, and for several generations there were no Herveys at Ickworth. It was not until the 15th century that the Herveys of Thurleigh in Bedfordshire renewed the links with Ickworth by a marriage with Jane Drury.

A Water Mill and a Wind Mill

At the time when Thomas Poley acquired Boxted, after the death of William Hervey around 1250, the manor was described in detail in an Inquisition Post Mortem. In addition to the old manor house we are told that there were two mills, a water mill and a wind mill. "The former is no longer there, but it existed in the

1630s, and the wind mill still exists", says Arthur Hervey writing in 1863. But that too has now disappeared.

Much of our present information comes from this article written for "The Proceedings of the Suffolk Institute of Archaeology and History". The writer, Arthur Hervey, presumably a descendant of the family, was drawing on the writings of the antiquarian and historian Simonds D'Ewes in 1630, but there are several differences of opinion. Each historian has his own ideas and wants to stick to them. As we are reminded by Alexander Pope:

> Tis with our judgements as our watches, none
> Go just alike, yet each believes his own.

Pope of course was writing before the days of quartz clocks and radio signals from Rugby!   .

Hervey even dares to challenge Burke's Landed Gentry with reference to the date of birth of John, the son of Richard Poley and Anne Clopton: "He says John was baptised at Boxted on September 27 1539. He might as well have said 1839. For he tells us himself that John's third son Giles married in 1534, five years before his father was born! That Giles had a son born in 1561, whose grandfather therefore was under twenty two! That his wife died in 1561, her husband therefore being between twenty one and twenty two, having borne him at least six children."

Presumably on this occasion Burke had got his Johns mixed up - there were rather a lot of them. But perhaps the rest of us can take comfort from the fact that even the professionals get it wrong sometimes!

The Badley Branch

To go back to Thomas Poley who acquired the manor in the 13th century, we find that his first marriage was to Maud (or Alice) Gislingham. Their grandson Simon married Margaret Allcocke of Badley, thus founding the Badley branch of the family. In subsequent generations there were marriages into the Gedding, Gurney and Wentworth families.

Two miles south of Stowmarket is Badley Hall, which in its grander days was approached by a mile-long avenue running straight up from the Gipping valley. There is evidence that the Hall dates back to the 16th century, and some features of the original building remain. An imposing, but now disused, main entrance with its brick piers and ornamental pineapples can still be seen.

Through the Gedding family the Poleys were related to Anthony Earl Rivers, the de la Poles, and the Hunts of Hunts Hall in Ashen, who in turn were related to the Knightons, Soames and Stutvilles.

Columbine Hall

The Columbine Hall connection is less well documented but again it was from Thomas's first marriage to Maud or Alice Gislingham. Four generations later the marriage to Constance Gedding produced two sons. The younger son, William, married Constance Rokewood of Euston Park, leading to the Stowmarket branch of the family. Edmund, the elder son, married Myrabella Gurney of Kenton. Again they had two sons: John who married Ann, the daughter of Lord Wentworth, and Edmund of Columbine Hall. We have no details of his marriage.

We know that Columbine Hall was occupied at various times by the Hotofts, Tyrells, Carys and Gardiners, but where Edmund Poley fitted in we do not know. The manors at this time were seldom sold, they nearly always passed down the family line and if there were no male heirs the names would change from generation to generation. This was almost certainly the case at Columbine Hall and the Poleys were part of the family network.

The Clopton and Waldegrave Connections

Back at Boxted Hall, Thomas Poley and his second wife Ann Badwell were to found the family which would remain at Boxted right up to the present day. Their son Thomas married Alice Rokewood of Wormingford. Alice inherited her father's estates which for a time descended with the manor of Boxted, before passing to a younger branch of the family.

Thomas died in 1461 and was succeeded by his son John, a man-at-arms in the retinue of Lord Hastings, whose son Richard married Anne, the daughter of Sir William Clopton of Kentwell Hall. He died in 1543 and there is a brass memorial on the north side of the altar in Boxted Church.

Now we come to their daughter, Elizabeth Poley, who married into another closely connected family - the Waldegraves of Hitcham, and to their son John, who was the next heir. It was this John whose date of birth was wrongly recorded in Burke's Landed Gentry. He would have been born between 1490 and 1500 and he died in 1580 as a "very old man".

John Poley - Kind, Sensitive and Thoughtful

John comes over as a lovely character - kind and sensitive and thoughtful. In 1561 when he was about 70 years old he obviously felt it was time to hand over to his son William. His wife had died, and he thought that his son and daughter-in-law really needed to take up their place as Lord and Lady of the Manor. In cases where the Lady survived her husband she would usually move into the Dower House, but while the Lord of the Manor lived on, the son would not be able to inherit the home or the title.

But John had his own solution to the problem. He handed over the property to his son, but asked to be allowed to live on in the Manor House. All he asked was that he should reserve to his own use the "parloure at the end of the hall, with the chamber within the said parloure, stabling for two horses in the stable at the end of the barn, liberty to fish in the moat, river, and other waters, with egress and regress to the said parlour for himself and servant and friends, and liberty to be in the walks, orchards and gardens etc, at all tymes mete and convenient."

He also asked that he might keep one servant to attend to his household needs and to look after his horses. William arranged to pay him £26 13s. 4d. each year to cover the cost of sufficient meat and drink "mete and convenient to his estate, degree and condition."

It is hoped that John lived happily in his parlour at the end of the hall, and finally died peacefully in the adjoining bedchamber.

The Building of Boxted Hall

After inheriting the manor in 1561, William Poley built the mansion house - Boxted Hall, which is the house we see today.

William was married to Alice, the daughter and heiress of Edmund Shaa of Horndon House in Essex. Edmund's father, Sir John Shaa, was Lord Mayor of

A present-day view of Boxted Hall

London in 1501, and his grandfather, also Edmund, held the same office in 1482. Arthur Hervey gives us some interesting details from an old manuscript describing Horndon House, the home of Edmund Shaa and his ancestors. It is quoted here with the spelling modernised: "Horndon House, called The Place ... is a very fair lofty and ancient house built of very good timber with a wondrous large dining parlour and a fair Chapel of brick ... and it was in the time of King

Edward IVth the mansion house of Sir John Shaa, Knight, then Lord Mayor of London, whose heir is the now owner of this house by right descent".

William Poley died in 1587 and in Boxted Church there is an altar monument on which lie the life-sized effigies of William and Alice. They are made of wood, but perfectly preserved.

Wooden effigies are very rare and Arthur Mee tells us "there are not more than a hundred ancient wooden figures in the land". However, we do know of at least one more example of wooden effigies in Suffolk - the memorials to Michael de la Pole and his wife Katharine Stafford, which can be seen in Wingfield Church.

The Jermyn Connection

William was succeeded by his son, also William, who was married to Ann, the daughter of Sir Robert Jermyn of Rushbrooke. William was Member of Parliament for Sudbury in 1623 and 1628. His eldest daughter Judith married Sir Humphrey May, Vice Chamberlain to King Charles I. Their daughter Isabella was the wife of Sir Thomas Hervey and the mother of John, Earl of Bristol.

William died in 1629 and was succeeded by another William whose second wife Elizabeth was the daughter of Paul D'Ewes of Stowlangtoft Hall and the sister of the celebrated antiquary Sir Simonds D'Ewes.

A Third Crop of Peasen

This William kept detailed records of the estate. In a document dated 1630 he lists all his properties including Boxted, Horndon Markets, Barrow Hall and Aldhams Fee, and he also names all his tenants. He states that the tenant of Boxted Hall Manor Farm is to have "all the Dovehouse muck out of the Dovehouse belonging to Boxted Hall" and "ten cart loads of wood for fire-bote." The tenant of the "water mill called Boxted Mill" is bound "to prevent the flowings of the lord's meadows by drawing up his gates, and at such time as the lord shall dwell at his manor house, shall bring the best and choicest fish which shall happen to get in the myll-damme and rivers".

He also instructs his tenants not to take more than two corn crops in succession, but to fallow and "summertyll" according to the custom of the county - "a third crop of peasen ... alone excepted". Another tenant is told to "mewe a cast of hawkes at Boxted Hall every year".

The Advowson of Boxted

Another interesting note in these documents refers to the advowson of the church. "The Advowson of Boxted did long since belong to the manor, but now is united to Hartest and the Bishop of Ely presents to both churches together, yet they be severall parishes to all other purposes". Then there is a note in another hand-writing, "Noe such thing: exchanged with him, and the King presents".

Sir William died in 1664 and the following entry appears in the Parish Register: "Sir William Poley of Boxted, in the County of Suffolk, Knight, dyed there May 17th about eight o'clock in the morning, and was buried the 18th of the same, in the night about eleven or twelve o'clock. Decessit desideratus".

Boxted Church

William was succeeded by his son John who lived at Boxted for over forty years. John had three marriages, and the eldest son of the first marriage, another John, was his successor.

Sir John Poley, The Last Knight

In his "Notices of Suffolk Families" Sir Richard Gipps speaks warmly of Sir John, the last Knight of this branch: "Sir John Poley was a gentleman of a sound understanding, a sincere heart, and a plain, primitive and open behaviour, a loyal subject, and a true lover of his country; he was chosen Burgess of Sudbury without his knowledge, and sat in the Convention against his inclination, where, in a memorable debate, January 28th 1688, whether the throne was vacant, he made the following short speech".

We know from other sources that John faced a dilemma in having to help decide whether the Prince and Princess of Orange (William and Mary) were lawful contenders for the throne. The speech, though short, is too long to quote in full, but it begins: "Mr. Speaker, I am sent hither to do the Church and Caesar Right, to vindicate the Doctrines of one and preserve the Majesty of the other; both which are in Danger from Gentlemen's Arguments in the Debate of this Day. Mr. Speaker, here is an Affair of the greatest Weight before us, both as we are Christians and Englishmen; no less than the deposing a King whom we have sworn Allegiance to. Will our Religion or our Laws justify such a Proceeding? I know they will not".

When they were declared King and Queen "contrary to our known laws", Sir John retired to his seat at Boxted and never acted in a public station again.

The Weller-Poley Family

Sir John was a first cousin to Isabella, Lady Hervey, and in her diary she records John's death: "13th September 1705 my cousin John Poley of Boxted died".

His only surviving son succeeded him, but he died in 1757 unmarried. The next heir, his nephew Richard, also died without issue and the inheritance passed to his sister Elizabeth, the wife of Robert Weller of Tunbridge Wells. They had a son George Weller, born in 1710, who took the name Poley, and since that time Boxted has continued as the home of the Weller-Poley family.

The house was extensively altered in the 18th century, but much of the old building still remains. Arthur Hervey quotes an extract from the Terrier of 1631, which gives an idea of its condition in the 17th century:

> The scite of the Manor or Mansion House called Boxsted Hall, with the buildings yards and garden within, the moate, the court yards within the bowling ground therein, lying right before the house, the stable, the dovehouse, and dovehouse garden, the high house, the old orchard encompassing the moat round about the Mansion House, with the fishpond therein, the meadowe behind the house, the new orchard and the church hill lying by to the church, with the warren of conies there conteyninge in the whole by estimation, fifteen acres.
>
> The newe dairie house belonging to the Mansion or Manor House called Boxsted Hall, with a little yard lying before the said house, and the stable adjoining to the end of the saide house, together with the barne and a shed at the end thereof, a hoggefroate and cartlodge, and the yards wherein the same doe stande, called the barne yarde.

"The most interesting features in Boxted Hall of today", says Hervey, "are its picturesque situation, its ancient moat with the bridge still preserving decided Tudor features and the spacious hall with its handsome oak wainscoting of the sixteenth century. The collection of family pictures too is unusually perfect ...".

Chapter 5 - The Poleys

There are memorials of the Poley family in several Suffolk churches - but mainly at Boxted, which has many rare and beautiful monuments. A recent historian remarked: "The family certainly thought well of itself". And why not? Each generation wished to honour its predecessors, and the family produced many notable characters worthy of honour.

Arthur Hervey pays an eloquent tribute to the family, who have "shown themselves as capable of maintaining the honour of an ancient name, in public life, at home and abroad, in the senate and in the field, as they were of fulfilling the more quiet duties of country life, in their extensive charities, in their intercourse with their tenantry, and in social gatherings under their own hospitable roof".

The memory of this ancient family of Poley will remain, we hope, for many years to come.

Chapter 6

The Tyrells of Suffolk and Essex

The name of Tyrell immediately brings to mind the sad story of the murder of the Princes in the Tower. It was Sir James Tyrell of Gipping Hall, near Stowmarket, who was said to have committed this evil deed, but there are many differences of opinion and it is possible that Sir James was completely innocent. He did in fact meet his death by execution but this was 20 years later, and for quite a different reason.

Nine generations previously it was a member of the same Tyrell family who is said to have shot the arrow which killed William Rufus in the New Forest.

Gipping Hall at the time of the Conquest was known as Rokewood Hall. In the reign of Henry VI it passed to the Tyrell family, who held the manor for more than six centuries. They were descended from Sir Walter Tyrell, a Norman

Gipping Hall

Knight who soon after his arrival in England became tenant of the manor of Langham in Essex, which he held in the Domesday Survey under Richard de Tonbrigg.

William Tyrell Lord of the Manor of Gipping

It was around 1422 that William Tyrell became Lord of the Manor of Gipping. He was the son of Sir John Tyrell of Heron Hall at East Horndon in Essex and he was married to Margaret, daughter of Sir Robert Darcy of Maldon. It is thought that the so-called Abbot's Tomb in Stowmarket Church, with effigies of a lady in mitre head-dress with five sons and eight daughters, is for this Margaret. William was Treasurer of the Household to Henry VI, and in 1446 he was High Sheriff of Suffolk and Norfolk. In 1447 and again in 1459 he was also a Member of Parliament for Suffolk.

The Chapel of St. Nicholas at Gipping

While William and Margaret settled at Gipping, it seems that one of their sons, Thomas, went back to live at the old family home at Heron Hall, because we hear of him again in connection with the Browne family at Abbess Roding.

But it was their their eldest son who made a name for himself as the famous (or infamous) Sir James Tyrell. It was James who built the beautiful Chapel in the grounds of Gipping Hall, and it was thought by some to have been a penance for his wicked deed.

Gipping Hall was pulled down in the 1850s and the family moved to one of their other estates at Haughley. But fortunately the Chapel remains, and is still used as a place of worship.

Master of the Horse to Richard III

Sir James Tyrell was Master of the Horse to the newly crowned King Richard III and was obviously anxious to please his royal master. The Princes, Edward aged 13 and his 10 year old brother Richard, were the sons of the late King Edward IV. On the death of his father Edward briefly became King Edward V, but there were some doubts about his legitimacy and his Uncle Richard took the opportunity to seize the throne. But while the princes were alive Richard felt vulnerable. He managed to abduct the boys as they travelled to London with their mother Elizabeth Woodville, and imprisoned them in the Tower. According to Sir Thomas More, King Richard sent a message to Sir Robert Brakenberry, the Constable of the Tower, asking him to do away with them, but Sir Robert refused, saying he would rather die himself.

But the King did manage to get hold of the keys for one night and persuaded James Tyrell to carry out his wishes. Tyrell hired two "ruffians" who proceeded to smother the boys as they slept. Their bodies were said to have been buried under the stairs leading down from their bedchamber.

The Princes at Gipping Hall

Other writers have said that Tyrell was not involved, and some say that the princes were not killed at all. There is a story that Tyrell brought them secretly to Gipping Hall and from there arranged for them to be taken to Flanders.

Another story suggests that the elder prince, Edward, died of natural causes, and that his brother was smuggled out and lived incognito in Kent for the rest of his life. He was said to have worked as a brick-layer, and suspicions were aroused when it was reported that there was a brick-layer who spoke Latin!

Sir James was never formally accused of murdering the Princes in the Tower, but he did eventually come to a sad end. He was arrested for communicating with William de la Pole, who was executed for treason after his defeat in the French wars and his surrender to Joan of Arc. James was imprisoned in the Tower and he too was finally executed for treason in 1502.

Sir James Tyrell was married to Ann, the daughter of Sir John Arundell of Lanherne in Cornwall, and they had two sons. Thomas, the elder son, was attainted for treason with his father, but was later pardoned and all his estates, including Gipping Hall, were restored to him. The younger son, James, was fortunate enough to marry an heiress, Ann Hotoft of Columbine Hall, founding another branch of the family.

The Tyrells of Columbine Hall

Columbine Hall, just a few miles away at Stowupland, fortunately survived the centuries and still remains today, a beautiful moated farmhouse, part of which dates back to the 14th century. Throughout its long history it has been the home not only of the Tyrells but also of many other important families, all distantly related to each other. They include the Gardiners, the Poleys and also the Carys, who were related to Ann Boleyn, and even more closely related to King Henry VIII - but that's another story!

At home in Gipping Sir James seems to have been highly respected as a good and caring Lord of the Manor. He would no doubt still have royal duties but he would have spent part of his time at Gipping planning and supervising the building of the magnificent Chapel of St Nicholas, where some members of the family were baptised or married.

Over the door of the Chapel there is an inscription: "Pray for Sir James Tirrel and Dame Anne his wife", which some people have connected with his guilt for having murdered the princes.

The main line of Tyrells descended through Sir James's eldest son Thomas, and continued without a break until 1891 when Lieut Col. Walter Tyrell, the last male descendant, died at Plashwood, Haughley.

Moat Hall, Parham

During that time there were many notable characters and many links with the other leading families of Suffolk. Thomas was married to Margaret Willoughby, the daughter of Christopher Willoughby of Moat Hall, Parham. They had a son John and a daughter Anne who married Sir John Clare.

It seems that Thomas was not altogether happy with this union and in his will he made some very scathing remarks about his son-in-law. Thomas died in 1551 and was succeeded by his son John who had undoubtedly returned to royal favour and high office.

John attended Mary Tudor at Kenninghall and was knighted in 1553. He was married to Elizabeth Mundy, whose father Sir John Mundy was Lord Mayor of London in 1522.

The Sulyards of Wetherden

In the next generation John Tyrell married into the Sulyard family and inherited some of their estates at Wetherden and Haughley. His second marriage was to Mary Drury, linking the family with the Corbetts and Waldegraves, but he died without producing an heir.

His brother Thomas inherited all the Gipping and Wetherden estates. There was also a sister, Margaret, who set up the memorial to her brother Thomas and his family in Stowmarket Church.

In the next generation another Thomas married Ann Keable of Stowupland, and in 1676 the Tyrells were linked once again with a well-known family, when Thomas Tyrell married Keziah, the daughter of Sir William Hervey of Ickworth.

Financial Problems

Thomas at this stage seems to have had some financial difficulties - probably leading the high life - and ran up debts of £1,060 - about £70,000 in today's money - and Gipping Hall, with all its wide-ranging lands and properties was mortgaged to his uncle Edmund Tyrell of Norwich.

Apparently Keziah's father, who must have been a wealthy man, was unable or unwilling to help his son-in-law. In the archives is an inventory made at the time of the settlement, which gives an idea of the contents of a grand house in 1678 and the values of the various items:

> In the Parlour - three tables and eleven
> cushion stools, one couch and nine
> cushion chairs   £5. 15s.
> Carpets cushions and chairs   £11. 00.
> Four large pictures   4s.
> Several books   £2. 10s.
> In his Lodging Chamber - one downe bed,
> 2 feather beds with curtains and other
> furnishings   £20. 00.
> In the Porters Lodge - an old bed and
> lumber   £2. 10s.

Beds seem to have been among the most expensive items. We read that in the Storehouse were "two beds as they stand with all the furnishings - £20". But a gun case of pistols and a sword were only £2. There is no mention of silver, but the 'plate' is valued at £11. Two carts, two tumbrells and harness for the horse were £7. The total value of all the goods was £398. 10s. 4d. and this included about 20 beds which together were worth about £150 - a large proportion of the total. The beds would no doubt have had elaborate curtains and covers.

It seems that Thomas never managed to redeem the mortgage and his two daughters appear to have lived in comparative poverty in Bury St Edmunds.

A Warning to Future Generations

Later the property descended to Uncle Edmund's son Thomas, who now owned all the estates. But he also seems to have been in difficulties and in 1698 mortgaged Gipping Manor to James Gibbs of Ipswich for £300. Thomas's son. however, another Edmund, evidently managed to redeem the mortgage once again. There is a note in the records of 1742 in which Edmund gives a solemn warning to future members of the family:

"Let these mortgage deeds which I have redeemed be a monument of Terrour to succeeding generations of the Tyrells never to involve their estates and heirs in such difficulties as my Father did me which often proves the Ruin and destruction of men and Familys and let them remember that if they do recover their ancient Inheritances after fresh involvements 'tis only and solely the Hand of Heaven which helps them out of such and all other difficulties. Laus Deo. Edmund Tyrell 1742".

Future generations obviously heeded this warning, and the property stayed in the Tyrell family for many years to come. In 1811 it passed to Charles Tyrell, who in 1815 was High Sheriff of Suffolk, and was a Member of Parliament for the county from 1830-34.

From the Parish Registers

From the Parish Registers we get more intimate details of family life during the last years at Gipping Hall. One entry in 1735 tells us: "Thomas Tyrell of Gipping, Esq. in his 69th year, dying at his house about the middle of the night of 26 March at his home at Stow Market was buried in his own aisle inherited from his ancestors". This refers to the North Aisle of Stowmarket Church with the Tyrell Chapel at the end.

In 1739 Duke, the son of Edmund Tyrell of Gipping Hall and of Mary his wife, was "baptised privately at the Hall on 24 June and on 30 Aug received more publicly into the Congregation of Christs Flock at the Chapel of Gipping". Sadly we read that on November 10th, "Duke, the son of Edmund Tyrell and Mary his wife was buried at Stow Market". In 1740 they had another baby,

Mary, who was "baptised in a private chamber at the Hall on 10 June, having been born the day before about six of the clock in the afternoon".

The following year we read that Mary, the late wife of Edmund Tyrell, died on the 2nd and was buried at Stow Market on the 6th of November, and that their son who had been born and baptised at the Hall on Oct 31st, died on 20 Nov. In 1744 Edmund remarried and in 1745 they had a little son Edmund who presumably survived.

The last entry was for John Downing, Coachman from Gipping Hall, who died of Smallpox in 1749 and was buried "in this churchyard". His headstone in Old Newton churchyard states that he died 29 July 1749 aged 39.

Memorials in Stowmarket Church

Although the Tyrells had their own family Chapel they looked upon Stowmarket as their Mother Church, and it is here that most of the members of the family are buried.

Thomas Tyrell and his family in Stowmarket Church

There are various Tyrell tombs and memorials, including an effigy of Margaret Tyrell mentioned earlier, together with her brother Thomas and his wife Mary, with their 6 sons and 4 daughters. Margaret, though twice married, had no children of her own. Her second husband was Edward English and the inscription reads "To the memory of Margaret English of the City of Westminster, one of the daughters of Sir John Tirell, Knight ....". Margaret left £100 to provide an annuity for the relief of the poor of Stowmarket.

All the Tyrells were very much involved with Stowmarket, which was part of their home territory. We can imagine them coming into the town on horseback, cantering through the woods and across the fields, down Stowupland Hill and across the river into the town. Then after stabling the horse at one of the inns, they would walk along the very same roads which we know so well today.

The Rev'd Thomas Young - Tutor to John Milton

Not many of the houses have survived from those early days but some of the Tyrells would have known and probably visited the Old Vicarage in what is now called Milton Road.

In the 17th century this was the home of the Rev'd Thomas Young, who had been tutor to the poet John Milton when he was at Cambridge. John Milton often came to stay at the Vicarage, and is said to have planted the mulberry tree which survived into the 20th century, and is probably still there today.

Abbot's Hall would also have been familiar to the early Tyrells. It was the Manor House of Stowmarket, built on

The Rev'd Thomas Young
Tutor to John Milton

the site which previously belonged to the Priory of St Osyth.

The Tyrells also had their own town house in Stowmarket, thought to have been Lynton House, which still stands on the corner of Gipping Way.

During these years the Essex branch of the family were at Heron Hall, but they were still in contact with their Gipping cousins. Sir James Tyrell's brother, Sir Thomas, was a friend of the Browne family of Abbess Roding, and his son John was betrothed as a child to Anne, the 4 year old daughter of William Browne, who was at this time Lord Mayor of London.

Anne and John were married in 1521 when Anne was 12 years old. John died without a male heir in 1540, but they had 2 daughters, Anne and Catherine. We know a great deal about Catherine because of a connection with the Petre family of Ingatestone Hall.

The Brownes of Abbess Roding were close friends and neighbours of the Petres of Ingatestone Hall. Little Anne Browne, who was betrothed at the age of 4 and married at the age of 12 to Sir John Tyrell of Gipping, was widowed at the age of 34. Two years later she married Sir William Petre, Deputy to Thomas Cromwell and Principal Secretary to Queen Mary. So Anne's daughters by her first marriage became Sir William Petre's step-daughters and went to live at Ingatestone Hall.

The Wedding of Catherine Tyrell at Ingatestone

The Petres kept detailed estate records which included all the household expenses, and we have the good fortune to know exactly what was provided at the wonderful feast for Catherine Tyrell's wedding in 1552.

In the week before the wedding they used 600 eggs and 8 gallons of cream for the puddings and custards, and on the feast day itself the dinner included a whole ox and a quarter, 4 veals, 6 lambs, 2 kids, 2 bucks, 22 geese, and dozens of rabbits, chickens, partridge and quails.

We are not told how many cooks and servants they employed but it must have been a vast number. For supper on the wedding day they consumed 5 muttons, 4 lambs, 1 kid, 1 buck, 15 capons, 3 pheasants, 3 dozen chickens, 36 rabbits, 20 pairs of pigeons, 4 peachickens and 2 dozen quails!

Sir James Tyrell - Guilty or Not Guilty?

Finally, going back once more to Sir James Tyrell. Did he really murder the Princes in the Tower? Certainly Sir Thomas More had no doubts whatsoever. He was quite convinced that Sir James was guilty.

Shakespeare, a hundred years later, also assumes the same - but of course he was writing to impress the public and needed to name the murderer for dramatic reasons. In his Richard III, Act IV, James Tyrell's soliloquy includes the following words:

> The tyrannous and bloody act is done
> The most arch deed of piteous massacre
> That ever yet this land was guilty of.

But there is no evidence that Sir James was an evil person. He was loyal to his friends and he spent his wealth to help the poor and to build the beautiful Chapel which gives pleasure and inspiration right up to the present day.

A Public Testimony of Respectful Regard

The Rev'd A G H Hollingsworth of Stowmarket writes: "He was not unpopular in the town and the stone laid over his grave and its brasses were paid for by both parishes [Stowmarket and Gipping] and the parishioners in this manner gave a public testimony of their respectful regard for his memory".

Even if he was responsible for this tragic episode it does not necessarily make him an evil man, in view of the harsh and ruthless customs of the times. The only person really to blame would have been the King himself, Richard III.

Many things have been done in the name of loyalty to a Leader or Cause, or simply because they were considered to be the will of God, things which might afterwards be regretted. We are reminded of Shakespeare's famous lines:

> The evil that men do lives after them
> The good is oft interred with their bones

So perhaps the people of Suffolk can be proud of the Tyrells, who did so much for their community and for the county, and if Sir James really did do that infamous deed, he must surely by now have repented and earned his forgiveness.

The remains of Heron Hall, Essex

Chapter 7

The Herveys of Ickworth Hall

The Harvey (or Hervey) family of Ickworth Hall is well known in Suffolk and possibly throughout the world for many reasons. But it may be surprising to know that, although the name was associated with Ickworth back in the 13th and 14th centuries, the Hervey family we know today had its roots in Bedfordshire. They came to Suffolk when Thomas Harvey of Thurleigh married Jane Drury, who inherited Ickworth on the death of her father around 1475.

The story begins with a certain John Harmer who held the manor of Wroxhill in Marston Moreteyne a few miles south of Bedford. He acquired it from Richard de Argentein for one quarter of a knight's fee in the year 1286.

The Marriage of Joan Harmer and John Harvey

John Harmer also owned the manor of Thurleigh just to the north of Bedford. His daughter Joan married John Harvey from the adjoining parish of Riseley, and when John Harmer died in 1297 Joan inherited Thurleigh, while her brother John inherited Wroxhill. So it was Joan Harmer and her husband John Harvey who founded the family which was later to become the Hervey family of Ickworth. Joan and John Harvey had a son William and a grandson John, who was a Justice of the Peace for Bedford in 1382 and was knighted in 1386. Two generations later Thomas Harvey married Jane, the daughter of William Paston of Norfolk. They had a son Thomas, who was Chamberlain of London, and also a daughter Elizabeth, who was Abbess of Elstow, and whose memorial can still be seen in Elstow Abbey Church.

A Suffolk Heiress - Jane Drury of Ickworth

In the next generation there were two sons - Thomas who was admitted to Lincoln's Inn in 1475, and John a Member of Parliament for Bedford in 1474. John's son George was the next heir, but unfortunately his wife bore him no sons. He did however have one 'natural' son, Gerard Smart, who was later adopted by his father and took the name of Harvey. He later inherited all the Thurleigh estates. His uncle Thomas, however, was lucky enough to marry a Suffolk heiress, Jane Drury of Ickworth, thus linking Ickworth once again with the Harveys, and founding the family which still has connections with Ickworth right up to the present day.

The Bedfordshire and Suffolk branches of the family continued to keep in close touch, reinforcing the links with frequent marriages between cousins. Some of the Hertfordshire families were also forming new links with the Harveys. In 1602 Mary Harvey of Thurleigh married Thomas Fairclough of Weston in Hertfordshire and a few years later one of the Harveys is mentioned in Rebecka Harmer's will. It seems therefore that the 13th century Harmers of Wroxhill Manor and Thurleigh were almost certainly ancestors or kinsmen of the Harmers and Faircloughs of Weston.

Ickwell Bury in Bedfordshire

In 1680 one of the Thurleigh Harveys acquired the manor of Ickwell Bury in Bedfordshire from his kinsman Robert Barnardiston, a relative of the Barnardistons of Suffolk. The Barnardistons had property at Northill in Bedfordshire, and also at Kedington or Ketton in Suffolk.

The Suffolk branch of the Harvey family now continued to flourish at Ickworth. (There seems to be no connection between Ickwell in Bedfordshire and Ickworth

Ickwell Bury, Bedfordshire

in Suffolk, but the similarity of the two names can sometimes be confusing). The Ickworth family around this time began to use the alternative spelling of their name, and from now on they became known as Hervey - although the pronunciation was still the same.

Thomas Hervey and Jane Drury had a son William, who like his father, studied law at Lincoln's Inn. He died in 1538 and was buried in St Mary's Church at Bury St Edmunds. His eldest son, Sir Nicholas Hervey, actually went back to live in Bedfordshire at Bakenloo Manor.

Nicholas was a member of the Royal Household at the time of Henry VIII, and ambassador to Emperor Charles V in 1530. He died in 1532, during his father's lifetime, and was buried at Ampthill in Bedfordshire. His youngest brother

Edward was also a member of the Royal Household, and at the time of the Dissolution he was granted part of the manor of Elstow, where his great-great aunt Elizabeth had once been Prioress.

The Poley and Darcy Connections

It was William's second son, John, who became the next Lord of the Manor at Ickworth and he was married to Elizabeth, the daughter of Henry Pope of Mildenhall. They had two sons, William and Francis, and six daughters. Francis was a Gentleman Pensioner to Queen Elizabeth. He was married first to Mary Nevill and secondly to Camilla Guicciardini of Florence, who was the widow of Thomas Darcy of Tolleshunt Darcy in Essex.

William Hervey, the elder son and heir, married Elizabeth, a member of another well-known local family, the Poleys of Boxted. William and Elizabeth again had a large family, four sons and three daughters, and their eldest son married Frances Bocking of Bocking in Essex. John was the next heir, followed by his son Sir William Hervey.

The Gage Family of Hengrave Hall

Here we have links with the Gage family of Hengrave Hall, when William Hervey married Penelope Darcy, daughter and co-heir of Thomas, Earl Rivers. Both Penelope and Sir William had been married before. Penelope was first married to Sir George Trenchard, but she was widowed at the age of 17. Her second marriage was to Sir John Gage by whom she had a large family. Her marriage to Sir William Hervey was her third marriage - and there were no children.

Sir William Hervey's first marriage was to Susan, the daughter of Sir Robert Jermyn of Rushbrooke. They were married in 1612 at St Mary's Church in Bury St Edmunds. Susan bore him 12 children - five sons and seven daughters. Their eldest son John, we are told, was Treasurer to Queen Catherine. This would have been Catherine of Braganza, the unhappy wife of Charles II. She had no children, but Charles had several offspring through his various mistresses including the famous Nell Gwyn.

John Hervey was married to Elizabeth, the daughter of Lord Hervey of Kid-brooke, but they had no children and the inheritance went to his brother, Sir Thomas Hervey, whose wife Isabella was the daughter of Sir Humphrey May, who had been Chamberlain of the Household to Charles I.

The next heir was their son John, born in 1665, who was married to another Isabella, the daughter and heir of Sir Robert Carr of Sleaford. John was a Member of Parliament, and he was a supporter of the Revolution of 1688 and the Hanoverian Succession. In this he would have strongly disagreed with his kinsmen, the Poleys, who were very definitely opposed to it, supporting the cause of James II's son, James Stuart - and the Roman Catholic faith. In March 1703 John was created 1st Earl of Bristol.

John had no children by his first wife, but his second wife, Elizabeth Felton of Playford, made up for it by producing 16 children - eight sons and eight daughters - plenty of potential heirs! In fact he did not need the extra 'spares' as his eldest son George succeeded him and became the 2nd Earl of Bristol. He was Ambassador to the Court of Spain and Lord Keeper of the Privy Seal, but he died in 1775 without issue.

Now the 'spares' came in useful after all. Augustus John Hervey succeeded his brother, but died five years later without producing any offspring. So it came about that the third and most remarkable son, Frederick Augustus Hervey, became the 4th Earl of Bristol, and he left his mark on the Suffolk landscape in a very dramatic way.

A Decidedly Eccentric Character

A decidedly eccentric character, Frederick Augustus was married to Elizabeth, daughter of Sir Jermyn Davers of Rushbrooke. He became a Doctor of Divinity and in 1768 was created Bishop of Derry in Ireland. From this time on he was generally know as the Earl Bishop.

Derry was the richest diocese in the whole of Ireland, and in addition to the wealth which this brought him, he also had the income from 30,000 acres of family estates in Suffolk and Lincolnshire. He was described as a part-time bishop, and he spent most of his life in Italy as a patron and collector of art. He did very little for his flock in Ireland, but strangely he seems to have been popular, and the poverty-stricken Irish country folk raised a memorial to him after his death.

Travelling in Italy and throughout Europe he accumulated a wonderful collection of paintings, sculptures and other treasures, but few of them found their way back to Ickworth. When Napoleon's army occupied Rome in 1798 the whole collection was seized before he could ship them back to England.

The Building of Ickworth Hall

It was this 4th Earl, Frederick Augustus, who was responsible for the building of Ickworth Hall, described by Eric Sandon as "one of the most ambitious Palladian houses in England". It seems that when the Earl inherited the manor in 1779 he had never been to Ickworth. Where he was born we do not know, but we do know that he spent part of his life in Ireland, but lived mostly in Italy.

When he visited Ickworth for the first time he was disappointed with the flat Suffolk landscape which was "totally unsuitable for sublime architecture", and particularly for the Italian style palazzo which he envisaged.

Apparently a new mansion house had already been proposed by one of the two brothers who preceded him, and plans for an entire new house with landscaped gardens had been drawn up by Capability Brown (for which he charged £105). But nothing came of these plans, which perhaps was rather unfortunate.

An Italian Architect, Mario Asprucci

The final project was for a rotunda with two curving wings, and was designed by a little-known Italian architect, Mario Asprucci. Eric Sandon writes "It is difficult to see the idea of a house in the form of an enormous central oval as anything but an eccentric design". Apparently the Earl had previously attempted a similar building in Ireland, though on a smaller scale, and this had proved disappointing.

The building of this vast house was a challenge in every way. A huge oval hole was dug out and within the oval was a basement storey, with some of the walls 7ft 6in thick. The house was built mainly of bricks which were made in kilns specially set up on the estate for this purpose. The large clay pits, now mainly filled with water, can still be seen to the west of the house.

Died in Rome, Buried at Ickworth

The work started in 1795 and was still nowhere near completion when the Earl died in Rome in July 1803 - without ever having seen his wonderful palazzo. He was buried - or presumably re-buried - at Ickworth in 1804. There is an interesting story about how the body was brought back to England. It is said that superstitious sailors were unwilling to have a dead body on board, so it had to be packed as an antique statue - presumably they encased it in some kind of stone shell. A fitting climax perhaps to the career of a man who spent his life collecting statues and similar works of art.

Frederick Augustus and his wife Elizabeth had three sons and three daughters. The first son, George, died at the age of 9 and the second son, Augustus, a Captain in the Royal Navy, died at 21, so it was Frederick William, the third son, who succeeded his father as Earl of Bristol. In 1826 he was created Marquess of Bristol and Earl Jermyn of Great Horningsheath; High Steward of the Liberty of St Edmund.

Frederick William, 1st Marquess of Bristol

Fortunately the Earl (later Marquess) had the courage to carry on with his father's eccentric project - he probably had no choice! The work was finished in 1829, but it never achieved its Palladian purpose - which would be for the rotunda to form the living area, and the wings with their curving corridors to be used as galleries for exhibitions of magnificent works of art.

The term "eccentric" has already been used on several occasions in connection with the Hervey family, and we are reminded that John Timpson in his book "Timpson's English Eccentrics" did include a member of the Hervey family. This was Sir Harvey Elwes of Stoke College at Stoke-by-Clare, mentioned in a another chapter. He was the son of Gervase Elwes and Isabella Hervey, and was one of the richest men in England. He owned most of the land in and around Ashen, but lived in unbelievable squalor. Sir Harvey and his nephew became known as the Misers of Ashen and they are described in more detail in "Forgotten Families of Hertfordshire and Bedfordshire".

Timpson also refers to the Hervey family in another of his books,"Timpson's Travels in East Anglia". He quotes one guide book which refers to Ickworth Hall as "the eighteenth century equivalent of one of the Pyramids of Egypt, a vast monumental edifice put up by a very rich man for his self-glorification".

Perhaps this is rather harsh. Frederick Augustus was trying to fulfil a dream which just didn't work out, and his son simply tried to make the best of a bad job out of loyalty to his father, and because there wasn't much else he could do.

A Little English Eccentricity

Timpson mentions that a French traveller reckoned that all the Harveys were a little mad, and quoted Voltaire as saying that in England he met three kinds of people - men, women and Harveys. "Such views from two Frenchmen put me on the side of the Harveys", says Timpson, "you can't beat a little English eccentricity". And I think I tend to agree with him. Perhaps you can either be boring and nice, or interesting and outrageous, although hopefully there could be a happy medium.

Frederick William Hervey, 1st Marquess of Bristol, who nobly continued and completed the building of Ickworth Hall, was succeeded by his son Frederick, born in 1800 and usually known as Earl Jermyn. Like many of his predecessors and successors he was a Member of Parliament for Suffolk. He was married in 1830 at St James' Westminster to Katherine Isabella, daughter of the Duke of Rutland. Three of his sisters, Augusta, Georgiana and Sophia were married into the families of Lord Seymour, Earl Grey, and William Windham of Felbrigg Hall in Norfolk. His son Frederick was to become the 3rd Marquess of Bristol. He was born in 1834 and was baptised at St Mary's

Detail from the frieze on the Rotunda

Putney, his Godfather being HRH the Duke of Gloucestor. But his daughter Adelaide went one better. Her Godmother was Her Majesty Queen Victoria!

The Pompeian Room at Ickworth

In 1859 Frederick was elected Member of Parliament for West Suffolk, and from 1886-1907 he was Lord Lieutenant of Suffolk. He created the famous Pompeian Room at Ickworth, with designs based on Roman wall paintings which were uncovered in 1777.

He died in 1907 and was succeeded by his nephew Frederick William Fane Hervey, the 4th Marquess, who was later Member of Parliament for Bury St Edmunds. When he died in 1951 his younger brother, Lord Herbert Hervey, became the 5th Marquess.

By the time we come to the 6th Marquess of Bristol, Victor Frederick Cochrane Hervey, the storm clouds are gathering for this ancient and illustrious family. There are rumours of the sale of arms to both sides in the Spanish Civil War, and of a bungled Mayfair jewel robbery as a result of a drunken bet.

But every great family has its black sheep. Sometimes their misdeeds are hidden away as 'skeletons in the cupboard'. And if they do eventually come to light they may even take on a certain glamour. The Bishop, Frederick Augustus, might perhaps have been considered a black sheep. It was not very honourable to neglect his duties in Ireland, and accept large sums of money to indulge his passion for art and Italy. And some people might even find it difficult to forgive him for Ickworth Hall!

Things are rather different now, with scandal-mongering newspapers and media outlets clamouring for a good story. But in spite of all the recent problems the Hervey family can be proud of its history - its many services to the Church, the Crown and the State - not forgetting the Harvey's Bristol Cream! The family which originated from John Harvey and Joan Harmer of Thurleigh 700 years ago, and has since been linked with many of the other distinguished families in Hertfordshire, Bedfordshire, Suffolk and Essex, will certainly survive the storms, and prove itself worthy of its illustrious past.

Ickworth Hall West Wing and Rotunda

Chapter 8

The Underhills of Little Bradley
Linked with Knighton, Soame and Daye

It might at first seem rather unfortunate to have an ancestor with the name of Underhill. The family is seldom mentioned in the history books, and when we find that they came from a rather remote little Suffolk village on the borders of Cambridgeshire and Essex, we might expect them to melt into oblivion.

The Underhill name does in fact disappear after two or three generations, but on further investigation we find that their family held the manors of Great and Little Bradley for over 400 years.

Working back from the Underhills we come to the Caldebeck, Aspall, Peche and Peverell families. From Sir Payne Peverell who lived around 1100 we can trace our way back step by step to Alfred the Great. We could go even further, but you have to draw the line somewhere!

Of course these early records are not always to be trusted, and even the later ones can be confusing. Different historians tell different stories according to their own ideas and perspectives.

In the early days following the Conquest the Bradleys were owned by the de Clares, one of the most powerful families in the country. In 1205 the manors were held by Sir John Botetout and his wife Matilda, who was the granddaughter of William de Beauchamp, Baron of Bedford. Later they came into the possession of Sir Payne Peverell.

The Peverell and Peche Families

The Peverells appear several times in the early stages of the family history. Ranulf Peverell held the manor of Aspall before 1066 and was an ancestor of the Brooke family. He was also an ancestor of the Piggots of Tewin in Hertfordshire and the de la Poles of Wingfield.

The daughter of Sir Payne Peverell married Hammond Lord Peche, who was succeeded by five generations of Peches all bearing either the name Hammond or Gilbert, which causes some confusion.

Gilbert, the 3x great grandson, we are told, held the manor of "Little Bradley, Overhall or Harveys" in 1322, and we know that the Peches already owned the manor of Great Thurlow. This Gilbert married the daughter of Sir Hugh Waterville and they had one daughter, Catherine, who was the sole heir.

Catherine Peche was married first to Sir John Aspall, of Aspall Hall (later the home of Edward Brooke, Lord Cobham). Her second marriage was to Sir Thomas Notbeame. There was no son by either marriage - so no male heir. Mirabel Aspall and her husband William Gedding, who already held lands in Great and Little Thurlow, inherited a small part of the manor, but Margaret Notbeame who married John Hinkley was the main heir.

In the next generation the descent is again through the female line, when Griselda (or Cecily) Hinkley married Henry Caldebeck. Their daughter Thoma-sine inherited the manor. She married into the Turnor family of Horseheath but had no children. Her second marriage was to Thomas Underhill who now inherited the property.

The manor at this time was known as "Harveys" - suggesting a link with the Harvey family of Ickworth, which is confirmed by the fact that the Harvey arms appear on one of the memorial brasses in Little Bradley Church.

The Underhills, like their predecessors, were apparently not very clever at producing male heirs, and the manors continued to descend mainly through the female line, giving us a wide variety of names, which included many of the leading families of Suffolk. There were also connections with Cambridgeshire and Essex but the strongest links were with Hertfordshire. The Underhills married into the Knighton and Bull families, leading us back in a direct line to the Harmers who were first recorded in Hertfordshire in 1555.

Thomas Underhill, Master of Northill College

But before we leave the Underhills (the family itself of course continues at Little Bradley for many more generations, but under different names) there are two more references which may at some time throw new light on the family. One is connected with Northill in Bedfordshire where a Thomas Underhill is recorded as Master of Northill College. Stanford, a neighbouring village, was the home of the Hunt family, and the area has many other family connections.

A second mystery yet to be solved is the reference to a certain Edward Underhill who was descended from the Mauvesin family and whose mother may have been one of the Herveys of Ickworth. This could well have been the Edward Underhill who is described as an "evangelical Yeoman of the Guard", who intervened to prevent the printer John Daye from being arrested for his scathing attacks on the Roman Catholic doctrines.

Memorials in Little Bradley Church

From now on much of the history of the Underhill descendants can be discov-ered from the memorials in Little Bradley Church. The Church, parts of which date back to the 11th century, stands quietly all by itself at the end of a narrow country lane. The exterior is comparatively plain and unadorned but it has a certain dignity of its own which is even more apparent as we go inside.

It is evident from the various effigies and inscriptions that this is a place which has been sacred to the memory of many ancient families. It is obviously still loved and cherished by the people who worship here today. It is beautifully kept, and has an air of peace and tranquillity.

We can imagine the Underhills and the Knightons, the Soames, the Hunts, and the Dayes, worshipping here with their families. We can feel their happiness at the baptism of a new baby, the joy of a newly married couple, and the sad farewells as loved ones are laid to rest under these ancient stones.

Sadly some of the memorials have been damaged over the years, but they still serve their purpose as reminders of the people who lived here long ago.

The earliest monument shows two kneeling figures and is presumably part of a much more elaborate brass. There is a stone shield with the arms of Underhill impaling Caldebeck, denoting the marriage between Thomas Underhill and Thomasine Caldebeck.

Next we have the headless knight in armour. This is Thomas Knighton, the son of Thomas Knighton of Bayford in Hertfordshire and Ann Underhill, the daughter of Thomas and Thomasine. The monument appears to be very well pre-served, but why has Thomas lost his head? It is thought to have been re-moved at the time of the Dissolution, when Henry VIII ordered all religious symbols in the churches to be destroyed. The soldiers who carried out the mutila-tion exceeded their orders. They were not instructed to interfere with family monu-ments - only the sacred ones.

Richard le Hunt and his family

The le Hunt monument suffered the same fate: the mother and all the children are headless. The father, Richard le Hunt, dressed as a knight in armour, has had his head returned, thanks to the initiative of Mr Robert Clifton-Brown, one of the present Churchwardens. When building work was going on some years ago Robert searched among the rubble and discovered the head which he ingeniously re-attached to the body.

The Knighton Family of Hertfordshire and Suffolk

In the early 1500s the manor of Bayford was bought by John Knighton from King Henry VIII for £317 13s. 9d, and it was John's son Thomas who married Ann Underhill of Little Bradley.

When his father died, Thomas Knighton inherited Bayford, but he chose to go and live on his wife's estate in Suffolk. All his children were born there, but his eldest son, Thomas, married a Hertfordshire lady, Alice Bull of Hertford. This Thomas is described in the Hertfordshire Visitations as Thomas Knighton of

Bayfordbury, the Hertfordshire home of the Knightons

Brickendon (a manor near Bayford which was later held by the Kympton family). But in the Suffolk Visitations he is described as Thomas Knighton of Harveys in Little Bradley, and as we know, his memorial is in Little Bradley Church.

There were still however strong links with Hertfordshire, and particularly with the Bull family. Thomas Knighton's sister Jane married Alice Bull's brother Charles, and while Thomas and Alice stayed in Suffolk, Jane and Charles lived in Hertford, where Charles was soon to inherit considerable estates from his father Richard Bull.

Both the Suffolk and the Hertfordshire Visitations describe the Knighton family arms. The Suffolk account is as follows:

> Quarterly, 1 and 4, Barry of eight Or and Azure on a
> canton Gules a ton of the first (Knighton) 2 and 3
> Underhill, impaling Browne.

This was obviously granted to Thomas the younger and included his mother's family, Underhill, which we now learn also included the Browne family. This was almost certainly the family from Abbess Roding in Essex, related to Ann Browne, the second wife of Sir William Petre of Ingatestone Hall.

Thomas Knighton and Alice Bull of Little Bradley had a daughter and two sons. The daughter, Ann Knighton, was married first to Richard le Hunt, of Hunt's Hall in Ashen, Essex, and secondly to Thomas Soame of Beetly in Norfolk. The eldest son of this marriage, also Thomas Soame, is pictured with his wife Elizabeth Alington and their seven children on another of the brasses in Little Bradley Church. One of the other sons of Ann Knighton and Thomas Soame was Sir Stephen Soame, Lord Mayor of London in 1598.

The Bull Family of Hertford

The Knightons were very closely connected with the Bull family of Hertford - in fact, as we discovered earlier, a brother and sister married a sister and brother. Thomas Knighton, the headless figure in Little Bradley Church, was married to Alice Bull, while his sister Jane Knighton married Alice's brother Charles.

Charles and Alice were the children of Richard Bull and Helen Skipwith of St Albans. Helen's father, William Skipwith, was High Sheriff of Hertfordshire and Essex in 1503 and 1504, and once owned many of the properties previously belonging to St Albans Abbey. The Bull family owned a large part of the town of Hertford and had several estates in the surrounding villages.

Charles and his wife moved back to Hertfordshire after their marriage at Little Bradley, and their grandson Richard Bull was later Mayor of Hertford. Richard Bull was married to Alice Hunt, whose brother Richard Hunt married Ann Knighton of Little Bradley.

With the cross-marriages between brothers and sisters in the Bull, Knighton and Hunt families this is all very confusing but maybe the pedigree at the back of this book will help to sort it out! The situation becomes even more complicated when we come to second marriages - as we are about to discover.

John Daye and Foxes Book of Martyrs

Alice Hunt, the daughter of Richard Hunt and Ann Knighton, had two marriages - the first to John Daye the printer, and second to William Stone of Segenhoe in Bedfordshire.

When John Daye married Alice Hunt he was already a widower and the father of 13 children. By his marriage to Alice he had another 13 children, who are shown on the memorial brass on the north wall of the chancel in Little Bradley Church.

John Daye was the foremost printer of his time. He produced the first English Church Book with tunes accompanying the words. He printed Queen

John Daye 1522-84

Elizabeth's prayer book in six languages and numerous other writings, including some by a certain Henry Bull of London. We do not know exactly who this Henry Bull might be, but it seems very likely that he was connected with John Daye's in-laws, who were part of the Bull family of Hertford. But his most famous book was Foxe's Acts and Monuments, which is usually known as Foxe's Book of Martyrs.

John Daye was born in Dunwich in 1522 and by the age of 25 he had set up his printing business in London and had his own house in Aldersgate.

He soon became the most highly respected printer in the country, having licences from members of the royal family and printing all the most important books of the period, including the complete works of William Tyndale, John Frith and Robert Burns.

He specialised in luxury editions, using top quality paper and elaborate bindings. They were very costly to produce as the paper had to be imported from the Continent, but they sold well and John became both famous and wealthy.

He had some influential friends who no doubt helped to further his career. They included William Cecil who later became Queen Elizabeth's First Minister, and Elizabeth's favourite, Robert Dudley. Daye frequently worked with John Foxe, not only on the many editions of the Book of Martyrs but on many other projects. He was not just a printer, but did a great deal of research and editing.

Church of England Versus Roman Catholicism

John Daye was a zealous supporter of the new Church of England, rather than the old church of Rome, and when Mary came to the throne he was in trouble for printing scathing comments about the Roman Catholic doctrines - especially the vexed question of transubstantiation. At last he had to go into hiding in Lincolnshire, but he managed to set up his own clandestine printing press, from which he continued to publish writings under the pseudonym of Michael Wood.

In October 1554 Daye was arrested as he came out of Norfolk, probably having been to Kings Lynn to receive a cargo of paper from the Continent. He was imprisoned in the Tower, but was released in June 1555 - possibly because he had friends in high places. But it also seems likely that there were conditions which he was obliged to meet. He and his former partner William Seres, both confirmed Protestants, spent the latter years of Mary's reign printing books of devotion for Catholic readers!

Family Problems

John seems to have had problems with Richard, his eldest son by his first marriage, who became a printer in his own right and threatened to rival his father. There was at this time the problem of piracy in the printing trade. Before the law of copyright it was possible for books to be copied and reprinted by competing companies and Richard seems to have been one of the competitors. At this time John's financial situation was uncertain and he could not afford to lose clients.

It all caused a great deal of bitterness. Richard, still a very young man, was forced out of business and decided to go to Cambridge to study for the priest-hood. There were recriminations on both sides. Richard was accused of stealing money from his father, and he in turn later accused his father of ruining his life once again by forcing him to leave King's College and return home to work as his father's "corrector of print". It emerged later that this was not true. Richard had personal reasons for leaving college. He had fallen in love with a young lady who lived near his father's printing house!

The Death of John Daye

No doubt all this family trouble saddened the final years of John's life. For some time he had been suffering from a very painful illness, and he was desperately struggling to produce one last de luxe edition of Foxe's Book of Martyrs. He succeeded in finishing the beautifully produced books just before his death in 1584. He died at Saffron Walden while travelling home from London, and his body was brought to Little Bradley for burial.

If John was disappointed with his offspring from his first marriage he did have the satisfaction of seeing the sons of his second marriage making their way in the world. The eldest son, John, fulfilled his father's hopes for a son who would grow up to be a godly cleric. He studied at Eton and Oriel College, Oxford, where he was later elected Fellow. He became a popular preacher in the diocese, spending the last five years of his life, 1622-7, as Rector of Little Thurlow.

After John's death his wife Alice set up the handsome brass which we see in the church today. It shows John and Alice kneeling with their thirteen children, including the two babies who were stillborn, who are shown in their shrouds on the end panel of the prayer desk.

The inscription includes a pun on the word Daye, and also refers to Alice's second marriage to William Stone:

> Heere lies the Daye that darkness could not blynd
> When popish fogges had over cast the sunne
> This Daye the cruell night did leave behind
> To view and shew what bloudi Actes weare done
> He set a Fox to wright how Martyrs runne
> By death to lyfe, Fox ventured paynes and health
> To give them light Daye spent in print his wealth
> But God with gayn returned his wealth agayne
> And gave to him as he gave to the poore
> Both wyves he had partakers of his payne
> Each wife twelve babes and each of them one more
> Als was the last encreaser of his stoore
> Who mourning long for being left alone
> Set upp this toombe her self turned to a Stone
> Obiit 23 July 1584

As well as this brass placed by Alice, there is also a memorial window in the nave given by The Stationers Company in 1880 as a mark of respect to John Daye, who was one of the first Masters of the Company.

The Hunts of Hunts Hall, Ashen

Before we go on to Alice's second marriage we return briefly to her own family, the Hunts of Hunts Hall in Ashen, just over the Essex border but not far away from Little Bradley.

Her mother was Ann Knighton, and Alice was the daughter of her first marriage - to Richard Hunt. This Richard Hunt also had a sister called Alice, and she was married to Richard Bull, who was a cousin of his wife Ann Knighton. Richard Hunt and Ann Knighton also had a son, John Hunt, who was married to Jane

Colte of Colte's Hall at Cavendish. The Coltes were connected by marriage with the Poleys of Boxted, and another Jane Colte, a member of the same family, was the wife of Sir Thomas More.

There is a memorial brass to John Hunt and Jane Colte on the floor of Little Bradley Church. The inscription reads as follows:

> Here lyeth buried the body of John le
> Hunt of Little Bradlye in the County
> Of Suffolke Esquire who married Jane
> Theldest daughter of Henry Colte
> Of Candish in the sayd Countye Esq
> And had issue by her one sone & two daugh
> Ters and departed this lyfe the XVI th
> Daye of Maye in the yeare of our Lord
> 1605

After Richard Hunt's death his widow Ann married Thomas Soame, so Alice and John Hunt had several Soame half-brothers and sisters (14 altogether).

The Soames were one of the most influential families in the 16th century. The eldest son, Thomas, was married to Elizabeth Alington and they produced a family which would continue to play an important part in the life of Little Bradley and the surrounding villages for many years.

The Alingtons, Cupbearers to the King

The Alingtons probably lived at their manor house in Horseheath, but they also held the lordship of Wymondley in Hertfordshire, and with it the title of "Cupbearers to the King".

The honour was originally granted to the Argenteins of Wymondley, who were descended from a Norman knight, David de Argentein, who served under William the Conqueror.

For 10 generations the Argenteins managed to produce a male heir but in 1427 John de Argentein died without offspring (he was only six years old!) and his sister Elizabeth was the sole heir. She married William de Alington of Horse-heath, who became Lord of the Manor of Wymondley and Cupbearer to the King. It is unlikely that the Alingtons ever lived at Wymondley, preferring their mansion house at Horseheath.

We are told that the ceremony of presenting the first cup of wine to the newly crowned monarch was last carried out at the Coronation of George IV in 1830. By this time Wymondley Manor had descended to the Wilshere family, who performed the last ceremony.

Thomas Soame died in 1606, having produced five sons and two daughters. Six years after his death his widow, Elizabeth Alington, erected a memorial brass which can still be seen on the south wall of the Chancel at Little Bradley.

The inscription reads: "Here lyeth buried ye bodie of Thomas Soame of Little Bradley in ye county of Suff: gent: died ye 12th of Octob: 1606 aetatatis sua [aged] 64. He married Elizabeth Alington daughter of Robert Alington of Horseheath in the county of Cambridge esquier by whom he had issue 5 sonnes and 2 daughters wch said Elizabeth erected this small monument for a perpetuall memorye of his name ye 15th of May An dni 1612
Quis est homo qui vivet et non videbit mortem?"

The Soames of Suffolk and Hertfordshire

The descendants of Thomas and Elizabeth lived on for many generations at Little Bradley, and the Soames continued as one of the most highly respected families in the area.

But it was Sir Stephen Soame, Thomas's younger brother, who was probably the most well-known member of the family. He had estates in Norfolk, Bedfordshire and Hertfordshire, but still retained his Suffolk links as Lord of the Manor of Little Thurlow, a neighbouring village to Little Bradley.

Stephen was a patron of St Andrew's Church in Hertford where he would have known his kinsmen Charles and Richard Bull, and in 1598 he was Lord Mayor of London.

His son, Sir Thomas Soame, had an equally illustrious career. In 1640 he was Sheriff of London, and Member of Parliament for the City of London. Thomas bought the Manor of Throcking in Hertfordshire, which had belonged to his distant cousins the Hydes. The Hydes were closely connected with the Court - Lucy Hyde being a Lady of the Bedchamber to the Queen. Later, Ann Hyde, a member of the same family, was to become the first wife of James II.

When Thomas Soame moved into Hyde Hall he would have discovered a rather unusual feature in his kitchen. When William Hyde was rebuilding the old manor house he is said to have paved his kitchen floor with gravestones from Throcking Church. A later historian writes "It is curious that no memorials to the Hydes now remain, although they were all buried in Throcking Church".

The Soames and Stones of Segenhoe

Sir Stephen Soame was married to Ann Stone, the daughter of William Stone of Segenhoe in Bedfordshire. Segenhoe, now part of the village of Ridgmont near Bedford, was once a thriving community, with a manor house and a church of its own. Only the ruins of the church now remain, but they are rather beautiful -

surrounded by green meadows and peacefully grazing sheep. William Stone was married to Massy Grey whose family had held the manor of Segenhoe since the 12th century, when Rougemont Castle was a stronghold of the Grey family. They also held Wrest Park and the Pelhams.

Sir Stephen Soame's mother, as we know, was Ann Knighton of Little Bradley, who had previously been married to Richard Hunt. Their daughter Alice Hunt (Stephen's half sister) was first married to John Daye the printer, and afterwards to William Stone, who was the nephew of her half-brother Stephen's wife Ann.

Members of the Soame family continued to live at Little Bradley for many years, and descendants of Stephen Soame remained at Little Thurlow until the end of the 19th century. We can be thankful for all these ancient families who left us so many memories of the past, and also for the people of Little Bradley who are still recording its history, and preserving its church and monuments for future generations.

All Saints Church, Little Bradley

Borley Church and Borley Place
Borley Place was originally the Rectory, but later the home of the Waldegraves.
The new Rectory, "the most haunted house in England", was just opposite.
It was mysteriously burnt down in 1939.

Chapter 9

The Waldegraves of Bures and Borley
in Suffolk and Essex

In the early years of the last century Borley Rectory was widely known as the most haunted house in England. And it was not only the Rectory but also the Church which was experiencing ghostly and terrifying phenomena. There were sounds of footsteps with no sign of any feet, keys turned mysteriously in the locks, bells rang all by themselves, and strange noises like falling earth were coming from the Waldegrave tombs.

The Waldegraves had lived at Borley and Bures since the 14th century or even earlier. Richard Waldegrave is first recorded in Bures in 1384, and later the manors of Overhall and Netherhall were added to the estate by his marriage to Joan, a member of the Silvester family. The manors had previously belonged to the ancestors of Elizabeth Woodville who was the wife of Edward IV and mother of the Princes in the Tower.

Smallbridge Hall

The main family home, known as Smallbridge Hall, was situated on the outskirts of the little town of Bures, on the Suffolk side of the river Stour. The Waldegraves also held estates just across the water at Wormingford in Essex. It is said that when the family decided to transform the gently sloping meadowlands of Wormingford into a deer park they built a wooden bridge across the river and the manor took the name of Small Brigg, which later became Smallbridge.

Borley Manor

A little further north, just beyond Sudbury, was the other Waldegrave family home - Borley Manor. It is not quite certain where the original manor house was situated, but it was probably on the site of the famous Borley Rectory, which was built by the Rev'd Henry Bull in 1863, and burnt down in 1939. The previous Rectory, later known as Borley Place, was just opposite.

According to some accounts the Waldegraves were in Suffolk and Essex long before the events recorded in 1384. We are told that they "came out of Germany" and were living in Northamptonshire before the Conquest. John de Waldegrave was Sheriff of London in 1205, and Richard Waldegrave of Bures was his great grandson.

Member of Parliament for Suffolk

Copinger tells us that Sir Richard Waldegrave of Smallbridge represented Suffolk in Parliament in the reigns of Edward III and Richard II, which confirms that he must have been at Smallbridge before 1384, since Edward III died in 1377. Sir Richard was recorded as Speaker of the House of Commons during the reign of Richard II. In 1383 he obtained a licence to crenellate his manor house, so it seems that he was well established at Smallbridge before his marriage to Joan Silvester.

We know very little about Richard and Joan and their family, except that they had a son Richard who, according to some records, succeeded his father in 1406. But we have conflicting accounts of the date of Richard's death and also of Joan's.

According to a copy of the inscription on their tombstone, Richard died in 1400 and Joan in 1406:

> Hic jacet Richardus Waldegrave miles qui obijta 2 die
> Maij. Anno Dom. 1400 et Joanna uxor ejus que obijt 10
> Junij 1406 Quorum animabus propitietur Deus. Amen.
> Qui pro alijs orat, pro se laborat.

Yet in his will, dated 22 April 1401 (when he was supposed to be already dead) he directs his body to be buried on the north side of the parish church of St Mary of Bures, "near Joan my wife", (who was not yet supposed to have died).

Information from the will confirms that Joan had died on 10th July 1397 and that Richard died on 2nd May 1401. Inscriptions on tombs, which were copied many years later, are notoriously inaccurate - but we can be fairly sure of the authenticity of wills and other written documents - provided they have not been attacked by insects or nibbled by mice!

By his will, Sir Richard gives "20s. to the High Altar, 3s. 4d. to the Chapel of the Virgin Mary, 3s. 4d. to the Chantry and 12d. to every priest praying for my soul on the day of my burial".

He also leaves a cope to the "parish church of Walgrave" and "a missal to the Chapel of St Stephen in the parish of Buers". To the Friars of the Convent of Sudbury he leaves 100 shillings to pray for his soul and the soul of Joan his wife and the souls of his benefactors. One hundred shillings (£5) was a great deal of money at that time.

Lord Bures of Silvesters

Sir Richard was succeeded by his son - also Richard, who is styled 'Lord Bures of Silvesters'. He was married to Jane, the daughter and heir of Sir Thomas Mountchancy of Edwardstone. Both Richard and Jane are buried in the Parish Church at Bures.

St Mary's Church, Bures

Richard and Jane had a son William, who was the next heir, and a daughter Agnes, who was married to William Hunt of Hunt's Hall in Ashen (who was also related to the Underhills and Soames of Little Bradley).

Sir William Waldegrave was married to Joan, the daughter of William Dorwood of Barking in Essex. Joan and William had two sons, Richard and Thomas, and a daughter who married John Mannock of Giffords Hall at Stoke-by-Nayland. The elder son Richard died without issue, and the estate went to his younger brother Thomas and his wife Elizabeth Fray (who later married Sir William Saye).

Links with the Mannock Family

Thomas and Elizabeth had a daughter Katherine who, like her aunt, married into the Mannock family, while another daughter, Jane, married Sir Edmund Arundell.

It is interesting to note that both Katherine Waldegrave and her aunt married into the Mannock family of Giffords Hall at Stoke-by-Nayland, and three generations later, Edward Waldegrave married Sarah the daughter of John Higham of Giffords Hall at Wickhambrook.

There were also three sons. Like so many of the aristocratic families the Waldegraves were ardent supporters of the 'old religion' and during the reign of Queen Elizabeth life was very difficult. The eldest son, Edward, was evidently far too outspoken about his views, and spent most of his adult life in the Tower, where he died "at an advanced age" in 1561. He did however have a son John, who took over the family estates at Borley. Edward's brother, Sir William, inherited Smallbridge.

William Waldegrave of Smallbridge

William was married to Margaret (or Margery) the daughter of Sir Henry Wentworth of Coldham Hall at Withersfield in Essex. They had a large family, seven daughters and two sons. One of the daughters, Margaret, married John Lord St John of Bletsoe Castle in Bedfordshire.

The St Johns were part of the family network and were related to the Herveys, the Lyttons of Knebworth, the Brownes and the Pelhams, as well as being closely related to Henry VIII, who as a boy spent long periods at Bletsoe with his St John cousins. Another daughter, Dorothy, married Sir John Spring of Lavenham and another was married to Robert Drury. One of the younger daughters, Jane, became a nun in the Minories in London, probably because there were no more eligible bachelors left by the time she came of age!

Fortunately the two Waldegrave sons both made good marriages. Anthony, the younger son, married Elizabeth, the daughter and heir of Ralph Grey of Burnt Pelham in Hertfordshire and Wrest Park in Bedfordshire. Anthony was one of the Barons of the Exchequer. The elder brother, George, was married to Anne, daughter of Sir Robert Drury of Hawstead, Speaker of the House of Commons, who is buried in an armorial altar tomb in St Mary's, Bury St Edmunds.

The Chapel of Jesu at Bures

William died on 30th January 1524. In his Will dated 26 January 1524/5 he appointed his body to be buried in St Mary's Church at Bures in the tomb he had caused to be made under the arch between the high altar and the Chapel of Jesu, and that his body should be buried within 24 hours of his decease. The 'Chapel of Jesu' is now used as the church vestry.

To his wife Dame Margery he gives all his jewels and his manors and lands in the counties of Suffolk, Essex and Northampton. He adds "Above all things I desire my Executors to pay my debts, and if I have wronged any man, to satisfy him: My wife has the manor of Edwardstone". Although William seems to be leaving all his manors and estates to his widow, this did not include Smallbridge, which he had presumably handed over to his son George before his death.

George Waldegrave and Anne Drury

George and his wife Anne Drury had five children, three sons and two daughters. Their daughter Ann married first Henry Bures or Bewers of Acton, and secondly Sir Clement Higham. The son of Ann and Clement was married to Ann Poley of Boxted. The other daughter, Phyllis, married Thomas Higham, the brother of Sir Clement. There are brasses to Sir Clement Higham and his family in Barrow Church.

The three sons all had interesting histories. The second son took his father's name, George. He married Mary Corbett of Assington and they lived at Witherton (or Wetherden) Manor at Hitcham. His monument can be seen on the wall in Hitcham Church. George and Mary were first cousins - their mothers were both Drurys. They had two sons who married into the Knighton and Poley families.

George Waldegrave of Hitcham

The youngest son of George Waldegrave and Anne Drury was Edward who married Joan, daughter of George Ackworth of Lawford and inherited Lawford Hall. Edward and his future wife were confined to the Tower during the trial of Queen Katherine Howard, accused of withholding information. There were reputed to be some important letters which they found in an old chest and foolishly failed to report to the appropriate authorities.

The eldest son, William, was knighted about 1543 and was Sheriff of Norfolk and Suffolk in 1549. He was married to Julian, the daughter of John Rainsford.

It seems that George, their father, died while still a comparatively young man, possibly as the result of a riding accident - one of the chief causes of death at that time when a severe wound or a broken limb often proved fatal. He made his will on 6th July 1528, and died a few days later.

George Waldegrave buried at All Saints, Sudbury

In his will George asks to be buried in Bures Church, near to the tomb of his father Sir William. Despite this request he was buried at All Saints Church, Sudbury.

This seems rather sad. George, of course, wouldn't know anything about it, but it does show a lack of respect to ignore his clearly expressed wishes. Maybe there was some good reason. But it was nearly 500 years ago - so we shall never know!

Anne, his widow, would also have been quite young when George died. She later married Sir Thomas Jermyn of Rushbrooke, and lived on for another 44 years. There is a memorial brass in Debden Church dedicated to Lady Anne Jermyn. Anne is also represented twice in Bures Church - once with each husband - George Waldegrave and then Sir Thomas Jermyn.

Sir William Waldegrave - Died in Calais

William, the eldest son of George and Anne, was an ardent supporter of Queen Mary when she came to the throne in 1553. However, he did not live to see her firmly established, as he died in Calais a year later. He was buried in Calais, but a brass memorial was set up in Bures Church:

> Of your charity pray for the soul of Sir William Wal-
> degrave, Knight, of Bures St. Mary in com. Suff., who
> died xii. December 1554 and left behynd one son and
> two daughters, on whose souls Jesu have mercy. The
> said Sir William Waldegrave died at Callys in France,
> where his body is buried in St. Marie's Church there.

On his father's death Sir William, the only son of William and Julian, inherited Smallbridge. He was Member of Parliament for Suffolk in 1559, 1563 and 1597. Sir William was married first to Elizabeth Mildmay of Moulsham in Essex, and secondly to Grissel, the daughter of Lord Paget.

A Royal Visit to Smallbridge

Sir William entertained Queen Elizabeth at Smallbridge in 1561 and again in 1579. At the time of her first visit Smallbridge Hall was newly built. The old manor house had been replaced by a handsome brick mansion modelled on

Hampton Court. The present Hall is probably just one wing of the original mansion, which was very extensive - having 44 hearths recorded! We know that there was an impressive Gatehouse and also a Chapel dedicated to St Anne.

A present-day view of Smallbridge Hall, Bures

The Queen arrived in August 1561 and stayed at Smallbridge for two days. She came from Colchester and travelled with 12 coaches and 300 baggage carts. Foot soldiers ran behind and local gentry followed on horseback. It cost Sir William £250 to entertain the Queen and all her entourage. Although this was a great deal of money in 1561, it was only a fraction of the amounts recorded at houses such as Hengrave and Rougham.

On her second visit, in 1579, the Queen avoided Colchester "where the small pox was very bad". She was entertained by a "divertissement" at Wormingford Park and she also visited other members of the family at Church Hall. Here she honoured her hosts by writing her initials on the window with her diamond ring. She may also have visited Great Bevills - another of the Waldegrave family homes.

Great Bevills, a few miles distant from Smallbridge, is described in the Listed Buildings Schedule as a fine early 16th century manor house. It was built by the Waldegraves to accommodate members of their family around the time when Smallbridge was being rebuilt.

The name is thought to have originated from the Beauvilles, a Norman family who held the manor in the 12th century. The Beauville arms were recorded by Tillotson as being in an earlier stained glass window in St Mary's Church at Bures.

Threat from the Spanish Armada

Between these two visits was the time of the threatened invasion of England by the Spanish Armada, and the County of Suffolk responded nobly by sending a large number of Knights and soldiers to join the army which was gathering at Tilbury. We are told that they were "All Choice men, well disciplined and singularly furnished. Amongst them was Sir William Waldegrave, Knight, who had 500 men in his band".

We have accounts of several members of the family who, like William Waldegrave, were Muster Captains. Among them was Henry Capell of Hadham Hall in Hertfordshire whose archives include the Muster Books of Hertfordshire and Essex. At the time when the Spanish invasion was imminent he was leading his men across Hertfordshire to gather with all the other militia at Tilbury. Their experiences would have been very similar to those of the Suffolk contingent.

The threat of war became apparent after the excommunication of Elizabeth in 1570, and following the execution of Mary Queen of Scots in 1587 an attack from Spain seemed inevitable. There was no regular army at this time, and the defence of the Kingdom was in the hands of the local militia. All able-bodied men between the ages of 18 and 45 were required to join and to meet four times a year for training. The armour was kept in the parish churches, where a large cupboard was often built specially for this purpose. The parish church at Mendlesham in Suffolk is one of the very few churches in the country where remnants of this 16th century armour are still stored.

The Suffolk Militia March to Tilbury

William Waldegrave would have gathered his men from Bures and the surrounding villages and set out on the long march to Tilbury. Once the soldiers crossed the county border they were entitled to a maintenance allowance, but while they were in their own county the Muster Captain had to beg or buy (out of his own pocket) their nightly board and lodging. In the case of the Hertfordshire contingent this meant 40 miles of travelling across the county, but at Bures they had only to cross the river into Essex to be eligible for payment.

Certain inns along the route had been licensed as suitable places to stop for rest and refreshment, and the soldiers were not allowed to stop at any other hostelry. Some of the inn-keepers (mainly women) are named in the Muster Books. It was their duty to make sure the men did not drink to excess, or indulge in any other behaviour which might affect their physical fitness. We are told that the Hertfordshire troops, like those assembled by William Waldegrave, were a particularly well-disciplined band of men, quite unlike the "rabble" which Shakespeare describes in some of his plays.

When they arrived at Tilbury the men were accommodated in tents and the horses were penned. Those responsible for looking after the horses were provided with "little wheele barrows to carry away their dung, so that their Camp is no lesse cleene and orderly than a Princes Stable". The sanitary arrangements for the men are not recorded!

The threatened invasion, of course, never happened, because the Spanish ships were intercepted in the Channel and destroyed by Drake and his fleet. This was perhaps rather fortunate.

The Navy was already a very prestigious and professional force, whereas the militia, with their four days training a year, would have been much more proficient with their axes and pitchforks than with their Cullivers, Corselets and Muskets.

Sir William's first wife, Elizabeth, died in 1581, and his second marriage was to Grissel, the youngest daughter of William Lord Paget. Grissel had been married previously to Sir Thomas Rivett, and her only daughter by her first husband was married to Henry Lord Windsor, who was buried at Stoke-by-Nayland, where his monument can still be seen.

A Waldegrave-Clopton Marriage

Sir William had no children by his second wife Grissel, who died in July 1600, but by his first wife he had a large family, six sons and four daughters. One of his daughters, Mary, was married to Thomas Clopton of Kentwell Hall.

Their son, Sir William Clopton, by his first wife Anne (the daughter of Sir Thomas Barnardiston) had a daughter Anne, who married the famous Suffolk antiquary Sir Simonds D'Ewes - and their story is told in another chapter.

Sir William died on 1 August 1613 and he and his first wife, Elizabeth Mildmay, were buried together at Bures with the following inscription:

> Here liethe buriede Sir William Waldegrave, Knight,
> and Dame Elizabeth his wife who lived together in
> godlie marriage 21 years and had issue 6 sonnes and 4
> daughters. The said Elizabeth departed this life the 10
> daye of may in the year of our Lord God 1581 and the
> said Sir William deceased the 1 daye of August in the
> year of our Lord God 1613.

Sir William Waldegrave was succeeded by his eldest son, William, who died just three months after his father - on 25th November 1613. He was married first to Judith, the daughter of Sir Robert Jermyn of Rushbrooke Hall, who died soon after the marriage, having produced just one daughter, Elizabeth.

His second marriage was to Lady Jennemache, the daughter of Sir Nicholas Bacon of Redgrave, and she was closely connected with the Court. She was a niece of Sir Francis Bacon, the Lord Chancellor, and was a Lady in Waiting to the Queen. By this second marriage he had a son William, and two daughters - one of whom, Philippa, married Gyles Barnardiston. The Barnardistons, as we know, were already linked with the family.

When Sir William (the father) died in 1613 his widow Jennemache retired to the Dower House - Wormingford Hall. Descendants of this branch of the family continued to live at Smallbridge until it was sold in 1693. The Hall was demolished during the 1700s but was later rebuilt. In 1932 it was restored by Lady Phyllis Macrae, daughter of the Marquess of Bristol.

The Waldegraves of Borley

The branch of the family which descended from Edward Waldegrave who "died in 1561 in the Tower at an advanced age" lived at Borley Hall and Borley Place, which was opposite the Rectory - "the most haunted house in England".

Edward had a son John and also two daughters. One daughter, Elizabeth (or Grissel), was married to Thomas Eden, Clerk of the Star Chamber. This was a surprising relationship because the Edens, who were also connected with the Martyns of Melford Place at Long Melford, were a Puritan family, while the Waldegraves were loyal supporters of the Roman Catholic church.

Edward's son John married Laura, daughter of Sir John Rochester. John is said to have died in 1514 , but if this date is correct he would have been a very young man. However, he managed to produce four sons and two daughters. His eldest son, another Edward, inherited Borley Manor, but like his grandfather he spent much of his adult life in the Tower.

Edward was married to Frances, daughter of Sir Edward Nevill, and they had three sons and three daughters. He was a staunch Roman Catholic, and at the time of the Reformation he was attached to the household of the young Princess Mary Tudor.

Even before she became Queen the young princess made no secret of the fact that she strongly disapproved of her father's break with Rome. Sir Edward Waldegrave was her trusted adviser and supported her when she insisted on observing the Roman Catholic rites and ceremonies. Edward was sent to the Tower for celebrating the Mass in his house, when it was strictly forbidden.

When Mary became Queen, Edward's loyalty was rewarded. He was knighted and made Chancellor of the Duchy, and a Privy Councillor to the Queen. He also represented Essex in Parliament in 1557.

Sir Edward Waldegrave - Died in the Tower

But on the accession of Queen Elizabeth, Edward was once again in trouble and was imprisoned in the Tower, where he died a few years later. He was buried in the Tower Chapel, but an imposing monument was erected in Borley Church.

It is often referred to as the Waldegrave tomb, but it is unlikely that it was ever used as a burial place. It does, however, indicate the importance of Sir Edward Waldegrave and the esteem in which he was held.

The monument commemorates Edward and his wife Frances, who survived him by 38 years. The effigies lie side by side and at Frances's feet is a squirrel, an emblem of thrift.

There is a stone canopy supported by six marble pillars, and the three sons and three daughters can be seen on the sides.

Some historians have asked why Edward was not brought home to Borley for burial. Perhaps there was some guilty secret here.

It was this Sir Edward who was reputed to be a suspect in the story of the murdered nun whose uneasy spirit was said to be haunting Borley Rectory and the Church during the early 20th century.

The Waldegrave Tomb

Perhaps the elaborate monument was significant. If Edward was being blamed for some evil deed, maybe his well-wishers wanted to show how greatly he was loved and honoured by his family and friends.

One of Edward's sons, Christopher (or Charles) was married to Jeromina the daughter of Sir Henry Jernagan of Costessey in Norfolk, while Nicholas, the eldest son, married into the Browne family of Abbess Roding. His wife Katherine appears on the pedigree of the Brownes of Essex.

Sir Edward also had a daughter Mary who married into another Essex family, the Petres of Ingatestone Hall. Her husband was Sir John Petre, later Lord Petre of Writtle. The story of Sir John is included in another chapter. We have a detailed account of his christening, and a picture of Thorndon Place, his magnificent house near Ingatestone in Essex.

The Whitbread Connection

In the next generation we have Philip the heir and two more sons and six daughters. One of the daughters, Magdalan, was married to John Whitbread of Writtle, a member of the well-known brewing family.

In the 18th century the Waldegrave name disappeared from Borley. The old manor house was pulled down and later the new Rectory was built on the site. It mysteriously burnt down in 1939, but even into the 1950s there were still reported to be strange happenings in and around the church and in the ruins of the Rectory.

Was there some ghostly connection with the Waldegrave family? We shall never know. It made a good story at the time, and several books have been written about it. Professor C.E.M. Joad, who was well known for his broadcasts on The Brains Trust, was among the people who came to investigate the manifestations.

But perhaps we should remember the Waldegraves for more positive reasons: for their public service as Sheriffs and Members of Parliament, their loyalty to their country, and their courage in facing disgrace and imprisonment, in order to hold firm to their religious beliefs.

Chapter 10

The Mannocks of Giffords Hall, Stoke-by-Nayland

Giffords Hall at Stoke-by-Nayland was the home of the Mannock family for nearly 400 years. It was acquired by Philip Mannock in 1428, but the family had been living in the area since the time of Edward III (1327-77).

They came originally from Denmark, and we are told that they "flourished under the Danish Kings" - presumably implying that they came to England with the Danish invaders in the 9th century.

Giffords Hall, Stoke-by-Nayland

There are two houses in Suffolk known as "Giffords Hall", one a beautiful timbered building at Wickambrook near Haverhill, and the other a more extensive house at Stoke-by-Nayland. Both manors were originally owned and built by the Gifford family.

The Gifford name first appears in the Patent Rolls of 1281, when there was an action between Roger le Chaumberleyn and Thomas Gifford concerning a dispute over a right of way which had been obstructed at Stoke.

A few years later William Gifford, possibly the son of Thomas, is recorded as Lord of the Manor, and on his death in 1310 the property passed to Thomas, and then to another William, who was Lord of the Manor in 1340. His son Richard Gifford was at Stoke until 1377, when it was taken over by the Burley family.

Peter Gifford, Lord of the Manor of Stoke

The old manor house is said to have been built by a certain Peter Gifford during the reign of Henry III, but we do not know exactly where he fits in. Henry III reigned from 1216 to 1272, so it would have been a very early building. Peter was perhaps the father of Thomas who obstructed the right of way - or was it Roger de Chaumberleyn who did the obstructing? It is not clear who was the guilty party.

Parts of the old manor house, including the Great Hall with its fine oak roof, were said by some historians to have been preserved and incorporated into the present house, which was built by the Mannocks 200 years later. But this seems to be unlikely, especially with regard to the 'fine oak roof'. There is certainly a fine oak roof in the present Giffords Hall, consisting of five double hammer beams with beautiful spandrel carvings, which according to Eric Sandon suggest a date of 1480-1500. This would confirm that it was part of the new building.

Opposite the entrance to Giffords Hall are the remains of an old Chapel, dedicated to St Nicholas. It is recorded in the "Proceedings of the Suffolk Institute" that "Richard Constable in the year 1216 built a Chapel close by his house. It was amply endowed by his son William Constable". It seems very probable that these were the ancestors of the famous painter John Constable of East Bergholt.

Giffords Hall at Wickhambrook

The original Giffords Hall at Wickhambrook has no connection with the Mannocks, but is of interest here because it was built by the same family who built Giffords Hall at Stoke-by-Nayland.

Giffords Hall, Wickhambrook

When they left Stoke in 1377, it seems likely that the Giffords moved to Wick-hambrook, and built a manor house there, similar to the house they left behind. This manor house was taken over about 100 years later by the Cloptons, who rebuilt it, but retained the name Giffords Hall. Further alterations were carried out around 1590 by Thomas Higham, and this is basically the house we see today.

The Cloptons also built another manor house in Wickhambrook, which is now known as Clopton Hall. It is quite usual to find two or more 'big houses' in close proximity, built no doubt to provide accommodation for new branches of the family, or for use as a Dower House for the widow, when she needed to move out to make way for the new Lady of the Manor.

Philip Mannock of Stoke-by-Nayland

Philip Mannock and his family arrived at Stoke in 1428 and they would have moved into the old manor house built by the Giffords. Though not as grand as the present Giffords Hall, there is evidence that it was a house of some signifi-cance. We know little of Philip or his family, except that they had lived in the area for some time.

We discover from the Visitations that he had a son John, who later inherited the manor and died in 1476. Presumably Philip was quite a young man when he came to Stoke, and it was not until 30 years later, when he had raised his family and assembled considerable wealth, that he started work on the new house.

The New Giffords Hall

It is now possible to date the building fairly accurately, because of a recent discovery of a contract for the supply of bricks dated 1459. This contract confirms the supposition that Giffords Hall was built with locally made bricks. On the estate there is still a site known as Kiln Field, and nearby in the parish of Shelley there is Brick Kiln Wood, but until this recent discovery there was no real evidence that the brick kilns existed at the time when the house was built.

Whoever chose the site of the original manor chose very well. The house itself was built on rising ground about 100 yards above the River Brett, which flows past it to the east, and it was protected by woods and rising ground to the north. It is still approached by a long drive, which is said to be of great antiquity.

There were high walls and a massive gateway which would help to deter unwelcome visitors. Its remote position, well away from the main London to Sudbury highway, would make it an ideal dwelling place for a family such as the Mannocks.

The Mannocks were one of the many recusant families of Suffolk, who held unflinchingly to their Roman Catholic beliefs throughout the long years of persecution following the Reformation. The comings and goings of priests and of other recusant family members were to be kept secret as far as possible.

The presumably reliable dating of the building, around 1460, would be consistent with other evidence. We have no record of the date of Philip's death, but we know his son John died in 1476. It seems likely therefore that the building was begun by Philip and continued or completed by John when he took over as Lord of the Manor.

The Mannock-Waldegrave Connections

John married into another closely connected family - the Waldegraves, his wife being the daughter of Sir William Waldegrave of Borley. The present owners of Giffords Hall have inherited from the previous owners two delightful portraits of John Mannock and his wife.

In the next generation their son George married his cousin Katherine Waldegrave, the daughter of Sir Thomas Waldegrave, who was related to the Brownes of Abbess Roding. George died in 1541 and the manor passed to his eldest son William.

At this point we read that William was acquiring various other properties, and when he died he held the manors of Holton Hall and Raynes, as well as Giffords Hall and Chaumberleyns at Stoke.

William was married to Audrey Alington, the daughter of John Alington of Horseheath. As we know from another chapter the Alingtons of Horseheath were also Lords of the Manor of Wymondley in Hertfordshire, and held the title of Cup-bearers to the King. Audrey's brother, Gyles Alington, was married to Margaret Spencer of Althorp, and her sister Mary was the wife of Robert Newport of Pelham - a kinsman of the Mannock family.

William's sister Elizabeth Mannock was twice married. Her first husband was Robert Dacre of Cheshunt, and the second was Thomas, a member of the Denny family. Thomas Denny was a relation of Thomas Roper (Viscount Baltinglass) and also the Nevill family (Abergavenny). William and Audrey had a son Francis, and it is this Francis whose memorial can be seen in the north aisle of the chancel in Stoke-by-Nayland Church. Francis was married first to Mary the daughter of William Fitch of Canfield in Essex, and it was their eldest son William who became the next heir. Francis died in 1590 but there is no record of the death of either his first or his second wife. His memorial brass bears this Latin inscription:

> Quid dant Divitiae Crassi, Craesive Talenta?
> Quid juvat immensus tantus et orbis honor?
> Omnia vilescunt, quae mors rapit ore voraci:
> Virtutis solidae Vita perennis erit.

The Martyns of Melford Place

In addition to their son William, Francis and Mary Mannock also had five daughters, and one of them, Elinor, was married to Richard Martin (or Martyn) of Long Melford. The Martyn family lived at Melford Place, an important house originating in the 14th century, but less well known than the other two grand houses - Kentwell Hall and Melford Hall. The Martyns were wealthy wool merchants, deeply religious and staunch Catholics. As we discover from other chapters there were strong links with the Waldegraves and also with the Edens, even though the Edens were one of the leading Puritan families in East Anglia. The Eden connection shows that religious differences did not necessarily mean antagonism between families on a personal level.

The Martyns did a great deal for the Church at Long Melford, including the building of the Martyn Chapel on the south side of the Church, where the effigies of Elinor Mannock and Richard Martyn can still be seen.

Francis's second marriage was to Ann Siscelton, and there were four children. One of the daughters, Bridget, was married to Thomas Sulyard, a member of another well-known Suffolk family. The Sulyards held the manor of Wetherden, and also had estates at Eye, Wilby and Kenton. Sir John Sulyard was Lord Chief Justice of the Common Pleas. In 1565 his daughter Margaret (or Ann) married John Tyrell of Herons in East Horndon - the son of Sir John Tyrell of Gipping. The Sulyards were also related to the Brownes of Abbess Roding, the Newports of Burnt Pelham and the Gages of Hengrave - all part of the network of related families.

William Mannock, the eldest son from Francis's first marriage, inherited the properties in 1590, but there were problems ahead. In 1596 Queen Elizabeth took away two thirds of his estates because of his recusancy. He was pardoned by James I in 1603 and his estates were returned to him, only to be taken away again in 1612, and he died four years later at the age of 60. William was married to Audrey, daughter of Ferdinand Parys of Linton in Cambridgeshire. There is a memorial to him in Stoke-by-Nayland Church.

Sir Francis Mannock - First Baronet

William's eldest son Francis was created Baronet by Charles I in 1627, a proud moment for the family. But sad times were to follow. Francis's wife Dorothy,

the daughter of William Sanders, died in 1632 after giving birth to their daughter Ann. Both Dorothy and Francis were recusants and most of their estates had been sequestered.

Francis died just two years after the death of his wife. He was only 49, but he had been through very difficult times - with the loss of his estates and finally the loss of his beloved wife Dorothy. There is a marble monument to Francis against the north wall of the church and a brass to Dorothy Sanders on the floor of the north chapel. The inscription above Francis's memorial is as follows:

> In pious and deserved memory of Sr. Francis Mannock Baronet Whose ancestors long since derived from Denmark and in England called Lords of Mannock's Manor (now called great Gravensden in the Countie of Huntington) the still continued Inheritance of theyr Families: have also for many ages been Lords and Inhabitants of this Manor of Giffords Hall in this Parish. Whose religious Conversation made him reverenced of all: whose Candor of mind, Sweetness of Manner, generous Hospitalitie, made his Life loved and honoured by the Rich: whose bountifull Charitie made his Death lamented by the Poor.

When Dorothy died in childbirth she was 42 years old, and had already provided Francis with three sons and one other daughter in addition to baby Ann, who died with her mother in 1632. Childbirth was always extremely hazardous at this time, particularly with first babies, and again towards the end when the mother was no longer young.

There had already been another sad event in the family when William, the eldest son and heir, died in childhood. But their surviving daughter Katherine lived to make a good marriage - renewing the links with the Newports of Brent Pelham by her marriage to John Newport, a well-known Royalist.

Francis, the second son of Francis and Dorothy, inherited the manor and the title, becoming the 2nd Baronet. But again times were very hard for Francis and his wife Mary, even though he was an important and highly respected member of the community. Most of their estates had been taken away, which meant they had scarcely any income, and in addition they had to pay heavy fines to avoid imprisonment.

Sir George Heneage of Lincolnshire

Fortunately Mary's father, Sir George Heneage of Hainton in Lincolnshire, was very generous, and we are told that he "provided for the younger members of the Mannock family left penniless by the sequestration".

Sir Francis was followed in succession by his son Sir William Mannock, 3rd Baronet, and his grandson Sir Francis, 4th Baronet. This Sir Francis had four sons: William, Francis, Thomas and George. When Sir Francis died, his eldest son Sir William Mannock became the 5th Baronet. The next heir was his only son - Sir Anthony, 6th Baronet, who died soon after his father.

Anthony was succeeded in turn by his three uncles. Sir Francis, 7th Baronet, died unmarried in 1778. Sir Thomas became 8th Baronet, but died 3 years later in 1781. He had been married for just one year, and had no children. His wife was Anastasia Browne, a descendant of Sir Anthony Browne, 1st Viscount Montague, a member of the Browne family of Sussex, who were almost certainly part of the same family as the Brownes of Abbess Roding. Finally came Sir George, 9th Baronet.

The Overturning of the Dover Coach

Poor Uncle George! Having lost his nephew Anthony and his three brothers, George himself came to a sad, but rather dramatic end. He was killed on 3rd June 1787 by the overturning of the Dover Coach!

When Sir George died in 1787, leaving no issue, the Baronetcy expired. The manor went to William Comyns who took the name of Mannock and died in 1819. It went to his kinsman (through a Strickland marriage) Patrick Power, who again took the title of Mannock by royal licence in 1830.

The beautiful mansion of Giffords Hall remains for us as a legacy, and also as a memorial to the Gifford and the Mannock families. It is still a family home, and the present owners are obviously continuing to cherish and care for it, fully aware of its illustrious history. It is good to know that such buildings can be preserved and maintained, even though it must be a daunting task.

The Mannocks will long be remembered, not least because of their many monuments and memorials in the church, which was supported and enhanced by their generosity. They suffered times of financial hardship because of their religious beliefs, but managed to hold on to their inheritance, and produce descendants through their marriages with many of the famous families of Suffolk and Essex who are no doubt still living amongst us today.

Giffords Hall - Inner Courtyard

Chapter 11

The Cloptons of Kentwell Hall, Long Melford

The Clopton family of Suffolk is usually associated with Kentwell Hall at Long Melford. In the church there is a Chantry dedicated to their memory, and there are many beautiful monuments and stained glass windows which indicate the importance of the family from the middle of the 15th century. According to one account there are 55 tombs, though many are now lacking their brass portraits.

But we first come across the Clopton name a century earlier at Wickhambrook, when they took over the manor of Giffords Hall from the Gifford family who

Clopton Hall, Wickhambrook

built it in the 14th century. The Cloptons also held the manor of Clopton Hall which was only about half a mile away to the east, so it is likely that the family was already well established in the area.

The Cloptons of Castlings Hall

Later we also find another branch of the Clopton family at Castlyns, or Castlings Hall at Groton near Kersey. Castlyns was held originally by a Knight called Sir Gilbert de Chastelyn who died in 1294. It passed through his descendants to the Knevett family and then to the Cloptons.

The Knevetts were connected to the Kentwell Hall family through William Clopton's third wife, Thomasine Knevett, who inherited Castlyns, which then descended to her son William. William (the father) would have been the grandson of Thomas and Katherine who founded the Clopton family of Melford in the 15th century. The present Castlings Hall was built by William Clopton around 1560, but there are remnants of an earlier manor house, probably the "tenement called Casteleins" mentioned in earlier documents.

Castlings Hall, Groton

Two generations later, in the early 17th century, William's grandson went to Virginia, founding the American branch of the Clopton family, who are now very interested in their Suffolk roots, and make regular visits to Long Melford and Castlings.

Katherine Mylde of Clare

Kentwell Hall came to the Clopton family through Katherine Mylde of Clare who married Sir Thomas Clopton in the early years of the 15th century. Katherine is commemorated in the north-west window of the nave of Long Melford Church.

The manor at this time was usually known as Lutons, and it had once belonged to the Abbots of Bury St Edmunds. There had been an earlier manor house which was almost certainly on the moated site where the present house now stands. It would have been unlikely that William Clopton would have created the moat when he built his new house in 1540.

Lutons, sometimes known as Kentwell, would have been just outside the moat, and was built soon after the manor passed from the church into secular ownership.

This account of the Clopton connection with Kentwell seems to be rather different from Copinger's version in his "Manors of Suffolk", in which he states that the manor was granted to William Clopton at the time of the Dissolution and he gives a date of 1545. According to other sources, William had already started building the new house by 1540 and Katherine Mylde, who brought the manor to the Clopton family by her marriage to Sir Thomas, is said to have died around 1400. Possibly there were two manors involved, and the Cloptons already owned Lutons when another adjoining manor was granted to them in 1545.

A Year of Hope and Tragedy

Thomas and Katherine had a son William who was married first to Margery, the daughter of Sir Roger Drury of Rougham. William and Margery had four daughters - Alice, Ann, Margery and Katherine, and at last they were overjoyed to have a son and heir, who took his father's name - William.

But tragedy was to follow. It seems likely that there was an outbreak of smallpox or some other deadly disease. We do not know exactly how old little William would have been, but he died in March 1420. This sad event was followed three months later by the death of his mother Margery, and four months after that came the deaths of two of his sisters, Ann and Margery, who both died in October 1420.

We hear no more about Katherine, but we know that Alice died in 1440 at the age of 30, so she would have been only 10 years old when she lost her mother, her brother and her two sisters. There is a memorial to William's wife Margery in the church, and his daughter Alice, who was married to John Harleston, is commemorated with a brass in the floor of the Clopton Chapel.

John Clopton, High Sheriff of Norfolk and Suffolk

Sir William's second marriage was to Margery Francis, and at last they had a son and heir to carry on the family name. This was John Clopton who largely rebuilt Long Melford Church and was High Sheriff of Norfolk and Suffolk in 1451. His mother, Margery Francis, died in 1424 while he was still a baby, and her heraldic effigy remains in the church.

John Clopton was married to Alice, the daughter of Sir Robert Darcy of Maldon in Essex. Alice's brother, also Sir Robert Darcy, names John Clopton his "brother" (actually his brother-in-law) in his will in 1449. John himself lived until 1494, when he must have been quite an old man.

John and Alice had a large family including Anne who was married to Thomas Rookwood of Coldham Hall. It would probably have been their grandson, Ambrose Rookwood (or Rokewood) who became famous for his alleged involve-

Chapter 11 - The Cloptons

ment in The Gunpowder Plot. Anne died in 1522 and her altar tomb is in Stanningfield Church.

John and Alice had another daughter, and three sons. The second son, Edmund, is described as Knight of the Rhodes, and we hear no more about him. The third son, Edward, lived at Glemsford. He had a daughter Elizabeth who was his sole heir, so the Clopton name would have died out in this branch of the family. But the succession of Kentwell was secure through John's eldest son, William.

Bountiful, Liberal, Skilled and Proficient

William had three wives, Joan, Katherine and Thomasine. Joan (or Johan) was the daughter of William Marrow, an Alderman of London, and it was John, the son of this marriage, who was the next heir. We are told that Joan is buried in Melford Church, but her brass and monumental inscription has gone.

William's second wife, Katherine, who apparently produced no offspring, is also buried in Melford Church. His third wife was Thomasine, the sister and co-heir to Edward Knevett of Stanway in Essex.

It was the family of William and Thomasine who founded the Clopton family of Castlyns at Groton. William, the husband of Joan, Katherine and Thomasine, died in 1530 aged 50. The epitaph on his memorial brass reads as follows:

> Bountiful and liberal and skilled and proficient in all the arts, famed
> for his gentle blood, William Clopton is confined in this narrow
> tomb, but all too straight for so great a friend of virtue.

Sir Simonds D'Ewes, who later married into the Clopton family, refers rather disparagingly to Sir William's first marriage: "The unworthiest match that ever any Clopton had was the alliance of Sir William Clopton of Kentwell with Johan daughter of Sir William Marrow Knt an alderman of the City of London in the time of Henry VII, and the noblest match was that of John Clopton, son and heir of the said Sir William Clopton, with Elizabeth, daughter of John Roydon Esq and Margaret his wife, daughter of Thomas Knevett Esq of Great Stanway, Essex, and the co-heir of many great and ancient families".

This was obviously the Knevett family who were already connected to the Cloptons by William's third marriage, of which Sir Simonds D'Ewes would no doubt have approved, though he himself did not marry into that particular branch of the family.

The Dilemma of Younger Sons

The wife of John Clopton mentioned above would have been the niece of William's third wife, Thomasine Knevett. In addition to his son John, William and his wife Joan Marrow had two more sons, William and Robert, and five daughters. Robert was a priest (possibly because there was no future for him at Kentwell Hall) but William was lucky enough to find a wealthy wife.

It was hard for younger sons who sometimes had very little to live on. They often went in for the Law or the Church, but it was even better to find a rich wife. William's wife was Elizabeth, daughter of Sir Thomas Saye of Lyston Hall in Essex and they went on to found the Clopton family of Lyston. One of the daughters, Elizabeth, was married to Sir Geoffrey Gates of Essex and her sister Anne married Richard Poley of Boxted.

Sir Stephen Peacock, Lord Mayor of London

John Clopton and his wife Elizabeth Roydon (who was the daughter of Margaret Knevett) had four sons and three daughters. The youngest son, George, who lived at Sudbury, was married to Alice, the daughter of Sir Stephen Peacock, Lord Mayor of London.

The eldest son and heir, William Clopton, was married first to Margaret, daughter of Sir Thomas Jermyn of Rushbrooke and secondly to Mary, the daughter of George Perient, who belonged to one of the Hertfordshire families who were part of the network. Mary later married into the Barnardiston family of Bedfordshire. Like the Perients, the Barnardiston family had links in Hertfordshire, Bedfordshire, Suffolk and Essex.

William inherited the manor when his father died in 1541, and he was then 32 years old. It was this William who was responsible for the building of Kentwell Hall, the beautiful house we see today.

Kentwell Hall was described later as "a very fair brick house with 12 wainscot rooms, the park stored with above 150 deer, a double dovehouse, fish ponds and other conveniencys, besides timber in the grounds and woods considerable".

The building was started about 1540, while the family were still living at Lutons, and we know it was finished before Sir William's death in 1562 because his mother's will, dated December 1st 1563, mentions "the new Mansion house of Kentwell Hall". There may have been traces of the ruins of the older house on the site where the new one was built, and there was certainly a timber framed barn, which is the building now known as the Moat House.

Lutons, the house which the family had occupied from the time they acquired the manor until the building of the new house, was pulled down a few years later.

The Waldegrave Connection

William and his first wife Margaret Jermyn had three sons. The eldest and youngest sons both died without issue, and the inheritance went to the second son, Francis, who was 23 years old when his father died in 1562.

Francis, however, died in 1578 without producing an heir, and it was Thomas, the son of the second marriage, who inherited the manor. He was married to Mary, daughter of Sir William Waldegrave of Smallbridge.

In the next generation we come across the Barnardistons again when Anne, the daughter of Sir Thomas Barnardiston of Clare, married Sir William Clopton, the eldest son of Thomas Clopton and Mary Waldegrave.

Sadly the marriage between William and Anne was to last for only five years. Anne, who would have been only 15 years old when she married, died in 1615 at the age of 20.

She left one daughter, also Anne, who was baptised at Clare on 2nd March 1612. After the death of his young wife William Clopton married again.

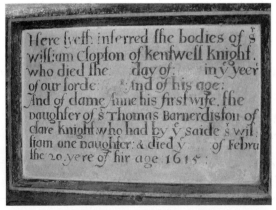

Plaque for William and Anne, Long Melford Church

His second marriage was to Elizabeth, the daughter of Sir Giles Alington whom we meet in the Underhill chapter. He lived at Horseheath, near Haverhill, but also held the manor of Wymondley in Hertfordshire.

William and Elizabeth had two sons but both died without producing any heirs. So the manor eventually descended to Anne, the only child of his first marriage, and to her husband Simonds D'Ewes.

The Barnardiston Family

Even before Anne Barnardiston married William Clopton in 1610 there had been many links between the two families. In 1520 Mary Walsingham, the daughter of Sir Edward Walsingham, Lieutenant of the Tower, married an earlier Sir Thomas Barnardiston. Later this lady, known as Lady Mary Barnardiston, married Francis Clopton, who afterwards married Sir Thomas Barnardiston's daughter from his first marriage. Then in the Parish Registers we find that a George Barnardiston married Mary Clopton at St Mary's, Bury St Edmunds in 1567, but exactly who they were, and where they fit in, is not clear.

The Barnardiston family was based at Kedington, sometimes known as Ketton, or Kediton, where they built a new nave in the church. There is the tomb of Lady Elizabeth Barnardiston who died in 1520, and is said to have "built the church roof new and covered it with lead". The Barnardistons, unlike many of the families we meet in our history, were Puritans - strongly opposed to the old Roman Catholic religion. There is a story that it was Sir Samuel Barnardiston whose handsome round head was noticed by one of the lady supporters of Cromwell's army, and from then on they were known as Roundheads.

The Puritans were generally averse to rich ornamentation in the churches but it seems that the Barnardistons were quite happy to erect monuments in Kedington Church to their own family. Arthur Mee tells us "inside we find as big a congregation in stone as many churches have of villagers on a Sunday, no less than nine men and women and eight children, all Barnardistons, of the family to which Kedington owes most of its treasures".

Sir Simonds D'Ewes, Historian and Antiquary

Sir Simonds D'Ewes, a distinguished lawyer and historian, wrote an autobiography and this, together with many of his letters, has been preserved, giving us a wonderful insight into the domestic life of a 17th century family.

Simonds D'Ewes was the eldest son of Paul D'Ewes of Stowlangtoft Hall, often referred to as Stow Hall. Paul died in 1631 and Simonds set up a fine monument in Stowlangtoft Church showing his father with his two wives and eight children. The monument was erected in 1624 and is the only known work of Jan Janson of St Martin-in-the-Fields.

Stowlangtoft Hall was demolished in the 19th century and a new house was built on a different site.

Close to the D'Ewes family home was Ixworth Hall, and much of the correspondence preserved in Simonds' memoirs was connected with his neighbours at Ixworth. It was later the home of his stepmother-in-law.

A Close and Loving Relationship

Anne Clopton and Simonds D'Ewes were married about 1630, when Anne would have been 16 years old, and it was obviously a very close and loving relationship.

Sir Simonds was a Member of Parliament and had to spend a great deal of time in London, but he wrote frequently to Anne telling her about his work in the 'House', or the 'Commons' and commenting on the details of family life which Anne had presumably mentioned in her letters to him.

He often refers to Lady Barnardiston. She was Anne's grandmother, and had been closely involved in her upbringing after Anne's mother had died when she was only three years old.

We find a great deal of information in these letters, but even more in the autobiography, and it becomes clear that Sir Simonds and his family were already closely acquainted with the Barnardistons.

Christmas at Kediton Hall

It was Christmas 1619, and Simonds had been invited to stay at Sir Nathaniel Barnardiston's dwelling at Kediton Hall. He had expected to see old Sir Thomas Barnardiston, Nathaniel's father, who usually came over at Christmas from Clare Priory, three miles distant. Simonds had visited him earlier in the year and described him as "a very aged man, yet he spoke so cheerfully and fed us so heartily, as verily I thought he had been a man of many years' continuance".

But when Simonds arrived for Christmas he was shocked and distressed to find that Thomas was newly deceased, and the next night he was an assistant at his burial, "which was at night, without any manner of solemnity befitting the antiquity of his extraction or the greatness of his estate".

Happier Memories

In spite of this sad event Simonds also has happy memories of this Christmas. He records, "I had my first sight of my dear and faithful wife, then in mourning apparel for her father and a mere child not full seven years old. She was the daughter of Sir William Clopton Knt., who died upon the 11th day of March last past in the year 1618".

It must have been a sad Christmas for Anne, having recently lost her father and now her grandfather. We also get the impression that her relationship with her stepmother was not particularly close. But her beloved grandmother, Dame Anne Barnardiston was still with them. Simonds describes her as "a woman of exemplary wisdom and piety who continueth alive, being very aged and blind".

A Student at the Middle Temple

Having described this very special Christmas, Simonds' autobiography goes on to tell us of his years as a student of Law at the Middle Temple. His training lasted for eight years, but he was evidently a keen scholar and enjoyed the law discussions:

> I cannot deny but the study of our common-law, which most men account to be very hard and difficult work, grew most delightful and pleasing unto me, especially after I was once called to the bar; and the rather because I had at one time fully resolved to have gone on with the most gainful and enriching practice of it; assuring myself by my studies and estate, to fit myself for the greatest places of preferment in England which were compatible to a common-lawyer.....

But he admits that soon after this his mind was turned to other things, "the serious cogitation of the initiated motion of my marriage with Anne, the sole daughter and heir of Sir William Clopton, Knt., late of Lutons Hall, commonly called Kentwell, in the county of Suffolk, in whom were met and conjoined all those qualifications I desired to meet with in a wife".

He goes on to say that Anne had been very religiously educated by her Grand-mother, Dame Anne Barnardiston, that she was the heir to a stately house in the town of Melford with an estate of about five hundred pounds per annum lying around it, which was not far distant from Lavenham where his own father had an estate. But he adds that she was "in every way so comely, as that alone, if all the rest had wanted, might have rendered her desirable".

Times of Joy and Times of Sadness

As we know the marriage did take place and they had about ten years of loving relationship - which included, as always, times of joy and times of sadness. They lost several daughters during their early childhood, and evidently there were also three sons who died at birth. At last, however, they had a little boy who survived.

But tragedy was to follow. Simonds writes: "One of the most sad and dismal occasions ... that ever befell me, ... the loss of my most dear, tender and only son, Clopton D'Ewes, being one year and nine months old. In July when he was born, by our pitching upon a proud, fretting, ill-conditioned woman for a nurse, it was doubtless the chief cause of his falling into fits and convulsions".

The doctor also comes in for criticism because of treatment "having been too violently and unskillfully applied by Dr. Despotine, an Italian physician in Bury".

Sir Simonds ends this chapter of his autobiography with a most touching reference to the death of his little son:

> We both found the sorrow for the loss of this child on whom we had bestowed so much care and affection, and whose delicate favour and bright grey eye was so deeply imprinted in our hearts, far to surpass our grief for the decease of his three elder brothers, who, dying almost as soon as they were born, were not so endeared to us as this was: and as I ended the third book of my life with the relation of the death of my father, so I will end this with the decease of my sweet and only son.

In 1641 a final tragedy was to befall the family when his beloved wife Anne died of smallpox. Her illness and death are recorded in detail, and again Sir Simonds is anxious to find someone to blame. Anne was staying with Lady Denton, her step-mother, at Ixworth Hall when she became ill. In spite of her serious condition, Lady Denton did not invite her to stay on, but allowed her to travel home to Stowlangtoft where she died shortly afterwards. There were many letters of condolence which are recorded in Sir Simonds' memoirs. Several were from members of the Stutville family, who were apparently neighbours, and who were also part of our group of related families.

Anne and Simonds had just one surviving child, a daughter called Cecilia. She was married to Sir Thomas Darcy of St Cleres Hall in Essex. Kentwell Hall descended to Cecilia and her husband and became their family home. Sir Thomas Darcy was created a baronet in 1660, and around this time he made considerable repairs to the interior of the house. Cecilia and Thomas had only one daughter, Anne, who died in infancy. Lady Darcy died on 29th May 1661 and was buried in the Clopton Aisle of Long Melford Church on 1st June.

On this rather sad but intimate note we must leave the Cloptons, but we can be thankful to Sir Simonds D'Ewes for allowing us to share some of the thoughts and aspirations, joys and sorrows, of this 17th century Suffolk family.

Kentwell Hall still stands today, very much the same as it was when Sir William Clopton built it in 1540. And because of the initiative and good will of the present owners, we are able to visit it and experience some of the aspects of life in a country house in the days of the Tudors and Stuarts. For one brief moment we can leave the 21st century, and enter the world of our distant kinsmen who lived here nearly 500 years ago.

Chapter 12

The Kytsons and Gages of Hengrave Hall

Hengrave Hall, situated about 3 miles north of Bury St Edmunds, is possibly the stateliest of all the stately homes in Suffolk. For 14 generations it was the home of the Kytson and Gage families, all of whom were descended from Sir Thomas Kytson who bought the estate from the Duke of Buckingham in 1521.

The Kytsons and Gages married into many of the leading families of Suffolk, and one of the lateral branches led down to George Washington - first President of America.

Hengrave Hall Gatehouse

Hengrave, originally in the possession of the Abbey of St Edmund, was held from the 12th to the 15th century by the de Hemmegrave family from whom it took its name. It was probably one of the Hemmegraves who built the church which stands in the grounds of the Hall. It was later rebuilt, but the original Saxon tower was left intact, and can still be seen today.

The Stafford family, Dukes of Buckingham, acquired the estate in the 15th century when Henry Lord Stafford married Margaret Countess of Richmond, who was to become the mother of Henry VII. Hengrave was part of the marriage settlement.

Satins, Laces and Cloth of Gold

Thomas Kytson was a very wealthy merchant, dealing in fine cloth and tapestries, including satins, laces, cloth of gold, furs and velvets. The family came originally from Lancashire where they made their fortune by exporting Kendal Cloth, made from the fine wool of the Lakeland sheep.

But at the time when he bought his Suffolk estate Thomas was probably living in London, where he was a much-respected citizen and a member of the Mercers Guild. He had a house in Milk Street and a Country House at Stoke Newington. He also had a grand house in Flanders, where much of his overseas trade was based. Thomas was married to Margaret, the daughter of John Donnington of

Stoke Newington. It seems likely that the 'Country House' would have been inherited from Margaret's family.

The building of Hengrave Hall began in 1524 and took 13 years to complete. Sir Thomas was determined to make it one of the grandest houses in the country, modelling it partly on Hampton Court which had recently been built by Cardinal Wolsey. One difference would be the colour of the bricks, which were to be white instead of red, in order to harmonise with the stonework. The bricks were locally made, probably from Elmswell, and the stone was quarried from Kings Cliff in Northamptonshire.

Other materials would have been brought from various monasteries which were being demolished at the time of the Dissolution.

The Strikingly Magnificent Gables

One important feature of the new Hall was to be the moat, to reflect the "strikingly magnificent gables" on the south front. We are told that the outbuildings included "dovecote, grange, great barn, mill, forge, great stable and various offices, separate kennels for the hounds and the spaniels and a mews for the hawks". In addition we know there was a vineyard, orchards, gardens, fish ponds, and a bowling alley. There would almost certainly have been a rabbit warren nearby, though this is not recorded. The manor house in Tudor times would have been completely self-sufficient except perhaps for the spices which were imported from the East. As was the custom at the time, the kitchen buildings were detached from the house, and connected by a covered passageway.

The building of this great house was a tremendous undertaking. The digging of the 50ft wide moat alone would have been a daunting task, involving vast numbers of workmen. Little did they know, as they laboured away with their picks and shovels, that in 200 years time another generation of workmen would be filling it all in again! The house itself was truly magnificent, and no expense had been spared. A recent account describes it in the following glowing terms:

> The south front, gatehouse and inner court are superb examples of sixteenth century domestic architecture, but the most breathtaking feature of the house is the oratory, which contains beautiful linen-fold panelling and a window of superlative stained glass. This was manufactured in Picardy in the 1520s and brought to Hengrave in three great chests by boat to Ipswich and thence by cart. The window depicts biblical scenes and is regarded as one of the finest examples of its type in Britain. Also notable is the banqueting hall, complete with minstrels' gallery, and the dining room, which has a superb Jacobean fireplace.

Sheriff of London and Master of the Mercers Guild

During the thirteen years when Hengrave Hall was under construction, Thomas was probably having a great time in London and Flanders, with frequent visits

to Hengrave to see his beautiful mansion taking shape. His career was at its height, and in 1533 he was Sheriff of London and Master of the Mercers Guild, after which, as was the custom, he was awarded a knighthood.

But what about Margaret - where was she during these years? She must have been very young when she married. She was born in 1509, so the marriage probably took place around 1525.

She would not have moved into the old Hall at Hengrave because this was gradually being demolished to provide timber for the new house, so she was probably living in London, or perhaps out in the country at Stoke Newington. Meanwhile she was giving birth to their children. They had four daughters, Catherine, Dorothy, Frances, and Anne. Catherine was later to marry into the Spencer family - ancestors of the Spencers of Althorp.

Sir Thomas Kytson

A New House and a New Baby

There would have been great rejoicing when Sir Thomas, Margaret, and the four little girls moved into their beautiful new home. And there would have been even more rejoicing when Margaret discovered she was pregnant once again. Surely this time it must be a son!

Early in 1540 the baby arrived - and it was a boy. But sadly Sir Thomas was never to have the joy of knowing that he now had a son and heir. He died a few months before the baby was born.

But life at Hengrave Hall went on. Margaret, as we shall discover later, was a strong and feisty lady, with a determination to live life to the full. She went on to have two further marriages and seven more children. The second marriage was to Sir Richard Long, by whom she had four children.

Finally she married John Bourchier, Earl of Bath. The Earl, by his first wife, had had a son John who was later to marry Margaret's daughter Frances Kytson. Obviously John and Frances were not blood relations so there was no problem on that count, but it would need a very gifted mathematician to work out their exact relationship!

Margaret Bourchier, Countess of Bath

Margaret was now Countess of Bath, a situation which she obviously found very pleasing. She liked to have her status acknowledged, and in later life her young Washington and Spencer relations always addressed her as "Great Aunt Bath". Their parents however still called her Cousin Kit, a reminder that she was first and foremost a member of the Kytson family.

The Washington connection came through Sir Thomas Kytson's sister Margaret who married John Washington from her father's home town of Warton in Lancashire. Margaret and John's son, Laurence Washington, moved to Sulgrave Manor in Northamptonshire,

Sulgrave Manor

creating the link which led by direct line, seven generations later, to the birth of George Washington, the first President of the United States of America.

Not far away at Wormleighton lived the Spencer family who were also related to the Kytsons. Catherine Kytson, the eldest daughter of Margaret and Thomas was, as already mentioned, married to Sir John Spencer, a wealthy sheep farmer and wool merchant.

The Washington and Spencer cousins grew up together and as they grew older some of the boys became involved in adventures which threatened to put them in great danger. They had several politically motivated and hot-headed young friends who narrowly avoided imprisonment.

Princess Elizabeth, Prisoner at Woodstock

According to Cynthia Harnett's (partly fictional) "Stars of Fortune" two of the young rebels, Tom Tresham (a relative of Sir William Parr) and Chris Hatton were planning to rescue the young and beautiful Princess Elizabeth from Woodstock, where she was being held after a plot to overthrow her sister Mary.

Why these young people with a strong Roman Catholic background would be trying to rescue Elizabeth we cannot tell. The Kytsons and Washingtons, like many of the leading families in the area, were staunch Catholics, having secretly, or defiantly, continued to follow the "old religion" through the reigns of Henry VIII and Edward VI. Now that Mary was on the throne things were easier, but they were soon to get very much worse. During these troubled times there were many courageous men and women who were prepared to die for their religion. But in the case of these youngsters it was probably the need to rebel against parental authority rather than religious zeal which spurred them on in their adventures.

As far as we know the young Washingtons and Spencers soon settled down, but Tom Tresham, later Sir Thomas, and Chris Hatton continued to lead very turbulent lives. Both were imprisoned at various times and had all their estates taken away, but were eventually pardoned and returned to royal favour. Chris Hatton later became Chancellor of England, and Sir Thomas Tresham had his estates at Rushton returned to him, and became Sheriff of Northamptonshire.

The Treshams and The Gunpowder Plot

But the Tresham family troubles were by no means over. Both Thomas's son Francis and his daughter Elizabeth were closely involved in the Gunpowder Plot. Elizabeth was married to Lord Monteagle, who received the famous 'Monteagle Letter' which inadvertently led to the exposing of the Plot, and the death or imprisonment of all the conspirators, including her brother Francis. Francis actually died in prison, but because he refused on his deathbed to admit his guilt, he was deemed to be a traitor. After his death he was decapitated, and his head displayed on a pole outside the family home at Rushton Hall.

The Greyhounds and the Earl of Pembroke

"Aunt Bath" continued to hold sway over her large family including the Washingtons and the Spencers, and continued to assert her authority both inside and outside the family circle. There is a story, supported by a letter in the archives, telling how she had the audacity to write to the Earl of Pembroke accusing him of stealing two prize greyhounds which she was sending as a present to the Queen. The accusation was denied, but the story goes on to relate how Laurence Washington, enjoying a day's hawking with Sir William Parr, was admiring a very fine pair of greyhounds. "Yes," said Sir William, "I recently received them as a gift from the Earl of Pembroke." Laurence Washington suddenly realised that they were very similar to the greyhounds he had seen at Aunt Bath's home - and drew his own conclusions!

The Cornwallis Family of Brome Hall

The Kytson line of descent now continued with Margaret's son Thomas, who was born just after his father's death. He took his father's title and in due course married Elizabeth, the daughter of Sir Thomas Cornwallis of Brome. In the archives is a letter written by Margaret Duchess of Norfolk to Anne Cornwallis - Elizabeth's mother - just before the marriage. The letter reminds us of the custom of sending young sons or daughters to live with other noble families as pages or maids, to give them experience and training for the role they would be expected to play in society.

Elizabeth (Bess) had obviously been living with the Duchess as her maid, and the Duchess would like to have her back again until her marriage if possible.

The Duchess writes: "I must desire you, good Madam, to let me have Bess Cornwallis agayne, because one of my women has desyred leave to go to London for a time, and soe I have very few here, an, if you will so like, I woulde gladly keep her with me, till her marriage, yet not meaning to seperate Mr. Kytson and her, for, yf he will not come to Kenninghall, you shall have her to you, when you will".

Later the Duke of Norfolk sent a message to Sir Thomas Cornwallis and to the Countess of Bath, suggesting that the marriage might be celebrated at His Grace's house.

No doubt it would have been a very grand wedding and the Earl and Countess of Bath (the bridegroom's mother and step-father) would have been suitably honoured.

Lady Elizabeth Cornwallis

Young Thomas Kytson, although still in his minority, was celebrating his second marriage. He had been briefly married to Jane, the daughter of William Lord Paget, who died without issue only a year after the marriage.

Thomas's mother died in 1561 just a year after her husband, John Bourchier. Great Aunt Bath, as she was affectionately known by the family, lies in state in the church at Hengrave with her three husbands.

The Royal Visit

In 1578 Thomas and Elizabeth were honoured by a visit from the Queen during her Royal Progress to Norfolk. Although the Kytsons were Roman Catholics they were powerful enough to warrant a visit, and it is said that when the Queen tried to persuade them to change their religion, they presented her with a very valuable pearl which she accepted graciously.

Thomas Kytson was amongst the nobility and gentry who welcomed the Queen on her arrival at Bury St Edmunds. We read that "there were two hundred young gentlemen, clad all in white velvet and three hundred … apparelled in black velvet coates and fair chaynes, all ready at one instant and place, with fifteen hundred serving men more on horseback …to receive the Queens Highness into Suffolk". The contemporary writer, a certain Thomas Churchyard, Gentleman, goes on to give more details:

> And near Bury, Sir William Drury, for his part, at his house, made the Queen's Highness a costly and delicat dinner; and Sir Robert Jermyn of Rooshbroke feasted the French embassadoures two several times; with which charges and courtesie they stood marvellously contented. The sheriffe, Sir William Spring, Sir Thomas Kytson, Sir Arthur Higham, and divers others of worship, kept great houses, and sundry, either at the Queen's coming or return, solemnly feasted her Highness, … from thence to Sir Thomas Kytson's, where in very deede, the fare and banquet did so exceede a number of other places that it is worthy of mention. A show representing the fayries, as well as might be, was there seene; in which show a riche jewell was presented to the Queen's Highness.

The Last of the Kytsons at Hengrave

Sir Thomas and Elizabeth were the last of the Kytsons of Hengrave. Their only son John died in infancy and their elder daughter Margaret, who was married to Sir Charles Cavendish, the son of the Countess of Shrewsbury (Bess of Hardwick), died without issue during her father's lifetime.

Their daughter Mary inherited the estate and married Thomas Darcy Earl Rivers, Viscount Colchester. They had one son, Thomas, and four daughters. Thomas died without issue and it was Penelope Darcy, their third daughter, who inherited all the Hengrave estates.

With the introduction of the Darcy family, the Kytson and Gage dynasty became even more closely linked with that amazing network of families in Hertfordshire, Bedfordshire, Suffolk and Essex who had been marrying into each other for more than ten generations. They included the Tyrells, Cloptons, Mordaunts, and Hunts, and the Mannocks, Petres and Waldegraves. One of the most distinguished members of the family was Sir Thomas More, whose daughter Elizabeth was married to Sir John Darcy.

Penelope Darcy and Three Adoring Suitors

Penelope had three adoring suitors all of whom were desperate to marry her. She told them, in jest, that if they were patient she would marry each in turn. As it happened, that is just what she did!

Her first marriage to Sir George Trenchard was a very brief one, and by the age of 17 she was a widow. Her third marriage, to Sir William Hervey of Ickworth, also seems to have been unproductive, so it was the second marriage, to Sir John Gage of Firle in Sussex, by which Penelope became the matriarch of the succeeding nine generations of Gages at Hengrave.

Penelope Darcy we are told was a great beauty, though it is said that her portrait at Hengrave does not bear this out. But it seems that she was a very loving and caring lady and a wonderful wife and mother.

In the "Baronetage of England" written in 1771 we read: "The lady Penelope, wife to Sir John Gage, of Firle, by whom she had four sons and five daughters; and being a lady of great fortune, and greater hospitality and tenderness to her children, as keeping most of them together in her house of Hengrave many years, in a family of above one hundred in number, and leaving out of her own estate, considerable estates to each of her sons, and further contributing to the marriage-portions of her daughters, out of her particular love for her third son, Edward, as above, and through her desire to raise another branch of the family of the Gages, she left to him, the said Edward, her house of Hengrave, with the bulk of her estate".

Family Life at Hengrave

Life at Hengrave would have been very comfortable, with a large, happy family, servants to cook and wash and clean, and a beautiful house and gardens.

Penelope would probably have taught the younger children to read and write, while the older boys would have had lessons from the family priest, studying Latin, theology, and philosophy.

**Sir John Gage,
First Baronet of Firle**

The Gages were a recusant family, true to their Roman Catholic principles, but outwardly conforming to the Church of England customs. Among the household accounts we find "£3 for teaching the children the Virginalls from Christmas to Easter". Another item in the same account book states "A buck and ½ a stag - 10 shillings".

John Wilbye, Master of Music

In 1595 the famous madrigal writer, John Wilbye, became the Master of Music at Hengrave and lived with the family for more than 30 years. Among his works, "Adieu Sweet Amaryllis" and "Draw on Sweet Night" are still remembered and performed by madrigal groups at the present day. Sir Philip Sydney was also a frequent visitor, and poet and musician must have met on many occasions.

Also in the family records and Parish Registers are many references to the fact that some members of the family were "buried in linnen and paid the fine". At this time it was the law that bodies must be buried in wool, presumably to boost the wool trade, but occasionally the aristocracy decided they would like to be buried in linen - a status symbol perhaps.

Another interesting note in the archives tells us that in 1674 Hengrave Hall was top of the list for the Hearth Tax in Suffolk, with no less than 51 hearths!

Penelope and John seem to have had a good marriage lasting for over twenty years. John died in 1633 and their son Edward inherited the estate. Penelope later married Sir William Hervey and died in 1661.

Edward, like so many other members of the Kytson and Gage families, had a large variety of wives. He was married first to Mary Hervey and afterwards to Frances Ashton; Anne Watkins; Elizabeth Fielding and Mrs Bridget Slaughter.

But it was from his first marriage that the line of succession continued. His grandson John married Elizabeth Rokewood, the sole heiress of Thomas Rokewood of Coldham Hall at Stanningfield, and in the next generation their son Thomas Rokewood Gage became the master of both Hengrave and Coldham Hall.

Ambrose Rokewood and The Gunpowder Plot

The merging of the Gage and Rokewood families created yet another link with the Gunpowder Plot. It was Ambrose Rokewood, Elizabeth's great grandfather, who was supposed to have acquired the gunpowder for the conspirators, though according to some accounts he was not actively involved at all.

But it was well known that he had some very fast horses at Coldham and these were used by the conspirators to make their get-away. This was enough to implicate him, and led to his arrest and execution.

John and Elizabeth seem to have lived mainly at Coldham Hall, possibly because Hengrave was undergoing various alterations during this period. The moat was filled in and one wing of the original house was demolished.

John died in 1728 at the early age of 40, while Elizabeth lived to be 76, and died in 1759. Both are buried at Stanningfield.

When his father died Sir Thomas Rokewood Gage inherited Hengrave and Coldham and married another heiress, Lucy Knight. Their son Thomas, the next heir, was to marry Mary Teresa Throckmorton. The Throckmortons were a very well-known recusant family and in Queen Elizabeth's reign Elizabeth Throckmorton was famous for her ability to hide Jesuit priests in her various country houses.

The End of an Era

Thomas and Mary provided a son and a grandson, both called Thomas, to carry on the family name. But the Gage connection with Hengrave was coming to an end. There were no more male heirs, and when Henrietta Gage died in 1887 the house was sold. Between 1887 and 1952 it went through many changes and

Hengrave Hall Courtyard

during the First World War it was used as a hospital. But never again was it to become a family home. In 1952 came the Big Sale which lasted for 8 days, when Hengrave Hall with all its contents, and all the estate farms, houses and other property came up for auction. The Hall itself was bought by the Sisters of the Assumption for use as a school, and later as an Ecumenical Centre.

It seems that the Gages must still have had some connections with Hengrave because various family items were included in the sale. There were many valuable pieces of furniture, works of art and pictures, and it has been said that the Holbein portrait of the first Sir Thomas Kytson was among them, but there is no record of this in the sale catalogue. Another interesting item was an embroidered shirt said to have belonged to King Henry VII which was sold for £55 (probably over £1,000 by today's values). This was almost certainly one of the Gage treasures.

On a less lofty plane, we do know that there were two large wooden boxes containing a collection of faded but rather beautiful curtains, and on the inside of the lid of each box was a Gage signature. One box also contained a sketch book with the inscription "T Gage 1839 Coldham". It contained a number of pencil sketches including one of Firle, the ancestral home of the Gage family in Sussex. Jotted down on the back page was a list of pheasants which had been caught on a day's shooting at Hengrave.

Grand Occasions Recalled

During the 300 years when Hengrave Hall was the home of the Kytson and Gage family it saw many grand occasions and had close contacts with various reigning monarchs. It is said that Queen Mary stopped briefly at Hengrave on her way to Framlingham Castle in 1553. While there is no definite evidence of this, it could well be true because King Henry VIII was Godfather to Margaret Kytson's son Henry (by her second marriage to Sir Richard Long) and we know that her third husband, the Earl of Bath, was a strong supporter of Queen Mary. And of course there was the Royal Visit in 1578. A room - "The Queens Chamber" - was named in her honour. In the next century King James II visited Hengrave on several occasions and attended the wedding of William Gage and Charlotte Bond.

But perhaps the thing for which the Gages will be most remembered is the greengage, the new kind of plum brought to this country by a member of the family in the 1800s. But no one seems to know exactly who was responsible. It could have been the botanist Sir Thomas Gage, a Fellow of the Linnaean Society. Or perhaps it was another botanist, John Gage, who is reported to have brought some new butterflies to England. If he was bringing butterflies, why not bring plum trees as well?

Unfortunately we do not often see greengages in the shops these days but if you do happen to find some, as you bite into the luscious juicy fruit, just think of the Gages of Hengrave, who made their mark in many ways, but not least by bringing us that delightfully flavoured fruit - the greengage plum.

Hengrave Hall

Pedigrees of inter-related families in Suffolk and Essex

Abbreviations

osp - obit sine prole (died without offspring). MI - Memorial Inscription
m - married; d - daughter or died (according to context)

The arms and blazons are reproduced from the Victoria County Histories
by permission of the General Editor

NOTE: Names from this section are not included in the indexes.
Some of the pedigrees were originally drawn up for a previous book. Any
references which are not relevant to the present book can be found in
A Hertfordshire Family 1555-1923

Descent of the Argenteins and Alingtons
Lords of the Manor of Wymondley and Cupbearers to the King

DAVID DE ARGENTEIN a Norman who served under William the Conqueror

JOHN DE ARGENTEIN, m.Ellen Fitzteck. Fought with King Stephen (1135-54) against the Empress Matilda, and is thought to have built Great Wymondley Castle. (Earthworks to the east of the parish church)

REGINALD DE ARGENTEIN d. c1217. A grave slab in Baldock Church possibly commemorates this Reginald, though some think it was his great-grandson

RICHARD DE ARGENTEIN. d.1246. Sheriff of Herts and Essex, Governor of Hertford Castle. In 1225 his name appears as one of the witnesses to the Statute of Magna Carta, which set out the provisions made in 1215. It was this Richard who founded the Priory of Austin Canons at Little Wymondley.

GILES DE ARGENTEIN, d.1283. Fought with Henry III in Wales, but later rebelled and fought against the King at Evesham. He was later pardoned and his lands restored. The Inquisition Post Mortem mentions his office as Cup-bearer to the King

ARGENTEIN. *Gules three covered cups argent.*

REGINALD DE ARGENTEIN 1240-1307. Inherited the family lands, including 17 manors in Cambs, Suffolk, Norfolk and Herts. m. Laura de Vere, sister to the Earl of Oxford. (This could be the Argentein commemorated in Baldock Church - opinions differ.)

JOHN DE ARGENTEIN. d.1318. Described as 2nd Baron Argentein. he m. Agnes Beresford. His tombstone was once on the floor of Little Wymondley Church, but was removed, or covered up, in the restoration of 1875. It is likely that John was originally buried in the Priory Chapel, but was re-buried in the parish church when the Priory was suppressed in 1537.

JOHN DE ARGENTEIN 1318-83. Performed the office of Cup-bearer at the Coronation of Richard II in 1377. He m. Margaret Darcy and had 3 daughters. He also had an illegitimate son William, who managed with difficulty to gain the right to inherit his father's property.

WILLIAM DE ARGENTEIN, d.1419. He re-built the Hall (Wymondley Bury) and this is mainly the building which we see today. His son John predeceased him and he was succeeded by his grandson John - 5 years old

JOHN DE ARGENTEIN, 1414-20. He only outlived his grandfather by one year, dying at the age of 6. He was the last of the Argenteins to be Lord of Wymondley. His two heirs were his sisters, Joan, aged 13 and Elizabeth, aged 12..

JOAN DE ARGENTEIN m. Robert Alington, osp, Joan's sister Elizabeth inherited the manor.

ELIZABETH DE ARGENTEIN m. William Alington. Inherited the manor of Wymondley

JOHN ALINGTON, d.1480. m. Mary Cheney

SIR WILLIAM ALINGTON, c1449-1485, m. Elizabeth Wentworth. Killed in the battle of Bosworth

SIR GYLES ALINGTON, 1483-1521. Until he came of age Wymondley was controlled by his guardians Richard Gardiner and Sir Gilbert Talbot. m① Margaret Spencer of Althorpe (see Spencer tree), m② Mary Gardiner, d. of his guardian

SIR GILES ALINGTON, 1500-86, m① Ursula Drury (see Soame tree), m② Alice Middleton. He outlived his son Robert and grandson Giles

SIR GILES ALINGTON, 1572-1638, succeeded his great-grandfather at the age of 14. m①, 1594, Dorothy Cecil, m② the daughter of his half-sister. For this "incestuous match" he was fined £32,000 by the Star Chamber and pardoned "on condition that he did not live with his niece of the half blood". His daughter Ann m. Sir Thomas Fanshawe of Ware Park (see Note (*2) on Soame tree)

WILLIAM ALINGTON 1610-48, m.Elizabeth Tollemache. Created Baron Alington of Killard by Charles I in 1642.

WILLIAM ALINGTON d.1684, Created Baron Alington of Wymondley by Charles II in 1682. m. Diana Russell (who later sold the manor of Wymondley).

HILDEBRANDE ALINGTON became 4th Baron of Killard on his nephew Giles' death. He bought back the manor in 1704. He died childless in 1722 and the manor went, in equal shares, to his 3 nieces.

GILES ALINGTON 1681-91. 3rd Baron of Killard & 2nd Baron of Wymondley. At his death, aged 10, the Wymondley title became extinct. His uncle Hildebrande inherited the Irish title. Due to a faulty will Giles' mother, was able to sell the land, which had been in the family since the Norman Conquest, to Elizabeth Hamilton (d. of Lord John Culpepper)

JULIANA ALINGTON m. Viscount Howe

DIANA ALINGTON m. Sir George Warburton. Their d. Diana (*1) m. Richard, Lord Grosvenor, who acquired the other two thirds of the manor

CATHERINE ALINGTON m. Nathaniel Napier

(***1**) Diana's husband Richard became Lord of the Manor but it is unlikely that members of the Grosvenor family ever lived at Wymondley. Sir Richard Grosvenor sold the manor in 1767. It went to the Wilshere family, and William Wilshere was the last to perform the ceremony of Cup-bearer at the Coronation of George IV in 1820. The house and land had already been sold (in 1806) to the Heathcote family, who were descendants of the Nodes family of Shephall.

The Barnardiston Family
of Suffolk and Bedfordshire

THOMAS de BARNARDISTON, of Barnardiston in Suffolk, lived in the reign of Edward II (1307-27). m. Margery, d. of William Willoughby of Suffolk

SIR THOMAS BARNARDISTON lived in the reign of Edward III (1327-77). m. Lucie, d. of Robert Havering of Norfolk

WALTER BARNARDISTON lived in the reign of Richard II (1377-99)m. Frances, d. of Thomas Kingsman

THOMAS de BARNARDISTON

JOHN BARNARDISTON of Keddington and Barnardiston. (osp)

ROGER BARNARDISTON of Grimsby, d. about 1440 m. Elizabeth, d. of Sir Edmund Perpoint

BARNARDISTON.
Azure a fesse dancetry ermine between six crosslets argent.

THOMAS BARNARDISTON of Suffolk. m. Joan Vavasour

WALTER BARNARDISTON - Clarke of the Church of Keddington, Suffolk at the time of Henry VI

SIR THOMAS BARNARDISTON of Keddington at the time of Edward IV, Edward V and Richard III. m. Elizabeth, d. of John Newport of Pelham in Hertfordshire (connected with Bulls and Casons)

SIR THOMAS BARNARDISTON of Ketton (Keddington). m. Ann, d. of Thomas Fitz Lucas of Saxham

A daughter, m. Thomas, Lord Audley, Chancellor of England

GEORGE BARNARDISTON, m. Elizabeth, d. of Thomas Burley of Lynn in Norfolk. In 1543 he acquired Ickwell Bury in Northill, Bedfordshire

SIR THOMAS BARNARDISTON, m. c1520, Mary, d. of Sir Edward Walsingham, Lieutenant of the Tower. (Mary later m. Francis Clopton of Kentwell)

JOHN BARNARDISTON of Ickwell Bury, m. Joan, d. of Thomas Mellor (or Miller) of Lynn in Norfolk. Joan d. 1568. John d. 1587 (buried in the aisle of Northill Church)

ELIZABETH BARNARDISTON m① ... Brookesbye. m② Francis Clopton (see note 1 below)	**SIR THOMAS BARNARDISTON** m① Elizabeth Hanchett m② Ann Bygrave (alias Warren) of Hertfordshire	**ANN BARNARDISTON** m.1610, William Clopton (brother of Elizabeth's second husband, Francis)	**GEORGE BARNARDISTON** of Ickwell Bury. d.1577. m. Mary, d. of Sir George Perient of Digswell	**MARGARET BARNARDISTON**, m. 1573, William Fyshe of Stanford Manor in Southill. The Old House at Ickwell Green came to the Fyshe family from the Barnardiston estate.	**SIGISMUND BARNARDISTON** m. 12th June 1582 at Northill to Mary Wynche (d. 1594)

SIR THOMAS BARNARDISTON m. Mary, d. of Sir Richard Knightly of Fawsley. ①

GYLES BARNARDISTON of Clare in Suffolk m. Philippa, d. of Sir William Waldegrave of Smallbridge in Bures, Suffolk (see Waldegrave Tree) ②

ROBERT BARNARDISTON of Ickwell Bury. m. Katherine, d. of George, son of John, the first Lord Mordaunt of Turvey

SIR WILLIAM FYSHE of The Old House, Ickwell Green m. Elizabeth, d. of Sir Thomas Barnardiston of Suffolk (his 3rd cousin once removed)

HANNA BARNARDISTON m. John Brograve of Hammels in Hertfordshire, (Related to the Leventhorpes of Shingle Hall and to the Brownes of Abbess Roding)	**SIR NATHANIAL BARNARDISTON** m. Jane, d. of Sir Stephen Soame (Lord Mayor of London in 1598) and grand-daughter of Ann Knighton and Richard Hunt. (see Soame and Hunt Trees)	**ELIZABETH BARNARDISTON** m. Sir William Fyshe (her 3rd cousin once removed)	**HENRY BARNARDISTON** of Ickwell Bury, d. 1640. m. Margaret, d. of Robert Hares of the town of Bedford	**RICHARD BARNARDISTON** of Ickwell. bapt 19th August 1604

NOTE 1: There were many connections between the Barnardistons and the Cloptons of Kentwell Hall. Around 1540 Francis Clopton married Lady Mary Barnardiston, widow of Sir Thomas Barnardiston, and afterwards he married Sir Thomas's daughter Elizabeth (the widow of ... Brookesbye). His brother William Clopton married Sir Thomas Barnardiston's other daughter Anne.

From the Parish Registers:
In 1567 George Barnardiston married Mary Clopton at St Mary's, Bury St Edmunds.
In 1610 Ann Barnardiston, d. of Sir Thomas Barnardiston, married William Clopton at Clare.

Note from White's History of Suffolk: Sir Thomas Barnardiston of Keddington was created baronet in 1663. In the reign of Queen Anne two baronets of the family sat in Parliament at the same time - Sir Samuel and Sir Thomas.

ROBERT BARNARDISTON, d. 1652. In 1680 his son George conveyed Ickwell Bury to John Harvey

The Brooke Family (Lords Cobham)
of Aspall Hall in Suffolk, Abbess Roding in Essex, Barkway in Hertfordshire, and Cobham Hall in Kent.

The manor of Aspall was held by ancestors of the Harmer family (the Peverells) from the time of Edward the Confessor. Later it passed to the Aspall family, who were descendants of the Peverells, and for a time it followed the descent of the manor of Little Bradley. The ancestral line comes down from Sir Payne Peverell, through Peche, Aspall, Notbeame, Gedding, Hinkley, Caldebeck, Underhill, Knighton, Bull and Harmer. The Brooke family acquired the manor of Aspall through the de la Poles. Catherine Brooke, who married George Kympton at Bengeo in 1568, almost certainly belongs to this family.

RANULF PEVERELL held the manor before 1066

↓

RALPH PEVERELL, Lord of the Manor of Aspall at the time of the Domesday survey (1086)

↓

EDMUND PEVERELL (*1) m. Alice, sister of Walter de Langton, Bishop of Lichfield and Coventry, who held part of the manor of Aspall in 1281. Edmund Peverell had probably inherited the other part of the manor, and by this marriage the two parts became united.

JOHN PEVERELL osp | **MARGARET PEVERELL** m. William de la Pole (de la Pole tree ↓)

BRAYBROOKE
Argent seven voided lozenges gules.

SIR JOHN de la POLE m. Joan, d. of John, Lord Cobham

JOAN de la POLE Baroness Cobham, d. 1433. m. Sir Reginald Braybrooke

JOAN BRAYBROOKE Baroness Cobham, d. 1442. m. Sir Thomas Brooke, d.1439, MP for Somerset 1417-27. Became 5th Lord Cobham

CECIL, MARQUESS OF SALISBURY
Barry of ten pieces argent and azure six scutcheons sable with a lion argent in each differenced with a crescent

EDWARD BROOKE of Aspall 6th Lord Cobham, d.1464. A zealous Yorkist who participated in the victory of St Albans in 1454. m. Elizabeth, d. of James, Lord Audley. | **REGINALD BROOKE**, d. 1482 m. Anne Everton. Inherited Aspall from his brother in 1464

JOHN BROOKE 7th Lord Cobham, m.① Eleanor Austell of Suffolk, osp; m② Margaret, d. of Edward Nevill Lord Abergavenny | **EDWARD BROOKE**, Lord of the Manor of Aspall. d. 1541. (*2), m. Florence, d. of Robert Ashfield of Stowlangtoft, Suffolk

| **THOMAS BROOKE** 8th Lord Cobham, d.1529. m.① Dorothy, d. of Sir Henry Heydon m.② Dorothy, widow of ... Sothwell m.③ Elizabeth Hart | **GEORGE BROOKE** of Aspall, d. 1554. m. Ann, d. of John Carew of Somerset | **EDWARD BROOKE** ------- **JOHN BROOKE** ------- **WALTER BROOKE** | **RICHARD BROOKE** ------- **FRANCIS BROOKE** ------- **REGINALD BROOKE** | **ROBERT BROOKE** m. Joan Pranell (see Brooke of Barkway tree) |

GEORGE BROOKE 9th Lord Cobham, KG, 1497-1558. m. Ann, d. of Edmund Lord Bray. They had a d. Catherine who was probably the Catherine Brooke who m. George Kympton at Bengeo in 1568 (*3). | **GEORGE BROOKE**, d.1557 m.① Alice, d. of Sir John Tyrrell of Gipping Hall near Stowmarket in Suffolk (related to the Browne family). Monument in Stowmarket church. | m.② Elizabeth, d. of Edmund Withypoole of Ipswich

WILLIAM BROOKE 10th Lord Cobham, 1527-1596. m.① Dorothy, d. of George Nevill Lord Abergavenny m.② Frances Newton, Lady of the Bedchamber. Their d. Elizabeth m. Robert Cecil 1st Earl of Salisbury (*4). | **GEORGE BROOKE**, d. about 1580. m.① Mary, d. of Edward Jobson son of Sir Francis Jobson of Doniland in Essex | m.② Katherine, d. of George Jernegan MP for Orford and Eleanor Spelman

| **HENRY BROOKE** 11th Lord Cobham, KG, 1564-1618, osp. Warden of the Cinque Ports. Imprisoned in the Tower with his brother George for complicity in the Raleigh conspiracy. m.1601, Frances, d. of Charles Howard 1st Earl of Nottingham. His nephew inherited. | **GEORGE BROOKE** Imprisoned in the Tower. Executed 1603. (*5) | **EDWARD BROOKE**, m. Agnes, d. of Thomas Fastolf of Pettaugh in Suffolk. (Brooke of Nacton tree ↓) (The Fastolf family probably built the famous 'Ancient House' in Ipswich in the late 15th century. Several members of the family served as MP for Ipswich.) |

SIR WILLIAM BROOKE 12th Lord Cobham. Only son of George. Succeeded his uncle when his titles and lands were restored. | **EDWARD BROOKE**, d. 1679, buried at Aspall. m. Rebecca Wiseman, who died 12th August 1699 and is buried at St Margaret's, Ipswich.

JOHN BROOKE, m. Mary, d. of George Green of Athlington. In 1702 John Brooke sold the manor of Aspall to Temple Chevallier of Jersey - a cider maker. Aspall Hall has since that time been famous for its cider.

The Brooke Family (Lords Cobham)
of Aspall Hall in Suffolk, Abbess Roding in Essex, Barkway in Hertfordshire, and Cobham Hall in Kent.

NOTES

(*1) Copinger states that Alice de Langton married Edmund Peverell, but the VCH suggests that she married Robert Peverell and Edmund was their son. Thomas Peverell DD (Oxford) and Bishop of Worcester was a member of this family. He died March 1419 and was buried in his own cathedral.

(*2) Edward Brooke d.1541 also held Abbess Roding in Essex and Barkway in Hertfordshire jointly with Sir John Petre of Ingatestone Hall ('Master John' whose baptism is mentioned in note (*1) of the Mordaunt tree). They sold Barkway to Henry Pranell whose daughter Joan was married to Robert Brooke, son of Edward, who appears on the Brooke of Nacton tree.

(*3) George Brooke 9th Lord Cobham had 2 daughters. Elizabeth who m. William Parr Marquess of Northampton, and Catherine who, according to the Visitations, m. John Jerningham. It seems likely however that this was the Catherine Brooke who married George Kympton (the other could have been a second marriage). The 2nd wife of William 10th Lord Cobham (brother of Elizabeth and Catherine) was Frances Newton, a Lady of the Bedchamber to the Queen. George Kympton's cousin Lucy was also one of the Ladies of the Bedchamber, so the two families would have been closely acquainted.

(*4) Elizabeth Brooke 1563-97 married Robert Cecil, Chief Secretary to Queen Elizabeth. In 1603 King James persuaded him to exchange his magnificent mansion of Theobalds near Cheshunt for the old brick palace of Hatfield. He was rewarded by being created Earl of Salisbury and Knight of the Garter. He became Lord Treasurer of England and Chancellor of the University of Cambridge.

(*5) The Brookes were one of the leading recusant families in the 17th century, related to the Mordaunts, Brownes, Throckmortons, and Wisemans. In 1603, two years before the Gunpowder Plot, Henry Brooke 11th Lord Cobham, and his brother George together with Lord Grey de Wilton and Sir Walter Raleigh, were involved in a plot (the treason of the Main) to eliminate King James and his 'Cubs' and put Arbella Stuart on the throne.

The Brooke and Pranell Families
of Nursells Manor and Rushdenwell in Barkway, Hertfordshire

HENRY PRANELL of Barkway in Hertfordshire, Alderman of London, d.1594. m. Ann Baxter. Bought the manor of Barkway from Edward Brooke and Sir John Petre in 1583.

HENRY PRANELL m. Frances, late Countess of Hertford. osp 1599	**JOAN PRANELL** m. Robert Brooke, a London merchant of Copfield, Essex (son of Edward Brooke from whom his father-in-law bought the manor). He held the manor in 1595 when Henry Pranell died.	**MARY PRANELL** m. John, son and heir of Sir Francis Clarke of Houghton, Beds.

ELIZABETH BROOKE m. Sir Robert Slingsby (He was made baronet by Charles II in 1660). Elizabeth inherited Barkway and sold it to Edward Chester.	**MARY BROOKE** m. Thomas, s. of John Saunders of Long Marston in Hertfordshire and Mary Coningsby (d. of Sir Henry Coningsby of North Mimms).	**HENRY BROOKE** inherited Barkway, m. the d. of Lord Maltravers, s. of Thomas Howard Earl of Arundel and Surrey

The Brooke Family of Nacton, Suffolk

THOMAS BROOKE of Leighton m. Joan, d. of John (or William) Parke of Copenhall, Chester.	**THOMAS FASTOLF**, MP for Ipswich in 1487

SIR RICHARD BROOKE, d.1529, Recorder of London, Chief Baron of the Exchequer, represented the City of London in several parliaments. Built Crows Hall in 1526, m. Ann Leeds who d.1547	**JOHN FASTOLF**, d.1506, MP for Ipswich 1494

ROBERT BROOKE 1495-1578, m. Elizabeth Holgrave of Sussex, owned lands in Nacton, Foxholes, Bucklesham and Levington. His grandson Robert Brooke (d.1626) was Sheriff of Suffolk in 1623. Two generations later Sir Robert m. Ann, d. of Sir Lionel Tollemache.	**BRIDGET BROOKE** m. **GEORGE FASTOLF** (the Thomas Fastolf of Pettaugh whose d. Agnes m. Edward Brooke of Aspall was almost certainly a son of George and Bridget) (Brooke of Aspall tree ↓)

The Browne Family
of Abbess Roding, Welde Hall and Ridley Hall in Essex

THOMAS BROWNE inherited the manor of Abbess Roding from his brother John in 1467. m.Joanne Kyrkham of Devonshire

THOMAS (or Robert) BROWNE of Abbess Roding, b.1488 m. Mary, d. of Thomas Carleton

---

SIR WESTON BROWNE of Rookwood. Knighted by the King of Aragon at the time of Henry VII, m. Maud (or Elizabeth) d. of William Mordaunt of Turvey. (see Mordaunt Tree)

WILLIAM BROWNE a London merchant Lord Mayor of London in 1507 and 1513/14. He died in 1514 during his term of office.

SIR HUMPHREY BROWNE of Ridley Hall , Essex Justice of the Common Pleas at the time of Henry VIII (1509-47)

m① Ann, d. of Henry de Vere. (They had one child, George, who died without issue)

m ② Ann, d. of John, Lord Hussey. Her sister, Bridget Hussey, was the wife of Francis Russell, 4th Earl of Bedford, d.1641.

JOHN BROWNE of Abbess Roding m. Audrey (or Etheldred) d. of Henry de Vere of Hedingham Castle in Essex and Great Addington, Northants. (Audrey was sister of Ann de Vere who m. Humphrey Browne and of Elizabeth who m. Lord Mordaunt)

SIR ANTHONY BROWNE 1510-67 of Welde Hall. Justice of the Common Pleas m. Joan Farrington (Sir Anthony was a guest at Catherine Tyrell's wedding)

KATHERINE BROWNE m. Francis Knighton, son of Alice Bull and Thomas Knighton of Brickendon. (see Underhill tree and Hunt tree)
———
JANE BROWNE m ① Thomas Scroggs of Patmore m ② Walter Bridges of Patmore

ANNE BROWNE b. 1509 m.① John Tyrrell of Heron Hall. (parents of Catherine Tyrell of Ingatestone Hall) m② Sir William Petre of Ingatestone Hall (See Tyrell tree and Petre tree)

ELIZABETH BROWNE m. John Hale who bought Harmer Green for his son John

CATHERINE BROWNE m① Richard Townsende m② Sir William Roper of Eltham, Kent, son and heir of Sir Thomas Roper, grandson of Sir Thomas More.

CHRISTIANA BROWNE m. John Tufton of Kent. Their son was Nicholas Lord Tufton.
———
MARY BROWNE m. Thomas Wilford , s. of Sir James Wilford

GEORGE BROWNE of Clovills Hall, m. Elizabeth Leventhorpe, d. of Sir John Leventhorpe of Shingle Hall, Albury, Herts and his wife Joan Brograve of Hammels, Braughing. Sir John Leventhorpe was Sheriff of Herts in 1510

HENRY BROWNE of London. d. 1558 m. Elizabeth Lambert, d. of Bartholemew Lambert

WILLIAM BRIDGES of Ickwell, osp.

THOMASINE PETRE KATHERINE PETRE JOHN PETRE (see Petre tree)

WESTON BROWNE d.1580 of Rookwood (or Clovills) Hall. m① Mary, d. of Sir Edward Capell of Hadham, Hertfordshire (osp). m ② Elizabeth, d. of Giles Pawlett

JOHN BROWNE of Wickham Hall m. Ann Stanton of Somerset

ANN BROWNE m. Rowland Elliott of Stortford

ELIZABETH BROWNE m. Sir Henry , s. of Sir George Jernagen of Somerleton, Suffolk

---

ANTHONY BROWNE osp 1583
———
CATHERIN BROWNE m. Nicholas, s. of Edward Waldegrave of Borley, Essex. (Waldegrave tree ↓)

JAYNE BROWNE m① Edward Wyatt of Tillingham, Essex m② Sir Gamaliell Capell, son of Sir Henry Capell. (Sir William Capell, gr. gr. grandfather of Gamaliell, was a native of Stoke by Nayland. He was Lord Mayor of London in 1503 and 1509 and an ancestor of the Earls of Essex. (Capell tree ↓)

SIR ANTHONY BROWNE of Welde Hall m.Elizabeth Pirton. They had John (son and heir), Elizabeth, Mary and Catherine.

WESTON BROWNE osp
———
WILLIAM BROWNE m. Mary, d. of Sir John Sulyard of Wetherden, Suffolk, widow of Thomas Tyrell

ANN BROWNE m..Thomas Perient of Burgh, Essex
———
SIBBEL BROWNE m. John Christmas of Colchester

ELIZABETH BROWNE m. Thomas Cheney of Chesham Boyes, Buckinghamshire
———
JANE BROWNE m. John Filleal of Rayne Hall in Essex

The Browne Family
of Abbess Roding, Welde Hall and Ridley Hall in Essex

The Manor of Abbess Roding (including Rookwood)

The manor of Abbess Roding or Abbess Hall belonged originally to Barking Abbey, but was taken over at the time of the Conquest by Geoffrey de Mandeville, one of the Norman barons. Later Barking Abbey regained part of the manor and held it until the Dissolution, when it was granted by Henry VIII to Thomas Cromwell. When Cromwell was disgraced and executed, Henry VIII gave the manor to Ann of Cleves. Richard Lord Rich (later Lord Chancellor) was her Steward. Later that year (1540), probably when Ann was divorced, the manor seems to have been in the possession of Richard Lord Rich and Oliver St John of Bletsoe. In 1541 it was acquired by Edward Brooke of Aspall Hall in Suffolk, a cousin of Lord Cobham. Edward Brooke also had estates at Barkway and St Pauls Walden in Hertfordshire which he held jointly with Sir John Petre, son of Sir William Petre of Ingatestone Hall.

The other part of the Abbess Roding estate, which was not regained by Barking Abbey, passed in 1086 to Aubrey de Vere, ancestor of the Earls of Oxford and also of the Browne family who later inherited it. It was known as Rookwood or Brownes. Thomas Browne was holding the manor in 1467, and it passed to his son Thomas (or Robert), then to Sir Weston Browne and to his son Sir Anthony Browne, Chief Justice of the Common Pleas. Here we have a great deal of confusion. This gentleman is referred to in some sources as Lord Montague, but Lord Montague was in fact an entirely different Anthony Browne, who lived at Cowdray in Sussex. To add to the confusion they were marrying into the same families. The Ropers of Eltham, Capells of Hertfordshire, and the Petres of Ingatestone Hall all had connections with both the Brownes of Sussex and the Brownes of Essex.

Around 1599 the manor of Rookwood (now sometimes referred to as Clovills), was acquired by the Capell family; presumably through the marriage of Sir Gamaliel Capell and Jayne, the daughter of Weston Browne and his second wife Elizabeth Pawlett. (His first wife was Mary Capell, Gamaliel Capell's niece). At this stage Nicholas Waldegrave, whose family had married into both the Brooke and the Browne families, seems to have had a share in the property, but finally the whole manor came to the Capells.

Mrs Sarah Capell, who was buried at Abbess Roding in 1698, was probably the last member of the family to live there. About 1700 Sir Gamaliel Capell, the great-grandson of the first Gamaliel, sold or mortgaged the manor to John Howland of Streatham, whose daughter and heir married Wriothes-ley Russell 2nd Duke of Bedford. His son, John 4th Duke of Bedford, sold Abbess Roding in 1739 to the Skinner family.

In the 19th century the Reverend Capel Cure, a descendant of the Capell family, bought the advowson of the Rectory. He did a great deal for the the parish at his own expense, providing a village school and restoring the church.

The Brownes, Lords Montague of Cowdray
and Battle Abbey in Sussex

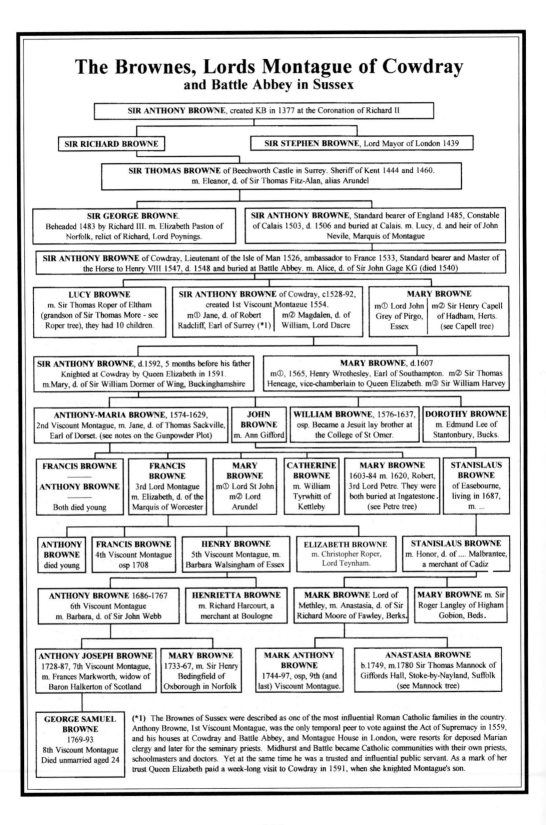

SIR ANTHONY BROWNE, created KB in 1377 at the Coronation of Richard II

SIR RICHARD BROWNE

SIR STEPHEN BROWNE, Lord Mayor of London 1439

SIR THOMAS BROWNE of Beechworth Castle in Surrey. Sheriff of Kent 1444 and 1460. m. Eleanor, d. of Sir Thomas Fitz-Alan, alias Arundel

SIR GEORGE BROWNE. Beheaded 1483 by Richard III. m. Elizabeth Paston of Norfolk, relict of Richard, Lord Poynings.

SIR ANTHONY BROWNE, Standard bearer of England 1485, Constable of Calais 1503, d. 1506 and buried at Calais. m. Lucy, d. and heir of John Nevile, Marquis of Montague

SIR ANTHONY BROWNE of Cowdray, Lieutenant of the Isle of Man 1526, ambassador to France 1533, Standard bearer and Master of the Horse to Henry VIII 1547, d. 1548 and buried at Battle Abbey. m. Alice, d. of Sir John Gage KG (died 1540)

LUCY BROWNE m. Sir Thomas Roper of Eltham (grandson of Sir Thomas More - see Roper tree), they had 10 children.

SIR ANTHONY BROWNE of Cowdray, c1528-92, created 1st Viscount Montague 1554. m① Jane, d. of Robert Radcliff, Earl of Surrey (*1) | m② Magdalen, d. of William, Lord Dacre

MARY BROWNE m① Lord John Grey of Pirgo, Essex | m② Sir Henry Capell of Hadham, Herts. (see Capell tree)

SIR ANTHONY BROWNE, d.1592, 5 months before his father Knighted at Cowdray by Queen Elizabeth in 1591. m.Mary, d. of Sir William Dormer of Wing, Buckinghamshire

MARY BROWNE, d.1607 m①, 1565, Henry Wrothesley, Earl of Southampton. m② Sir Thomas Heneage, vice-chamberlain to Queen Elizabeth. m③ Sir William Harvey

ANTHONY-MARIA BROWNE, 1574-1629, 2nd Viscount Montague, m. Jane, d. of Thomas Sackville, Earl of Dorset. (see notes on the Gunpowder Plot)

JOHN BROWNE m. Ann Gifford

WILLIAM BROWNE, 1576-1637, osp. Became a Jesuit lay brother at the College of St Omer.

DOROTHY BROWNE m. Edmund Lee of Stantonbury, Bucks.

FRANCIS BROWNE ――― **ANTHONY BROWNE** ――― Both died young

FRANCIS BROWNE 3rd Lord Montague m. Elizabeth, d. of the Marquis of Worcester

MARY BROWNE m① Lord St John m② Lord Arundel

CATHERINE BROWNE m. William Tyrwhitt of Kettleby

MARY BROWNE 1603-84 m. 1620, Robert, 3rd Lord Petre. They were both buried at Ingatestone. (see Petre tree)

STANISLAUS BROWNE of Easebourne, living in 1687, m. ...

ANTHONY BROWNE died young

FRANCIS BROWNE 4th Viscount Montague osp 1708

HENRY BROWNE 5th Viscount Montague, m. Barbara Walsingham of Essex

ELIZABETH BROWNE m. Christopher Roper, Lord Teynham.

STANISLAUS BROWNE m. Honor, d. of .... Malbrantee, a merchant of Cadiz

ANTHONY BROWNE 1686-1767 6th Viscount Montague m. Barbara, d. of Sir John Webb

HENRIETTA BROWNE m. Richard Harcourt, a merchant at Boulogne

MARK BROWNE Lord of Methley, m. Anastasia, d. of Sir Richard Moore of Fawley, Berks.

MARY BROWNE m. Sir Roger Langley of Higham Gobion, Beds.

ANTHONY JOSEPH BROWNE 1728-87, 7th Viscount Montague, m. Frances Markworth, widow of Baron Halkerton of Scotland

MARY BROWNE 1733-67, m. Sir Henry Bedingfield of Oxborough in Norfolk

MARK ANTHONY BROWNE 1744-97, osp, 9th (and last) Viscount Montague.

ANASTASIA BROWNE b.1749, m.1780 Sir Thomas Mannock of Giffords Hall, Stoke-by-Nayland, Suffolk (see Mannock tree)

GEORGE SAMUEL BROWNE 1769-93 8th Viscount Montague Died unmarried aged 24

(*1) The Brownes of Sussex were described as one of the most influential Roman Catholic families in the country. Anthony Browne, 1st Viscount Montague, was the only temporal peer to vote against the Act of Supremacy in 1559, and his houses at Cowdray and Battle Abbey, and Montague House in London, were resorts for deposed Marian clergy and later for the seminary priests. Midhurst and Battle became Catholic communities with their own priests, schoolmasters and doctors. Yet at the same time he was a trusted and influential public servant. As a mark of her trust Queen Elizabeth paid a week-long visit to Cowdray in 1591, when she knighted Montague's son.

The Bull Family
of Hertford, Stapleford and Tewin

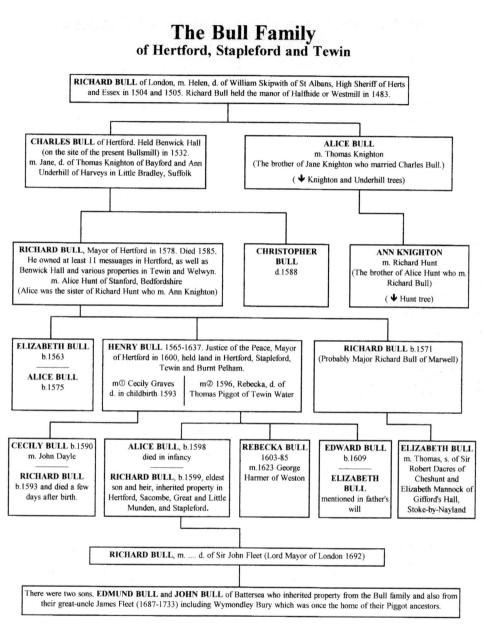

RICHARD BULL of London, m. Helen, d. of William Skipwith of St Albans, High Sheriff of Herts and Essex in 1504 and 1505. Richard Bull held the manor of Halfhide or Westmill in 1483.

CHARLES BULL of Hertford. Held Benwick Hall (on the site of the present Bullsmill) in 1532. m. Jane, d. of Thomas Knighton of Bayford and Ann Underhill of Harveys in Little Bradley, Suffolk

ALICE BULL
m. Thomas Knighton
(The brother of Jane Knighton who married Charles Bull.)
(⬇ Knighton and Underhill trees)

RICHARD BULL, Mayor of Hertford in 1578. Died 1585. He owned at least 11 messuages in Hertford, as well as Benwick Hall and various properties in Tewin and Welwyn. m. Alice Hunt of Stanford, Bedfordshire (Alice was the sister of Richard Hunt who m. Ann Knighton)

CHRISTOPHER BULL d.1588

ANN KNIGHTON
m. Richard Hunt
(The brother of Alice Hunt who m. Richard Bull)
(⬇ Hunt tree)

ELIZABETH BULL b.1563
ALICE BULL b.1575

HENRY BULL 1565-1637. Justice of the Peace, Mayor of Hertford in 1600, held land in Hertford, Stapleford, Tewin and Burnt Pelham.
m① Cecily Graves d. in childbirth 1593 | m② 1596, Rebecka, d. of Thomas Piggot of Tewin Water

RICHARD BULL b.1571
(Probably Major Richard Bull of Marwell)

CECILY BULL b.1590 m. John Dayle
RICHARD BULL b.1593 and died a few days after birth.

ALICE BULL, b.1598 died in infancy
RICHARD BULL, b.1599, eldest son and heir, inherited property in Hertford, Sacombe, Great and Little Munden, and Stapleford.

REBECKA BULL 1603-85 m.1623 George Harmer of Weston

EDWARD BULL b.1609
ELIZABETH BULL mentioned in father's will

ELIZABETH BULL m. Thomas, s. of Sir Robert Dacres of Cheshunt and Elizabeth Mannock of Gifford's Hall, Stoke-by-Nayland

RICHARD BULL, m. .... d. of Sir John Fleet (Lord Mayor of London 1692)

There were two sons, **EDMUND BULL** and **JOHN BULL** of Battersea who inherited property from the Bull family and also from their great-uncle James Fleet (1687-1733) including Wymondley Bury which was once the home of their Piggot ancestors.

NOTES: Henry Bull held the manor of Burnt Pelham (or Brent Pelham) jointly with Edward Cason (a descendant of Ann Hyde and Thomas Bowles). The Casons held the manor of Astonbury and Furneaux Pelham. Edward Cason's mother was Susan Oxenbridge of Hurstbourne Priors. The Casons had connections with Sir Francis Mannock of Gifford's Hall, Stoke-by-Nayland, who also had connections with the Bull family.

William Bull Clk, MA., Rector of St Andrew's Hertford from 1643 to 1660, was almost certainly a member of the family. Rebecka Harmer (née Bull) was baptised, married and buried in St Andrew's Church and the Bull family home was in this parish.

The Capell Family
of Little Hadham in Hertfordshire, and Abbess Roding and Raynes in Essex

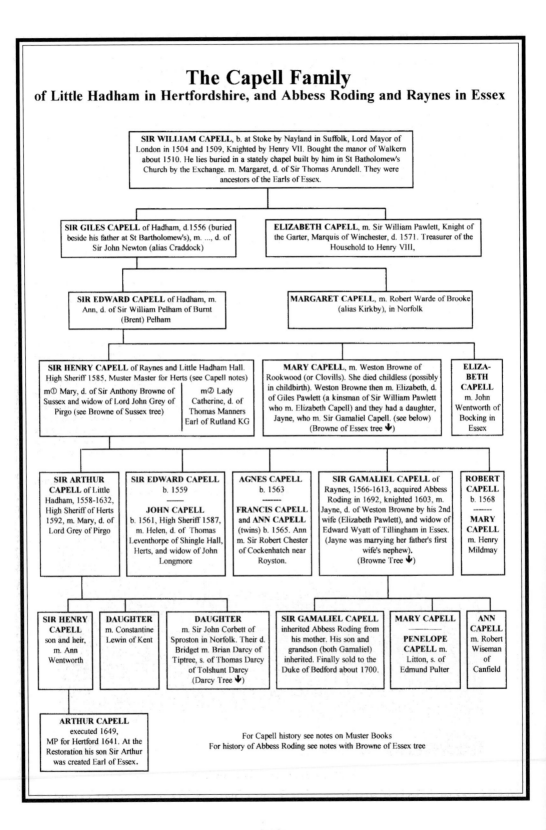

SIR WILLIAM CAPELL, b. at Stoke by Nayland in Suffolk, Lord Mayor of London in 1504 and 1509, Knighted by Henry VII. Bought the manor of Walkern about 1510. He lies buried in a stately chapel built by him in St Batholomew's Church by the Exchange. m. Margaret, d. of Sir Thomas Arundell. They were ancestors of the Earls of Essex.

SIR GILES CAPELL of Hadham, d.1556 (buried beside his father at St Bartholomew's), m. ..., d. of Sir John Newton (alias Craddock)

ELIZABETH CAPELL, m. Sir William Pawlett, Knight of the Garter, Marquis of Winchester, d. 1571. Treasurer of the Household to Henry VIII,

SIR EDWARD CAPELL of Hadham, m. Ann, d. of Sir William Pelham of Burnt (Brent) Pelham

MARGARET CAPELL, m. Robert Warde of Brooke (alias Kirkby), in Norfolk

SIR HENRY CAPELL of Raynes and Little Hadham Hall. High Sheriff 1585, Muster Master for Herts (see Capell notes)
m① Mary, d. of Sir Anthony Browne of Sussex and widow of Lord John Grey of Pirgo (see Browne of Sussex tree)
m② Lady Catherine, d. of Thomas Manners Earl of Rutland KG

MARY CAPELL, m. Weston Browne of Rookwood (or Clovills). She died childless (possibly in childbirth). Weston Browne then m. Elizabeth, d. of Giles Pawlett (a kinsman of Sir William Pawlett who m. Elizabeth Capell) and they had a daughter, Jayne, who m. Sir Gamaliel Capell. (see below)
(Browne of Essex tree ↓)

ELIZABETH CAPELL m. John Wentworth of Bocking in Essex

SIR ARTHUR CAPELL of Little Hadham, 1558-1632, High Sheriff of Herts 1592, m. Mary, d. of Lord Grey of Pirgo

SIR EDWARD CAPELL b. 1559
_____
JOHN CAPELL b. 1561, High Sheriff 1587, m. Helen, d. of Thomas Leventhorpe of Shingle Hall, Herts, and widow of John Longmore

AGNES CAPELL b. 1563
_____
FRANCIS CAPELL and **ANN CAPELL** (twins) b. 1565. Ann m. Sir Robert Chester of Cockenhatch near Royston.

SIR GAMALIEL CAPELL of Raynes, 1566-1613, acquired Abbess Roding in 1692, knighted 1603, m. Jayne, d. of Weston Browne by his 2nd wife (Elizabeth Pawlett), and widow of Edward Wyatt of Tillingham in Essex. (Jayne was marrying her father's first wife's nephew). (Browne Tree ↓)

ROBERT CAPELL b. 1568
_____
MARY CAPELL m. Henry Mildmay

SIR HENRY CAPELL son and heir, m. Ann Wentworth

DAUGHTER m. Constantine Lewin of Kent

DAUGHTER m. Sir John Corbett of Sproston in Norfolk. Their d. Bridget m. Brian Darcy of Tiptree, s. of Thomas Darcy of Tolshunt Darcy (Darcy Tree ↓)

SIR GAMALIEL CAPELL inherited Abbess Roding from his mother. His son and grandson (both Gamaliel) inherited. Finally sold to the Duke of Bedford about 1700.

MARY CAPELL
_____
PENELOPE CAPELL m. Litton, s. of Edmund Pulter

ANN CAPELL m. Robert Wiseman of Canfield

ARTHUR CAPELL executed 1649, MP for Hertford 1641. At the Restoration his son Sir Arthur was created Earl of Essex.

For Capell history see notes on Muster Books
For history of Abbess Roding see notes with Browne of Essex tree

Notes on the Muster Books 1580-1605
with reference to the Capell and Pulter families

Sir Henry Capell was Captain of the North and East Herts foot soldiers, and was responsible for recruiting and training a band of able men, who could be called upon at any time for the defence of the kingdom. The Captains or Commissioners of Array were also required to provide armour, arms and ammunition, sometimes at their own expense. Sir Henry's son, Sir Arthur Capell, was one of the Commissioners of Array, and was responsible for recruiting and helping to train the soldiers.

At this time there was no regular army, and the country relied on the County Militia, selected from the various bands of men between the ages of 18 and 45 who were required to do four days training a year under the command of the local Muster Captain. In 1588, when the country was threatened with invasion by the Spanish, a special levy was raised for the Defence of the Kingdon.

To give warning of invasion there was a chain of beacons along the south coast and across the country. They were guarded and maintained by specially trained and trustworthy Beacon Keepers and there was a very severe penalty for unauthorised firing. There were four beacons in Hertfordshire: on the tower of St Peter's in St Albans, on Hertford Heath, at Graveley, and at Therfield. Just across the county border there was a beacon on a high peak in the village of Ivinghoe. Four hundred years later Ivinghoe Beacon is a well-known local landmark, reminding us of the 16th century 'Early Warning System' which has now been replaced with rather more sophisticated methods!

The Hertfordshire Muster Books have been transcribed and published by the Hertfordshire Record Society. The earlier books in particular were meticulously kept, and were probably written by a professional scribe in the Capell household at Little Hadham Hall. They show that Henry Capell had at least 39 male servants. Some were probably sons of the gentry, who had been to university and were taking a year out to learn the skills of estate management before going on to the Inns of Court to complete their education.

The Hertfordshire Commissioners of Array, whose names appear in the Muster Books, were almost all related to each other, and several were related to the Queen herself, ensuring a high degree of loyalty and commitment. There are many familiar names including: Boteler, Bowles, Brocket, Coningsby, Docwra, Horsey, Hyde, Leventhorpe, Lytton, Pulter and Shotbolt.

Sir Henry Capell was succeeded as Muster Captain by Edward Pulter of Cottered and Wymondley. He was Muster Captain for 22 years. Like Henry Capell he received no pay for this public service, and willingly gave his time and money as one of the duties which went with privilege and wealth. We are told however that he was (understandably) a little resentful when asked to pay the extra levy which was demanded of all wealthy landowners in 1588. Later that year Edward Pulter had to march his selected band of soldiers to Tilbury, where an army was gathering in readiness to resist the expected Spanish invasion. Once the soldiers crossed the county boundary they were entitled to a maintenance allowance from the government, but during the 40 mile march through the Hertfordshire countryside Edward had to beg or buy their nightly board and lodging.

The Pulters were related by marriage to the Capells. Sir Henry Capell's granddaughter Penelope was married to Litton Pulter, the son of Captain Edward Pulter and his wife Mary who was the daughter of Sir Rowland Lytton of Knebworth.

Little Hadham Hall, Hertfordshire

The Cary Family
of Aldenham, Hertfordshire

THOMAS CARY of Chilton in Devon, 2nd son of Sir William Cary, m. Margaret, d. of Sir Robert Spencer of Cople (see Spencer tree)

JOHN CARY of Hackney, m. Martha, d. of Edmund Denny of Norwich and sister of Sir Anthony Denny of Herts (Privy Councillor to Henry VIII)

WILLIAM CARY, Esquire for the Body of Henry VIII. Died 1528. m. 1520 Mary, d. and heir of Thomas Bullen (Boleyn) Earl of Wiltshire, and sister of Ann Boleyn (2nd wife of Henry VIII and mother of Queen Elizabeth I). **(see important footnote)**

WYMOND CARY of Hackney. He had two daughters: Elizabeth, who m. George Dacres of Cheshunt, and Prudence, who m. Anthony Bridges of West Ham in Essex.

SIR EDWARD CARY Master of the Jewell House. m. Catherine, d. of Sir Henry Knevett and widow of Henry, Lord Paget. She was the sister of Thomasine Knevett who m. Sir William Clopton of Kentwell Hall in Suffolk. (see Clopton tree)

SIR HENRY CARY 1524-96, Baron of Hunsdon, Lord Chamberlain (and first cousin) to Queen Elizabeth. m. Ann, d. of Sir Thomas Morgan of Kent

CATHERINE CARY, a first cousin to Queen Elizabeth, m. Sir Francis Knollys (*1), counsellor and close friend of the Queen. Their d. Catherine m. Sir Philip Boteler.

FRANCES CARY m. Ralph Bashe of Stanstead Bury, Herts.

SIR ADOLPHUS CARY, m. Ann, d. of Sir Robert Corbett of Salop, osp. Buried at Aldenham.

SIR PHILIP CARY, m. Elizabeth, d. of Richard Bland of Yorkshire. They had 2 sons and 2 daughters. There were five other daughters: **ELIZABETH; MURIEL CATHERINE; ANNE** and **ANNE.** who all married.

SIR HENRY CARY, Viscount Faulkland in Scotland, Died at Theobalds after breaking his leg in a fall. m. Elizabeth, d. of Sir Lawrence Tanfield, Lord Chief Baron of the Exchequer.

SIR GEORGE CARY, b.1556, Lord Hunsdon, m. Elizabeth, d. of Sir John Spencer. (see Spencer tree) He was Lord Chamberlain at the time of Queen Elizabeth's death. He died later the same year (1603). His brother John inherited the title. (*1)

SIR JOHN CARY 1563-1617, Lord Hunsdon, m. Mary, d. of Leonard Hyde of Throcking and widow of John Paston of Norfolk. There is a memorial plaque in Hunsdon church.

SIR EDMUND CARY (*2) m① Mary Coker of Devon; m② Judith, d. of Lawrence Humphrey, DD, and widow of Sir John Rivers.

SIR ROBERT CARY (*3) Earl of Monmouth, m. .... Trevanion.

PHILADELPHIA CARY m. Thomas, Lord Scroop of Bolton.

MARGARET CARY m. Sir Edward Hobby, Gentleman of the Privy Chamber

CATHERINE CARY m. Charles Howard, Earl of Nottingham and Admiral of England

LUCIUS CARY

LAWRENCE CARY

EDWARD CARY

CATHERINE CARY

VICTORIA CARY

ANNE CARY

ELIZABETH CARY

ELIZABETH CARY b.1576.. Queen Elizabeth was one of her Godmothers. m. Thomas Barkley, s. and heir of Henry, Lord Barkley

HENRY CARY, Lord Hunsdon, Viscount Rochford and Earl of Dover (*4) m. Judith, d. of Sir Thomas Pelham of Laughton, Sussex

(*1) Sir Francis Knollys, who had the task of looking after Mary Queen of Scots, tried to marry her to his nephew George Cary, hoping it would solve some of the problems, but unfortunately Mary was not interested.

(*2) Sir Edmund Cary had 5 children: Robert, Ferdinando, Thomas, Anne and Catherine.

(*3) Sir Robert Cary had 2 sons: ① Sir Henry Cary, Knight of the Bath at the creation of Charles, Prince of Wales, and ② Thomas Cary, died 1634, one of the Gentlemen of the Bedchamber to King Charles I. He m. Margaret, sole heir of Thomas Smythe, Clarke of the Parliament and Counsell. Sir Robert also had 3 daughters: Philadelphia, Frances and Elizabeth.

(*4) Henry had no male heir so in 1617 King James granted the title to Sir John Boteler. It then went to Sir Thomas Dacres and in 1635 to the Earl of Elgin (the Bruce family, Lord Ailesbury).

Important footnote.

New discoveries resulting from research by Anthony Hoskins, Librarian of the Newberry Library, Chicago, have been recorded in the official journal of the Society of Genealogists (report in The Daily Telegraph, 27th May 1997). Historians have always agreed that Henry VIII did have an affair with Mary Boleyn, the wife of William Cary, but hitherto the relationship was thought to be childless. Now there is strong evidence that Catherine and Henry Cary were in fact the children of Henry VIII. Catherine married Sir Francis Knollys, and their daughter Lettice (not shown on our tree) was an ancestor of Queen Elizabeth the Queen Mother. This would mean that Henry VIII's descendants did not die out with Queen Elizabeth I, but continued in an uninterrupted line to Queen Elizabeth II. From our own family point of view it means that the niece of our ancestor Lucy Hyde was married to the grandson of Henry VIII.

The Clopton Family
of Kentwell Hall, Long Melford and Kedington, Suffolk

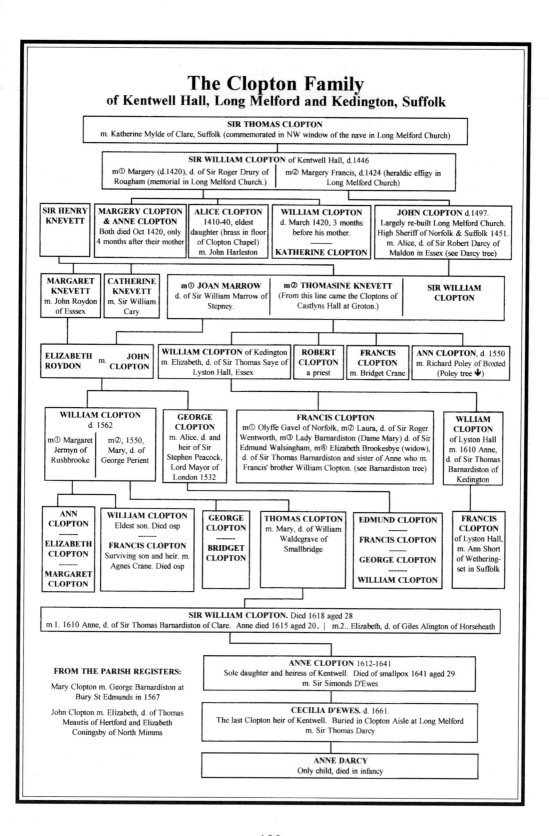

SIR THOMAS CLOPTON
m. Katherine Mylde of Clare, Suffolk (commemorated in NW window of the nave in Long Melford Church)

SIR WILLIAM CLOPTON of Kentwell Hall, d.1446
m① Margery (d.1420), d. of Sir Roger Drury of Rougham (memorial in Long Melford Church.) | m② Margery Francis, d.1424 (heraldic effigy in Long Melford Church)

SIR HENRY KNEVETT

MARGERY CLOPTON & ANNE CLOPTON
Both died Oct 1420, only 4 months after their mother

ALICE CLOPTON
1410-40, eldest daughter (brass in floor of Clopton Chapel)
m. John Harleston

WILLIAM CLOPTON
d. March 1420, 3 months before his mother.
——
KATHERINE CLOPTON

JOHN CLOPTON d.1497.
Largely re-built Long Melford Church. High Sheriff of Norfolk & Suffolk 1451. m. Alice, d. of Sir Robert Darcy of Maldon in Essex (see Darcy tree)

MARGARET KNEVETT
m. John Roydon of Esssex

CATHERINE KNEVETT
m. Sir William Cary

m① JOAN MARROW
d. of Sir William Marrow of Stepney.

m② THOMASINE KNEVETT
(From this line came the Cloptons of Castlyns Hall at Groton.)

SIR WILLIAM CLOPTON

ELIZABETH ROYDON m. **JOHN CLOPTON**

WILLIAM CLOPTON of Kedington
m. Elizabeth, d. of Sir Thomas Saye of Lyston Hall, Essex

ROBERT CLOPTON
a priest

FRANCIS CLOPTON
m. Bridget Crane

ANN CLOPTON, d. 1550
m. Richard Poley of Boxted (Poley tree ⬇)

WILLIAM CLOPTON
d. 1562
m① Margaret Jermyn of Rushbrooke | m②, 1550, Mary, d. of George Perient

GEORGE CLOPTON
m. Alice, d. and heir of Sir Stephen Peacock, Lord Mayor of London 1532

FRANCIS CLOPTON
m① Olyffe Gavel of Norfolk, m② Laura, d. of Sir Roger Wentworth, m③ Lady Barnardiston (Dame Mary) d. of Sir Edmund Walsingham, m④ Elizabeth Brookesbye (widow), d. of Sir Thomas Barnardiston and sister of Anne who m. Francis' brother William Clopton. (see Barnardiston tree)

WLLIAM CLOPTON
of Lyston Hall
m. 1610 Anne, d. of Sir Thomas Barnardiston of Kedington

ANN CLOPTON
——
ELIZABETH CLOPTON
——
MARGARET CLOPTON

WILLIAM CLOPTON
Eldest son. Died osp
FRANCIS CLOPTON
Surviving son and heir. m. Agnes Crane. Died osp

GEORGE CLOPTON
——
BRIDGET CLOPTON

THOMAS CLOPTON
m. Mary, d. of William Waldegrave of Smallbridge

EDMUND CLOPTON
——
FRANCIS CLOPTON
——
GEORGE CLOPTON
——
WILLIAM CLOPTON

FRANCIS CLOPTON
of Lyston Hall, m. Ann Short of Wetheringset in Suffolk

SIR WILLIAM CLOPTON. Died 1618 aged 28
m.1. 1610 Anne, d. of Sir Thomas Barnardiston of Clare. Anne died 1615 aged 20. | m.2.. Elizabeth, d. of Giles Alington of Horseheath

FROM THE PARISH REGISTERS:

Mary Clopton m. George Barnardiston at Bury St Edmunds in 1567

John Clopton m. Elizabeth, d. of Thomas Meautis of Hertford and Elizabeth Coningsby of North Mimms

ANNE CLOPTON 1612-1641
Sole daughter and heiress of Kentwell. Died of smallpox 1641 aged 29
m. Sir Simonds D'Ewes

CECILIA D'EWES. d. 1661.
The last Clopton heir of Kentwell. Buried in Clopton Aisle at Long Melford
m. Sir Thomas Darcy

ANNE DARCY
Only child, died in infancy

The de la Pole Family of Suffolk
showing links with the Brookes of Aspall and the Enderbys of Bedfordshire

WILLIAM DE LA POLE
Merchant of Hull

RICHARD DE LA POLE
Butler to the King [Edward III]

WILLIAM DE LA POLE, Merchant of Hull, d.1356, m. Catherine, d. of Sir John Norwich. (Effigy in the Church of the Holy Trinity, Hull)

WILLIAM DE LA POLE
m. Margaret, d. of Edmund Peverell and Alice Langton (sister of Walter de Langton, Bishop of Lichfield and Coventry)

MICHAEL DE LA POLE
1st Earl of Suffolk, Chancellor of England, d.1389, m. Katherine, d. and heir of Sir John Wingfield of Wingfield Castle in Suffolk.

JOHN DE LA POLE
succeeded to the manor of Everton in Bedfordshire in 1358, m.1362, Joan, d. of John 3rd Lord Cobham

KATHERINE DE LA POLE
m. John Bullok

MICHAEL DE LA POLE
2nd Earl of Suffolk, slain at Harfleur 1415 m. Katherine, d. of Hugh, Earl of Stafford (Effigy in Wingfield Church)

JOAN BARONESS COBHAM,
b. about 1378, d.1433 m. Sir Reginald Braybrooke, d.1405

ROBERT BULLOK
m. ... 1419

MICHAEL DE LA POLE
3rd Earl of Suffolk, slain at Agincourt 1415, m. Elizabeth, d. of Thomas Mowbray of Bedfordshire, Duke of Norfolk.

WILLIAM DE LA POLE
1st Duke of Suffolk, beheaded 1450, m. Alice, d. of Sir Thomas Chaucer of Studham in Hertfordshire [now in Bedfordshire], and granddaughter of the poet Geoffrey Chaucer. Alice was previously married to the Earl of Salisbury.

JOAN BRAYBROOKE
Baroness Cobham, d. 1442, m. Sir Thomas Brooke of Aspall (d.1439), who became 5th Lord Cobham. (↓ Brooke tree)

ELIZABETH BULLOK
m. William Furtho of Furtho

JOHN DE LA POLE
2nd Duke of Suffolk, d.1491, buried at Wingfield, m. Elizabeth, d. of Richard Plantagenet, Duke of York, and sister of Edward IV. (Effigy in Wingfield church)

ALICE FURTHO
m. John Enderby of Edworth and Astwick, Beds, and of Kingswoodbury Herts, d.1457

JOHN DE LA POLE
Earl of Lincoln, m. Margaret, d. of Thomas Lord Arundel. Heir presumptive to the throne but when Richard III was killed at Bosworth in 1485, Henry VII became King.

EDMUND DE LA POLE
The last Earl of Suffolk, beheaded in 1513 because of his royal blood. m. Margaret, d. of Richard, Lord Scrope.

Wingfield Castle about 1925

A 20th Century de la Pole Connection

When Thomas Harmer married Mercy Galbraith in 1923 it was quite by chance that they came to live in the Suffolk village of Wingfield. Thomas immediately became interested in the historical connections with the de la Pole family, but was quite unaware that they were his direct ancestors.

At this time the Vicar, the Rev'd Samuel Aldwell, was working on a history of Wingfield and Thomas Harmer soon became involved in the project. He drew up the ground plans of the church and college, and he also discovered the piscina which Mr Aldwell had hitherto been unable to locate. This is described in a note which was added just as the book was going to press:

> The old piscina in the Lady Chapel has at last been discovered and opened up. I had read in some old record of the Church that it was somewhere in the sill of the easternmost window on the south side of the Lady Chapel; so I asked Mr Harmer of Wingfield to remove the plaster and bricks with which the sill had been filled in. This he did most carefully, and we discovered that the window sill was originally flat, not sloping as it is now, but could not find any traces of a piscina. However, a few days after, Mr Harmer measured the distance of the piscina in the Chancel from the east wall, and then marked the spot on the Lady Chapel window sill a similar distance from the east wall; he went to work here and shortly after came across the piscina. It was uncovered on December 15th 1925 and is now being used for its original purpose.

The book, entitled 'Wingfield: Its Church,Castle and College', was published a few weeks later. It is now out of print, but a few precious copies remain.

Thomas and Mercy spent the first three years of their married life at Wingfield, in the cottage called 'Buntings', on the hill overlooking the church and college. It was here that their daughters Mercy, and Evelyn, the author of this book, were born. Buntings is now better known as the Swingletree Stables, and is the home of the famous Norwich Union coach and its equally famous driver John Parker.

In 1926 the family moved to Laurel Farm,Brundish, where they lived for the next eleven years. Laurel Farm, to the author, is still the most wonderful place in the world.

Harvest at Laurel Farm, Brundish in 1927

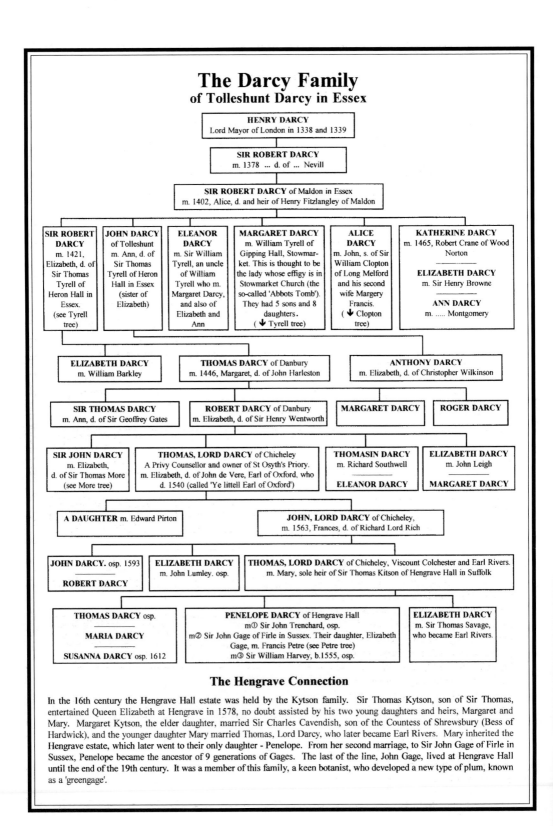

The Darcy Family
of Tolleshunt Darcy in Essex

HENRY DARCY
Lord Mayor of London in 1338 and 1339

SIR ROBERT DARCY
m. 1378 ... d. of ... Nevill

SIR ROBERT DARCY of Maldon in Essex
m. 1402, Alice, d. and heir of Henry Fitzlangley of Maldon

SIR ROBERT DARCY m. 1421, Elizabeth, d. of Sir Thomas Tyrell of Heron Hall in Essex. (see Tyrell tree)

JOHN DARCY of Tolleshunt m. Ann, d. of Sir Thomas Tyrell of Heron Hall in Essex (sister of Elizabeth)

ELEANOR DARCY m. Sir William Tyrell, an uncle of William Tyrell who m. Margaret Darcy, and also of Elizabeth and Ann

MARGARET DARCY m. William Tyrell of Gipping Hall, Stowmarket. This is thought to be the lady whose effigy is in Stowmarket Church (the so-called 'Abbots Tomb'). They had 5 sons and 8 daughters. (↓ Tyrell tree)

ALICE DARCY m. John, s. of Sir William Clopton of Long Melford and his second wife Margery Francis. (↓ Clopton tree)

KATHERINE DARCY m. 1465, Robert Crane of Wood Norton

ELIZABETH DARCY m. Sir Henry Browne

ANN DARCY m. ..... Montgomery

ELIZABETH DARCY m. William Barkley

THOMAS DARCY of Danbury m. 1446, Margaret, d. of John Harleston

ANTHONY DARCY m. Elizabeth, d. of Christopher Wilkinson

SIR THOMAS DARCY m. Ann, d. of Sir Geoffrey Gates

ROBERT DARCY of Danbury m. Elizabeth, d. of Sir Henry Wentworth

MARGARET DARCY

ROGER DARCY

SIR JOHN DARCY m. Elizabeth, d. of Sir Thomas More (see More tree)

THOMAS, LORD DARCY of Chicheley A Privy Counsellor and owner of St Osyth's Priory. m. Elizabeth, d. of John de Vere, Earl of Oxford, who d. 1540 (called 'Ye littell Earl of Oxford')

THOMASIN DARCY m. Richard Southwell

ELEANOR DARCY

ELIZABETH DARCY m. John Leigh

MARGARET DARCY

A DAUGHTER m. Edward Pirton

JOHN, LORD DARCY of Chicheley, m. 1563, Frances, d. of Richard Lord Rich

JOHN DARCY. osp. 1593

ROBERT DARCY

ELIZABETH DARCY m. John Lumley. osp.

THOMAS, LORD DARCY of Chicheley, Viscount Colchester and Earl Rivers. m. Mary, sole heir of Sir Thomas Kitson of Hengrave Hall in Suffolk

THOMAS DARCY osp.

MARIA DARCY

SUSANNA DARCY osp. 1612

PENELOPE DARCY of Hengrave Hall m① Sir John Trenchard, osp. m② Sir John Gage of Firle in Sussex. Their daughter, Elizabeth Gage, m. Francis Petre (see Petre tree) m③ Sir William Harvey, b.1555, osp.

ELIZABETH DARCY m. Sir Thomas Savage, who became Earl Rivers.

The Hengrave Connection

In the 16th century the Hengrave Hall estate was held by the Kytson family. Sir Thomas Kytson, son of Sir Thomas, entertained Queen Elizabeth at Hengrave in 1578, no doubt assisted by his two young daughters and heirs, Margaret and Mary. Margaret Kytson, the elder daughter, married Sir Charles Cavendish, son of the Countess of Shrewsbury (Bess of Hardwick), and the younger daughter Mary married Thomas, Lord Darcy, who later became Earl Rivers. Mary inherited the Hengrave estate, which later went to their only daughter - Penelope. From her second marriage, to Sir John Gage of Firle in Sussex, Penelope became the ancestor of 9 generations of Gages. The last of the line, John Gage, lived at Hengrave Hall until the end of the 19th century. It was a member of this family, a keen botanist, who developed a new type of plum, known as a 'greengage'.

The Hunt Family
of Suffolk and Essex

JOHN LE HUNT lived in Suffolk at the beginning of the 13th century. His son **SIR WARREN LE HUNT** succeeded him, followed by **EUSTACE LE HUNT** and **ROBERT LE HUNT** who was succeeded in 1310 by his son **JOHN LE HUNT.**

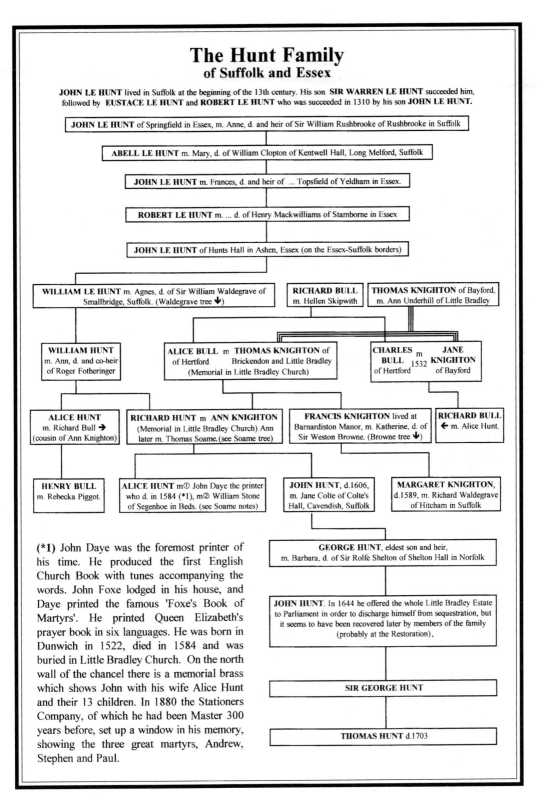

JOHN LE HUNT of Springfield in Essex, m. Anne, d. and heir of Sir William Rushbrooke of Rushbrooke in Suffolk

ABELL LE HUNT m. Mary, d. of William Clopton of Kentwell Hall, Long Melford, Suffolk

JOHN LE HUNT m. Frances, d. and heir of ... Topsfield of Yeldham in Essex.

ROBERT LE HUNT m. ... d. of Henry Mackwilliams of Stamborne in Essex

JOHN LE HUNT of Hunts Hall in Ashen, Essex (on the Essex-Suffolk borders)

WILLIAM LE HUNT m. Agnes, d. of Sir William Waldegrave of Smallbridge, Suffolk. (Waldegrave tree ↓)

RICHARD BULL m. Hellen Skipwith

THOMAS KNIGHTON of Bayford, m. Ann Underhill of Little Bradley

WILLIAM HUNT m. Ann, d. and co-heir of Roger Fotheringer

ALICE BULL m THOMAS KNIGHTON of of Hertford Brickendon and Little Bradley (Memorial in Little Bradley Church)

CHARLES BULL of Hertford m 1532 JANE KNIGHTON of Bayford

ALICE HUNT m. Richard Bull → (cousin of Ann Knighton)

RICHARD HUNT m ANN KNIGHTON (Memorial in Little Bradley Church) Ann later m. Thomas Soame. (see Soame tree)

FRANCIS KNIGHTON lived at Barnardiston Manor, m. Katherine, d. of Sir Weston Browne. (Browne tree ↓)

RICHARD BULL ← m. Alice Hunt.

HENRY BULL m. Rebecka Piggot.

ALICE HUNT m① John Daye the printer who d. in 1584 (*1), m② William Stone of Segenhoe in Beds. (see Soame notes)

JOHN HUNT, d.1606, m. Jane Colte of Colte's Hall, Cavendish, Suffolk

MARGARET KNIGHTON, d.1589, m. Richard Waldegrave of Hitcham in Suffolk

(*1) John Daye was the foremost printer of his time. He produced the first English Church Book with tunes accompanying the words. John Foxe lodged in his house, and Daye printed the famous 'Foxe's Book of Martyrs'. He printed Queen Elizabeth's prayer book in six languages. He was born in Dunwich in 1522, died in 1584 and was buried in Little Bradley Church. On the north wall of the chancel there is a memorial brass which shows John with his wife Alice Hunt and their 13 children. In 1880 the Stationers Company, of which he had been Master 300 years before, set up a window in his memory, showing the three great martyrs, Andrew, Stephen and Paul.

GEORGE HUNT, eldest son and heir, m. Barbara, d. of Sir Rolfe Shelton of Shelton Hall in Norfolk

JOHN HUNT. In 1644 he offered the whole Little Bradley Estate to Parliament in order to discharge himself from sequestration, but it seems to have been recovered later by members of the family (probably at the Restoration).

SIR GEORGE HUNT

THOMAS HUNT d.1703

The Harvey Family
of Thurleigh and Northill in Bedfordshire and Ickworth in Suffolk

All the Harveys (or Herveys) of Thurleigh and Ickworth are said to be descended from **DE HARVEY, DUKE OF ORLEANS** who came to England with William the Conqueror. **HENRY HARVEY** was settled in Bedfordshire in the reign of Richard I (1189-99). He had a son **HENRY**, who lived in the reign of King John, and a grandson **OSBERT DE HERVEY** who died 1206. Osbert's son **ADAM** m. Julien, d. and heir of John Fitzhugh.

JOHN HARVEY (Hervic de Risely), son of Adam and Julien, died 1297, m. **JOAN**, d. and co-heir of **JOHN HARMER** of Thurleigh

WILLIAM HARVEY of Thurleigh, died 1376, m. Mary, d. and heir of Richard Folliot

SIR JOHN HARVEY of Thurleigh, m. Margaret (or Joan), d. and heir of Sir John Neyrnute of Fleetmarston, Bucks. John Harvey was Knight of the Shire 1386, Justice of the Peace for Bedford 1382-94.

JOHN HARVEY died 1426, m. Margery, d. of Sir William Calthorpe of Norfolk

THOMAS HARVEY died 1475, Master of the King's Ordnance 1461, m. Jane, d. of William Paston of Norfolk

ELIZABETH HARVEY, Abbess of Elstow, d.1500

THOMAS HARVEY of Thurleigh, m. Christian, d. of John Chicheley, Chamberlain of London

THOMAS HARVEY, admitted to Lincoln's Inn 1475, m. Jane, d. and heir of Henry Drury of Ickworth in Suffolk. Inherited the Suffolk estate which had previously belonged to the Harveys in the 13th century. (Harvey of Ickworth in Suffolk tree ↓)

JOHN HARVEY, Member of Parliament for Bedford 1472, died 1474, m. Alice, d. of Nicholas Morley. Alice later m. one of the Pastons of Norfolk

SIR GEORGE HARVEY 1474-1522, m. Margaret (or Elizabeth) Stanford

GERARD SMART died 1569, natural son (and heir by adoption) of Sir George Harvey, changed his name to Harvey, MP for Bedford 1554.

m① Elizabeth (widow), sister of John Lord Williams of Thame.

m② Ann (widow), d. of Nicholas Luke

HARVEY OF THURLEIGH
Gules a bend argent with three trefoils vert thereon.

JOHN HARVEY m. Mary, d. of Sir John St John of Bletsoe. She was the sister of Margery St John who m. Francis Piggot of Gravenhurst, and also of Oliver Lord St John. (see St John tree)

MARY HARVEY b.1580, m.1602 Thomas Fairclough of Weston	OLIVER HARVEY 1568-1627, eldest son and heir, m. Ann Browne of London. In 1605 King James I stayed with him for two nights at Thurleigh	SIR GERARD HARVEY of Cardington, 2nd son b.1569, knighted at Caddes by the Earl of Essex being the first to enter the town, m.Dorothy, d. of John Gascoigne of Cardington	JOHN HARVEY, 3rd son 1572-1619, described in the parish register of Thurleigh as 'Mr John, steward to ye Earle of Bullingbrooke, died at Knebworth at Sir William Litton's house there in the County of Hertford'	SAMUEL HARVEY of Shenfield, 5th son b.1576, m. Dorothy, d. of George Wingate

LITTON FAIRCLOUGH m.1637 his cousin Mary Harvey	MARY HARVEY m.1637 her cousin Litton Fairclough	ELIZABETH HARVEY 1606-78, left a bequest to her sister Mary Fairclough and her children. (*1)	JOHN HARVEY heir, m. his cousin Elizabeth, d. of Stephen Harvey of London. (clandestine marriage) (*2)	ELIZABETH HARVEY m. Cecil (d.1632 aged 27), s. of Andrew Bussy of Cheshunt and Milliscent Fairclough (sister of Thomas who m. Mary Harvey)	GEORGE HARVEY b.1627

JOHN HARVEY (*3), 1632-1715, left a cottage & land at Thurleigh for the poor (rents given at Christmas), sold Thurleigh to the Holts (*4).

(*1) Elizabeth's godparents were: her uncle, Sir Gerard Harvey; the Countess of Bollingbrooke (sic); and the Lady Becher.

(*2) The ceremony was at St James's, Duke Place, where about 40,000 clandestine marriages took place between 1664 and 1694.

(*3) In 1680 a John Harvey acquired Ickwell Bury from his kinsman, Robert Barnardiston, and the family lived there for nearly 200 years. They sold it in 1860 and bought The Old House on Ickwell Green from their kinsmen the Fish-Palmer family. At Northill there are several memorials to Harveys who are buried in the family vault beneath the church. But although they were related to the Barnardistons and to the Fyshe family the connection with the Harveys of Thurleigh is unclear.

(*4) In 1790 Rowland Holt sold it to the Duke of Bedford for £1,796. The next Duke sold it in 1880 to William Thompson.

The Harvey (or Hervey) Family
of Ickworth in Suffolk

THOMAS HARVEY of Thurleigh, admitted to Lincoln's Inn 1475, m. Jane, d. and heir of Henry Drury of Ickworth, Wordwell and Sapiston

WILLIAM HERVEY, admitted to Lincoln's Inn 1479/80, died 1538, buried in St Mary's Church, Bury St Edmunds (M.I.), m. Joan Cokett of Ampthill

SIR NICHOLAS HERVEY of Bakenloo Manor, Bedfordshire, member of the royal household (Henry VIII), ambassador to Emperor Charles V in 1530, died 1532, buried at Ampthill, Beds. m① Elizabeth Fitzwilliam; m② Bridget Wiltshire (*1)

JOHN HERVEY d.1556 m.1511, Elizabeth, d. of Henry Pope of Mildenhall

EDMUND HERVEY d. before 1560, member of the royal household (Henry VIII) granted part of the abbey of Elstow, Beds.in 1541

WILLIAM HERVEY, eldest son and heir, d.1592, m.1554 Elizabeth, d. of John Poley of Boxted

14 OTHER CHILDREN including two named John - known as John the Elder and John the Younger

JOHN HERVEY, eldest son and heir, born about 1550, buried at Ickworth 1620, m.1582 Frances Bocking of Ashbocking

SIR WILLIAM HERVEY b.1555 — m① Susan Jermyn of Rushbrooke | m② Penelope, d. of Thomas Lord Darcy (Earl Rivers) of Hengrave Hall. (no issue)

8 OTHER CHILDREN including another William (b.1557) known as William the Younger. The older children were baptised at Boxted, the later ones at Ickworth.

SIR THOMAS HERVEY m. Isabella, d. of Sir Humphrey May and Judith Poley (see Poley tree)

ISABELLA HARVEY 1659-97 m. Gervase Elwes of Stoke by Clare (*2)

JOHN HARVEY 1st Earl of Bristol

(*1) Bridget was the d. of Sir John Wiltshire of Stone Castle in Kent. She was the widow of Sir Richard Wingfield of Kimbolton Castle, a descendant of Sir John Wingfield of Wingfield Castle.

(*2) Isabella and Gervase had a son, Sir Harvey Elwes who, with his nephew, John Elwes, were known as 'The Misers of Ashen' and are mentioned in John Timpson's 'English Eccentrics'.

Ickworth Hall
Home of the Suffolk branch of the Harvey family from about 1475 until the rebuilding in 1795

The Knighton Family
of Bayford in Hertfordshire and Little Bradley in Suffolk

JOHN KNIGHTON d.1559. In 1545 he received from Henry VIII the manor of Bayford, for which he paid £317. 13s. 9d.

THOMAS KNIGHTON of Bayford, m. Ann, d. and co-heiress of Thomas Underhill of Harveys in Little Bradley, Suffolk

THOMAS KNIGHTON of Brickendon. d.1582. m. Alice, d. of Richard Bull of Hertford and Helen Skipwith of St Albans. Thomas inherited his mother's estates in Suffolk and went to live there. (⬇ Knightons of Suffolk on Hunt tree)	**JOHN KNIGHTON** of the Inner Temple. d.1585. Lived at Aldbury. Acquired the manor of Kimpton in 1579 (*1) m. Alicia Copwood of Totteridge, Herts.	**JANE KNIGHTON** m. Charles, s. of Richard Bull of Hertford and Helen Skipwith of St Albans, and brother of Alice Bull who m. Thomas Knighton (Bull tree ⬇)

DOROTHY KNIGHTON _____ **URSULA KNIGHTON** d.1605	**JOYCE KNIGHTON** _____ **RALPH KNIGHTON**	**SIR GEORGE KNIGHTON** of Bayford. 1537-1613. (*2) m.① Johanna Cadwell / m.② Susan White (no issue)	**DIANIS KNIGHTON** d.1616 _____ **PHILIPPA KNIGHTON** m.1559

JOHN KNIGHTON 1564-1635 m. Elizabeth Vaughan osp	**GEORGE KNIGHTON** eldest son and heir. d.1607 (pre-deceased his father - estate went to his nephew Knighton Ferrers)	**ANN KNIGHTON** 1586-1630 m. 1604, Sir John Ferrers of Markyate (Gentleman of the Privy Chamber to Queen Elizabeth. and James I - memorial in Bayford Church)	**A DAUGHTER** m. ... Spring of Norfolk

KNIGHTON FERRERS m. Katherine, d. of Sir William Walter. Knighton Ferrers died 1628, just before his d. Katherine was born, and his widow m. Thomas, Viscount Fanshawe of Ware Park (who may previously have been m. to Ann Alington - see Soame note 2)

KATHERINE FERRERS m. 1640 (at the age of 12) Symon, Viscount Fanshawe (her step-father's son). Katherine became famous as The Wicked Lady.

(*1) Clutterbuck tells us that the Manor of Amwell Bury, alias Rushden, in the parish of All Saints, was held in the 19th year of Queen Elizabeth (1577) by John Knighton of Aldbury, his wife Alicia, and his son George. He also held the manor of Revell's Hall in Bengeo, and gave this to Henry Gardiner and his wife Mary (John's sister's daughter). John and George Knighton at this time also held Kimpton, Bayford and Brickendon.

(*2) There is a memorial to George Knighton in Bayford Church showing a knight in armour on an altar tomb.

The Kympton (or Kimpton) Family
of Westminster, Clothall and Weston

Held land in Herts and Beds, including the manor of Kimptons in Stanbridge, from the 14th century. By the 16th century they were also city merchants, but still held their estates in Hertfordshire. There is no apparent link with the manor of Kimpton Hoo in Hertfordshire.

EDMUND KYMPTON of Westminster, held land in Clothall, Yardley, Rushden and Astwick. He was probably related to the Poley and Sheldon families, from whom he acquired Astwick in 1539.

WILLIAM KYMPTON, Merchant Taylor, b. about 1515, m. 1539 Joan Mayman at St Margaret's Westminster, became Freeman of the Merchant Taylors Company in 1544 and Master of the Company in 1570. (*1)	**EDMUND KYMPTON** of Clothall, 1527-51, m. 1546 (at Weston) Lucy, d. of George Hyde of Throcking and Alice Roper of Well Hall, Eltham in Kent. When Edmund died his wife held court until her son George came of age.

WILLIAM KYMPTON, Merchant Taylor, Freeman of the Company 1575, m. 1577 Cecily Burse at St Margaret's Westminster. Possibly m. first to Jane Nodes of Shephallbury	**EDWARD KYMPTON**, bapt. 1556. Merchant Taylor, Master of the Company 1596.	**GEORGE KYMPTON** c.1546-1608, of Clothall and Weston (Howells). m.1568 at Bengeo, Catherine Brooke of High Cross (see Brooke tree). George and his cousin William also held the manor of Brickendon near Hertford

EDMUND KYMPTON m. 1619 Joanna Chaukell at St Margaret's Westminster	**JANE KYMPTON** 1573-98 m. Thomas Harmer of Weston	**ANNE** b.1574; **LEONARD** b.1576; **GEORGE** b.1577; **GEORGE** b.1580; and **ANNE** b.1581. All died young.	**GEORGE KYMPTON** b. 1583, only surviving son and heir, m. Dorothy, d. of Sir William Becher of Howbury Hall, Renhold, and lived at Clothallbury. He sold Astwick in 1420 for £2,100 to John Hudson (or Hodgeson) of London.

WILLIAM KYMPTON bapt. 1621 at St Margaret's Westminster.

(*1) One of the most well-known local members of the Merchant Taylors Company was Sir William Harpur of Bedford, who was Master in 1553 and Lord Mayor of London in 1561.

The Kytsons and Gages of Hengrave

ROBERT KYTSON of Warton, Lancashire

SIR THOMAS KYTSON of Hengrave 1485-1540.
m. Margaret, 1509-61, daughter of John Donnington of Stoke Newington. Margaret later married Lord Bath.

MARGARET KYTSON
m. John Washington of Warton, Lancashire

SIR THOMAS KYTSON of Hengrave 1540-1602. m. c.1560 Elizabeth, daughter of Sir Thomas Cornwallis of Brome, Suffolk d. 1628

CATHERINE KYTSON
m. Sir John Spencer of Wormleighton

LAURENCE WASHINGTON of Sulgrave, 1500-83
m. Amee Pargiter of Greatworth
(5x great grandparents of George Washington, the first President of the USA)

JOHN KYTSON 1562-63

MARGARET KYTSON m. Sir Charles Cavendish. osp

MARY KYTSON of Hengrave d. 1644. m. 1583 Thomas, Lord Darcy, Earl Rivers who died 1639 St Osyth

4 Sons
1. JOHN SPENCER 2. THOMAS SPENCER
3. WILLIAM SPENCER 4. RICHARD SPENCER

JOHN GAGE of Firle b.1570, Created 1st Baronet of Firle 1622. d. 3 Oct 1633, Sussex   m.   **PENELOPE DARCY** b.1593 St Osyth Essex. d.Jul.1661 Inherited Hengrave, Suffolk. Her 2nd marriage. Previously married to Sir George Trenchard, widowed. After John Gage died, she married Sir William Hervey of Ickworth.

SIR THOMAS GAGE, 2nd Baronet of Firle. Inherited Sussex estate.

JOHN GAGE m.Mary Baker

EDWARD GAGE 1617-1707 Inherited Hengrave. Created Baronet of Hengrave 1662. Had 5 wives.
m.1. 25 Jul 1648 Mary, d. of Sir William Hervey of Ickworth | 2. Frances Ashton. 3. Anne Watkins: 4. Elizabeth Fielding: 5. Mrs Bridget Slaughter

HENRY GAGE m.Henrietta, d. of Thomas Jermyn of Rushbrooke

5 daughters
FRANCES m. William Tresham:
ELIZABETH m. Sir Francis Petre:
PENELOPE m. Henry Merry:
ANNE m. Henry Petre:
DOROTHY unmarried

WILLIAM GAGE (2nd Bart.) 1701-1727 d. 8 Feb 1727, buried at Hengrave
m.1 1675 Mary Charlotte, daughter of Sir Thomas Bond of Peckham, Surrey | m.2 Merelina, daughter of Thomas, Lord Jermyn

PENELOPE GAGE m. Edward Sulyard of Haughley, Suffolk

MARY GAGE m.William Bond of St. Edmundsbury. d. 1719. Buried at Hengrave

---

THOMAS GAGE 1684-1716, m. Delariviere, eldest daughter of Simonds D'Ewes of Stow Hall, Suffolk, by Delariviere, daughter of Thomas, Lord Jermyn d.1 Mar 1716, aged 32, in his father's lifetime.

WILLIAM GAGE d.1685 osp

JOHN GAGE 1688-1728 m. Elizabeth (1685-1759) d. of Thomas Rokewood of Coldham Hall, Stanningfield, by Tamworth, daughter of Sir Roger Martin, Bart. of Melford Place, Long Melford.

6 daughters
CHARLOTTE m. Fitznun Lambe. d. 1733
HENRIETTA unmarried. d. 1757
MARY m. Henry Huddleston. d. 1770
PENELOPE a nun at Bruges. d. 1772 aged 85.
CATHARINE m. 1730 Henry Sorrel. d. 1733.
Buried in St Mary's Church, Bury St Edmunds.
ANNE unmarried. d. 1760.

THOMAS GAGE (3rd Bart.) succeeded his grandfather in 1726 and d. unmarried in Sept 1741 when the estate went to his brother William.

WILLIAM GAGE (4th Bart.) d.17 May 1767 m.Jun. 1741 Frances, widow of Robert Harland

THOMAS GAGE (5th Bart.) 1719-96 Later became Sir Thomas Rokewood Gage. Inherited Rokewood/Coldham estaes from John and Elizabeth and the Hengrave Estates (by Will) from his cousin William. m.1747 Lucy Knight of Lincolnshire.

JOHN GAGE 1720-90 A priest at Bury St Edmunds.

SIR THOMAS GAGE (6th Bart.) 1751-1798
m. 22 Nov 1779 Charlotte, (1756-90) daughter of Thomas Fitzherbert of Swinnerton, Staffordshire, by Mary Teresa, daughter of Sir Robert Throckmorton, Bart. d. 1 Dec 1798, buried at Hengrave.

SIR THOMAS GAGE (7th Bart.) 1781-1820
m. 9 Jan 1809 Mary Anne, daughter of Valentine Browne, Earl of Kenmare. d. 27 Dec 1820, buried in Rome.

SIR THOMAS ROKEWODE GAGE (8th Bart.) 1810-1866 Assumed the additional surname and arms of Rokewode by royal sign-manual in 1843. m. 16 Sep 1850 Adelaide, youngest daughter of Henry Drummond of Albury Park. d. 7 Jun 1866 in Paris, buried at Hengrave.

SIR EDWARD ROKEWODE GAGE (9th Bart.) b.1812 m. Aug 1842 Henrietta Mary, youngest daughter of Lord Frederick Beauclerk

The Mordaunt Family of Turvey and Drayton Park
with connections in Suffolk, Essex and Hertfordshire (Kimpton)

The manor of Mordaunts in Turvey was held by the Mordaunt family from the early 13th century.

EUSTACE MORDAUNT named in 1225 in an assize of Morte d'ancestor

WILLIAM MORDAUNT succeeded and his son WILLIAM held the manor in 1278

ROBERT MORDAUNT inherited the manor before 1346

EDMUND MORDAUNT, d. 1372. The Sunday before the feast of St Simon and St Jude he was seized with homicidal mania, killed his wife Ellen and drowned himself in a pool at Turvey.

ROBERT MORDAUNT. United the two manors of Mordaunt and Ardres. Died before 1397.

ROBERT MORDAUNT, a supporter of the house of York in the Wars of the Roses. Died 1448, having considerably impoverished the estate to support the Yorkist army.

WILLIAM MORDAUNT and his wife were 'frugal and provident' and the family became prosperous again.

MORDAUNT
Argent a cheveron between three stars sable.

MAUD (or Elizabeth) MORDAUNT
m. Sir Weston Browne of Abbess Roding
(Browne tree ↓)

SIR JOHN MORDAUNT succeeded about 1475. He was wounded when fighting on the Lancastrian side in the battle at Barnet. Made King's Sergeant in 1495 and is said to have been instrumental in arranging the marriage between Margaret Tudor and James IV of Scotland in 1503. He was Speaker of the House of Commons 1487. Died 1504.

JOHN LORD MORDAUNT, created baron in 1533. He accompanied Henry VIII to the Field of the Cloth of Gold. He received Anne Boleyn at the Tower when she came to be crowned and took part in her trial three years later. He lived at Drayton in Northamptonshire and used Turvey Park as a Dower House. Died 1561.

JOHN 2ND LORD MORDAUNT. Lived at Thorndon, West Horndon, near Ingatestone Hall. Died 1571. A supporter of Queen Mary who made him a Privy Counsellor. Inherited part of the manor at Kimpton in Hertfordshire by his marriage to Elizabeth, d. of Henry de Vere and sister of Ann and Audrey de Vere who were both married into the Browne family. John was a friend and kinsman of the Petres of Ingatestone Hall and made a gift of an ox at the wedding of Catherine Tyrell. Lady Mordaunt sent presents for the christening of Master John Petre in 1549 (*1).

GEORGE MORDAUNT
(3rd son)
His daughter Katherine married Robert Barnardiston of Northill.
(see Barnardiston tree)

LEWIS LORD MORDAUNT of Northill, Bedfordshire, d.1601. A judge who took part (unwillingly) in the trial of Mary Queen of Scots and also of Thomas Duke of Norfolk. Sold the manor of Kimpton to Thomas Hoo of St Paul's Walden. He m. Jane Nedham of Wymondley Priory.

HENRY 4TH LORD MORDAUNT. A Roman Catholic. Was sent to the Tower under suspicion of being involved in the Gunpowder Plot (1605). Released after long imprisonment. Died 1608 and in his will he states that his conscience is clear, and that he had no knowledge of the Gunpowder Treason (*2). When Sir Henry died his widow lived on at Turvey. The government took away her eldest son so that he should be brought up as a Protestant, but Lady Turvey remained a determined Roman Catholic. From 1625-31 she even had resident in her house at Turvey the Vicar Apostolic who travelled round the county in a coach with four horses, accompanied by 9 or 10 priests (*3). The jurisdiction of the Vicar Apostolic extended over Roman Catholics in the whole of England and also in the American plantations.

JOHN MORDAUNT, made Earl of Peterborough in 1628 but took the Parliamentarian side in the early part of the Civil War. Died 1642.

HENRY MORDAUNT 2nd Earl of Peterborough, was a Royalist (unlike his father). Wounded at Newbury and several times imprisoned. His estates sequestered in 1648 and recovered in 1655 at a cost of £5,106 - 15s. At the Restoration he was made a member of the Privy Council, and conducted negotiations for the marriage of the then Duke of York (later James II) and Mary of Modena. Became a Roman Catholic and was impeached for High Treason, but later released. Created Earl of Monmouth in 1689. He died at an advanced age in 1697 without male issue. His only daughter Mary died unmarried in 1705.

↓

CHARLES MORDAUNT 3rd Earl of Peterborough, d.1735, nephew of the 2nd Earl, General in the Spanish War of Succession.

↓

CHARLES MORDAUNT 4th Earl of Peterborough, grandson of the 3rd Earl. Died 1774.

CHARLES MORDAUNT 5th (and last) Earl of Peterborough. In 1786 he sold the property, including Turvey Abbey, to Claude Higgins, Sheriff of London for that year. The estates remained in the Higgins family until the 19th century (*4).

The Mordaunt Family of Turvey and Drayton Park
with connections in Suffolk, Essex and Hertfordshire (Kimpton)

(*1) For the christening of Master John Petre at Ingatestone Hall in 1549, Lady Mordaunt of Thorndon (previously Elizabeth de Vere) sent: 'a guinea fowl, a mallard, a woodcock, two teals, a basket of wafers and other cakes'. Her husband, John Lord Mordaunt, often came to play backgammon with Sir William Petre at Ingatestone Hall.

(*2) See pages on Family Connections with the Gunpowder Plot.

(*3) Lady Mordaunt's house at Turvey, about 1644, is described by Joyce Godber. It had three parlours, one of them wainscotted, the drawing room, where the chairs were of Turkey-work, the red room and the gallery and 14 bedchambers - her own containing a white wrought bed.

(*4) Until the 17th century the Mordaunt estate at Turvey was known as Mordaunts Manor. Another manor belonging to the Dudleys (later Earls of Leicester) was generally known as Turvey Manor and the two were united in 1660 by the Mordaunts who were related to the Brownes and Knightons of Little Bradley in Suffolk, and to the de Vere family of Kimpton in Hertfordshire. Another branch at Northill married into the Barnardiston family. The Oakley branch married into the Booth family of Shrublands in Suffolk and the Snagges of Marston Morteyne. The house now known as Turvey Abbey was occupied by another Roman Catholic family - the Brands, who were kinsmen of the de Veres and Brands of Kimpton.

Turvey Abbey, Bedfordshire

The Mordaunt Family of Oakley

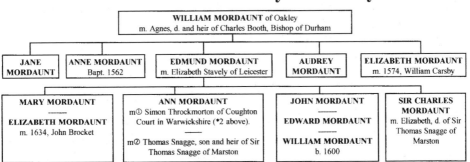

WILLIAM MORDAUNT of Oakley
m. Agnes, d. and heir of Charles Booth, Bishop of Durham

JANE MORDAUNT	ANNE MORDAUNT Bapt. 1562	EDMUND MORDAUNT m. Elizabeth Stavely of Leicester	AUDREY MORDAUNT	ELIZABETH MORDAUNT m. 1574, William Carsby

MARY MORDAUNT ----- ELIZABETH MORDAUNT m. 1634, John Brocket	ANN MORDAUNT m① Simon Throckmorton of Coughton Court in Warwickshire (*2 above). ----- m② Thomas Snagge, son and heir of Sir Thomas Snagge of Marston	JOHN MORDAUNT ----- EDWARD MORDAUNT ----- WILLIAM MORDAUNT b. 1600	SIR CHARLES MORDAUNT m. Elizabeth, d. of Sir Thomas Snagge of Marston

The Mannock Family
of Giffords Hall, Stoke-by-Nayland, Suffolk

PHILIP MANNOCK acquired the manor in 1428. The family had resided in the area since the time of Edward III. They came originally from Denmark and flourished under the Danish kings.

JOHN MANNOCK died 1476, m. ... d. of Sir William Waldegrave of Borley. (see Waldegrave tree)

GEORGE MANNOCK died 1541, m. Katherine, d. of Sir Thomas Waldegrave. (related to the Brownes of Abbess Roding)

WILLIAM MANNOCK d. 1558
m. Audrey, d. of John Alington and sister of Sir Gyles Alington of Horseheath, Cambridge (who m. Margaret Spencer of Althorpe) and of Mary Alington (who m. Robert Newport of Pelham), (see Spencer and Soame trees)

ELIZABETH MANNOCK
m① Robert Dacres of Cheshunt (great-grandfather of Elizabeth Dacres who m. Richard Hale of Tewin) | m② Thomas Denny of Cheshunt related to Thomas Roper (Viscount Baltinglass) and the Nevill family (Lord Abergavenny)

FRANCIS MANNOCK

THOMAS MANNOCK

FRANCIS MANNOCK 1523-90
Memorial in N aisle of chancel in Stoke-by-Nayland church
m① Mary, d. of William Fitch of Canfield, Essex | m② Ann Siscelton, widow, d. of ... Wentworth (d. 1620). There were four children of this marriage: John; Elizabeth (m. to Nicholas Bedingfield); Frances (m. to Giles Green) and Bridget (m. to Thomas Sulyard of Wetherden).

GILES MANNOCK

WILLIAM MANNOCK

A DAUGHTER
m. ... Cornwall of Essex

A DAUGHTER
m. ... St Clere of Essex

WILLIAM MANNOCK, eldest son and heir. In 1596 Queen Elizabeth took away two thirds of his estates because of recusancy. Pardoned by James I in 1603 and estates returned, but taken away again in 1612. m. Audrey, d. of Ferdinand Parys of Linton, Cambs. Memorial stone in Stoke-by-Nayland Church

MARGARET MANNOCK
m. Thomas Crawley of Maldon, Essex

MARY MANNOCK

ANN MANNOCK
m. Thomas Gaudy Everard of Linsted in Suffolk

ELINOR MANNOCK
m. Richard Martin of Long Melford. (Effigy in Melford church)

SIR FRANCIS MANNOCK, d. 20 Nov 1634 aged 49, m.1608, Dorothy, d. of William Sanders of Welford, Northants. Sir Francis was created Baronet by Charles I in 1627. Dorothy died 1632 aged 42, after the birth of her daughter Ann. Both Dorothy and Francis were recusants and most of their estates were sequestered. There is a memorial to Francis in the N wall of church at Stoke-by-Nayland, and a brass to Dorothy Sanders on the floor of the N chapel.

WILLIAM MANNOCK
b. 1611, eldest son and heir, died young.

JOHN MANNOCK

SIR FRANCIS MANNOCK, 2nd baronet, d. 1687, m. Mary, d. of Sir George Heneage of Hainton, Lincs (who provided for the younger members of the Mannock family left penniless by the sequestration).

KATHERINE MANNOCK
m. John, s. of Edward Newport of Brent Pelham

ANN MANNOCK
b.1632

SIR WILLIAM MANNOCK, 3rd baronet

SIR FRANCIS MANNOCK, 4th baronet

SIR WILLIAM MANNOCK
5th baronet

SIR FRANCIS MANNOCK
7th baronet, d. 1778

SIR THOMAS MANNOCK 8th baronet, d. 1781, m.1780, Anastasia Browne (2nd wife) descendant of 1st Viscount Montague.(see Browne of Sussex tree)

SIR GEORGE MANNOCK, 9th baronet, killed 3rd June 1787 by the overturning of the Dover coach (*1).

SIR ANTHONY MANNOCK, 6th baronet, d. 1776. His three uncles succeeded in turn to the title.

(*1) When Sir George died in the Dover coach accident in 1787, leaving no issue, the baronetcy expired. The manor went to William Comyns who took the name Mannock and died in 1819. It then went to his kinsman (through a Strickland marriage) Patrick Power, who again took the name of Mannock by royal licence in 1830. The mansion house of Giffords Hall remains, the oldest part, built by Peter Gifford, dating back to the time of Henry III. The main part is Tudor, built by the Mannock family. Nearby are the ruins of an old chapel built by Richard Constable in 1216 and endowed by his son William. Since this is 'Constable country' this is almost certainly the family of John Constable the painter. The Mannock family were related by marriage to the Chapmans of Hitchin (George Chapman the Elizabethan poet).

Sir Thomas More
of More Hall or Gobions at North Mimms, Hertfordshire

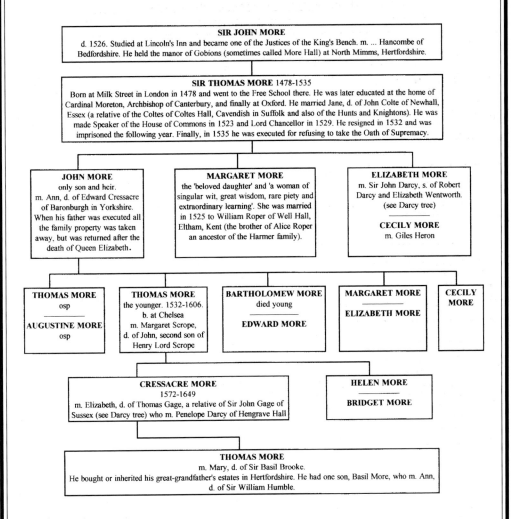

SIR JOHN MORE
d. 1526. Studied at Lincoln's Inn and became one of the Justices of the King's Bench. m. ... Hancombe of Bedfordshire. He held the manor of Gobions (sometimes called More Hall) at North Mimms, Hertfordshire.

SIR THOMAS MORE 1478-1535
Born at Milk Street in London in 1478 and went to the Free School there. He was later educated at the home of Cardinal Moreton, Archbishop of Canterbury, and finally at Oxford. He married Jane, d. of John Colte of Newhall, Essex (a relative of the Coltes of Coltes Hall, Cavendish in Suffolk and also of the Hunts and Knightons). He was made Speaker of the House of Commons in 1523 and Lord Chancellor in 1529. He resigned in 1532 and was imprisoned the following year. Finally, in 1535 he was executed for refusing to take the Oath of Supremacy.

JOHN MORE
only son and heir.
m. Ann, d. of Edward Cressacre of Baronburgh in Yorkshire. When his father was executed all the family property was taken away, but was returned after the death of Queen Elizabeth.

MARGARET MORE
the 'beloved daughter' and 'a woman of singular wit, great wisdom, rare piety and extraordinary learning'. She was married in 1525 to William Roper of Well Hall, Eltham, Kent (the brother of Alice Roper an ancestor of the Harmer family).

ELIZABETH MORE
m. Sir John Darcy, s. of Robert Darcy and Elizabeth Wentworth.
(see Darcy tree)

CECILY MORE
m. Giles Heron

THOMAS MORE
osp
___
AUGUSTINE MORE
osp

THOMAS MORE
the younger. 1532-1606.
b. at Chelsea
m. Margaret Scrope,
d. of John, second son of
Henry Lord Scrope

BARTHOLOMEW MORE
died young
___
EDWARD MORE

MARGARET MORE
___
ELIZABETH MORE

CECILY MORE

CRESSACRE MORE
1572-1649
m. Elizabeth, d. of Thomas Gage, a relative of Sir John Gage of Sussex (see Darcy tree) who m. Penelope Darcy of Hengrave Hall

HELEN MORE
___
BRIDGET MORE

THOMAS MORE
m. Mary, d. of Sir Basil Brooke.
He bought or inherited his great-grandfather's estates in Hertfordshire. He had one son, Basil More, who m. Ann, d. of Sir William Humble.

SIR THOMAS MORE probably spent much of his early life at Gobions, his country estate in Hertfordshire, but later lived mainly at Chelsea, where some of his younger children were born. His 'Utopia' is thought to have been written at Gobions. It was illustrated by his friend Hans Holbein, who also painted several portraits of Thomas More.

There was a large family portrait by Hans Holbein, probably commissioned by his son-in-law William (the brother of Alice Roper), which hung in the Great Hall at the Roper family home in Eltham, Kent. The original painting was lost when the home was sold in the 18th century but several variant copies still exist.

In the Frick Collection in New York there is a Holbein portrait of Thomas More, which seems to have been painted from the original sketch which he did for the family group. The Mores had several links with the family through the Ropers, Scroops, Darcys, Brookes and the Colte family of Coltes Hall in Cavendish, Suffolk.

The Petre Family
of Ingatestone Hall in Essex

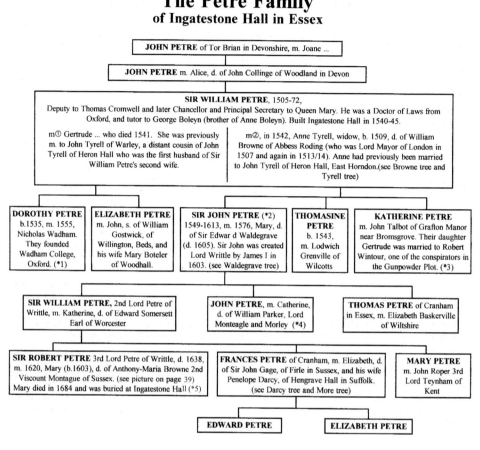

JOHN PETRE of Tor Brian in Devonshire, m. Joane ...

JOHN PETRE m. Alice, d. of John Collinge of Woodland in Devon

SIR WILLIAM PETRE, 1505-72,
Deputy to Thomas Cromwell and later Chancellor and Principal Secretary to Queen Mary. He was a Doctor of Laws from Oxford, and tutor to George Boleyn (brother of Anne Boleyn). Built Ingatestone Hall in 1540-45.

mⒶ Gertrude ... who died 1541. She was previously m. to John Tyrell of Warley, a distant cousin of John Tyrell of Heron Hall who was the first husband of Sir William Petre's second wife.

mⒷ, in 1542, Anne Tyrell, widow, b. 1509, d. of William Browne of Abbess Roding (who was Lord Mayor of London in 1507 and again in 1513/14). Anne had previously been married to John Tyrell of Heron Hall, East Horndon.(see Browne tree and Tyrell tree)

DOROTHY PETRE
b.1535, m. 1555, Nicholas Wadham. They founded Wadham College, Oxford. (*1)

ELIZABETH PETRE
m. John, s. of William Gostwick, of Willington, Beds, and his wife Mary Boteler of Woodhall.

SIR JOHN PETRE (*2)
1549-1613, m. 1576, Mary, d. of Sir Edward Waldegrave (d. 1605). Sir John was created Lord Writtle by James I in 1603. (see Waldegrave tree)

THOMASINE PETRE
b. 1543, m. Lodwich Grenville of Wilcotts

KATHERINE PETRE
m. John Talbot of Grafton Manor near Bromsgrove. Their daughter Gertrude was married to Robert Wintour, one of the conspirators in the Gunpowder Plot. (*3)

SIR WILLIAM PETRE, 2nd Lord Petre of Writtle, m. Katherine, d. of Edward Somersett Earl of Worcester

JOHN PETRE, m. Catherine, d. of William Parker, Lord Monteagle and Morley (*4)

THOMAS PETRE of Cranham in Essex, m. Elizabeth Baskerville of Wiltshire

SIR ROBERT PETRE 3rd Lord Petre of Writtle, d. 1638, m. 1620, Mary (b.1603), d. of Anthony-Maria Browne 2nd Viscount Montague of Sussex. (see picture on page 39) Mary died in 1684 and was buried at Ingatestone Hall (*5)

FRANCES PETRE of Cranham, m. Elizabeth, d. of Sir John Gage, of Firle in Sussex, and his wife Penelope Darcy, of Hengrave Hall in Suffolk. (see Darcy tree and More tree)

MARY PETRE m. John Roper 3rd Lord Teynham of Kent

EDWARD PETRE

ELIZABETH PETRE

(*1) When Nicholas Wadham died in 1609 he left his vast fortune to endow a college at Oxford. Nicholas and his wife Dorothy were dedicated to the cause of education and had already planned to build a new college. When Nicholas died it was his widow Dorothy, then 75 years old, who took over the responsibility of seeing that the work was completed. She added some of her own money to the endowment, and kept a strict control on the building and organisation.

(*2) The Christening of 'Master John' in 1549 is described in 'Tudor Food and Pastimes' (see (*1) on Mordaunt tree).

(*3) Robert Wintour and his brother Thomas were two of the 8 main conspirators in the Gunpowder Plot. They were hung, drawn and quartered on 30th January 1606.

(*4) William Parker Lord Monteagle (later Lord Monteagle and Morley) was married to Elizabeth Tresham, a first cousin of the conspirator Robert Catesby. On 26th October 1605 Lord Monteagle received an anonymous letter (now known as the 'Monteagle Letter') warning him not to attend Parliament on 5th November. The letter led to the discovery of the Gunpowder Plot. Lord Monteagle was one of those who searched the cellars under the Houses of Parliament and discovered the barrels of gunpowder.

(*5) The Petres were closely connected with both the Brownes of Abbess Roding, who were close friends and neighbours, and the Brownes Lords Montague, of Sussex, who were connected with the family by this marriage and by other 'network' links.

The Petre Family of Ingatestone Hall

At the time of the dissolution of the monasteries Sir William Petre was one of the King's Visitors and Chief Deputy to Thomas Cromwell. He travelled all over the country, obtaining the surrender of a large number of Abbeys and Priories. We are told that, unlike many of the royal agents, 'Petre emerged with no stain and even earned a few econiums on his leniency and honesty in this arduous task'. The nuns at Barking Abbey were very happy with the terms he offered them, and he was able to buy one of their most important properties, the manor of Gyng Abbess or Abbess Hall, afterwards known as Ingatestone Hall. (This is not to be confused with the Abbess Hall which was an alternative name for Abbess Roding, the home of the Browne family).

It is emphasised that Petre paid the full market price for the property (£849 12s. 6d to be paid over 4 years). The Abbess of Barking and thirty nuns assembled on 14th November 1539 to hand the deed of surrender to Dr Petre. Among them were ladies from many of the leading families in Suffolk and Essex, including the Mordaunts, Tyrells, Wentworths, Drurys, Sulyards and Kempes, who all appear on the family pedigrees. All were very happy with their annuities, Abbess Barley's being £133 13s. 4d.

Sir William Petre was married first to Gertrude, the widow of Sir John Tyrell of Warley Hall in Essex, and secondly to Anne Tyrell, the widow of another John Tyrell, a distant cousin of Sir William's first wife. Anne was the daughter of William Browne of Abbess Roding, (who died in 1514 during his second term as Lord Mayor of London, when Anne was only 4 years old). It was Catherine Tyrell, the daughter of Anne's first marriage, whose wedding feast is described in 'Tudor Food and Pastimes' by F G Emmison.

Sir Anthony Browne who appears on the Browne pedigree is mentioned as one of the guests at Catherine Tyrell's wedding. We are told that three oxen were given for the wedding feast, one by Sir John Mordaunt, one by Sir Harry Tyrell, and one by Sir Anthony Browne. (The Petres were also connected with the Brownes Lords Montague of Cowdray in Sussex, but there seems to be no obvious link between the Brownes of Sussex and the Brownes of Essex).

Sir Richard Rich, later Richard Lord Rich, who was related to the Piggots of Gravenhurst and the St Johns of Bletsoe, was a frequent visitor to Ingatestone Hall. He lived at Leigh's Priory in Essex (another property which previously belonged to Barking Abbey). Lord Rich later founded Felsted School on his estate.

William Byrd, the Court musician and composer, spent as much time as possible on his manor at Stondon, which was not far from Ingatestone Hall, and Sir William Petre and his son John were his very good friends and patrons.

Another frequent visitor to Ingatestone Hall was Lady Darcy. She was the wife of Thomas Lord Darcy, who owned St Osyth's Priory. He was a Privy Councillor, and was treated with great respect when he visited Ingatestone Hall. Lady Darcy was previously Elizabeth de Vere, daughter of John Earl of Oxford (known as 'ye little Earl of Oxford'). The grandson of Lord and Lady Darcy (another Thomas Lord Darcy), became Earl Rivers and married Mary Kitson of Hengrave Hall. Their descendants (through the 2nd marriage of their daughter and heir Penelope), were the Gage family, who held Hengrave for nine generations, until the late 19th century. Sir John Petre's grandson Francis Petre married Elizabeth, daughter of Sir John Gage.

Ingatestone Hall, Essex

The Poley Family
of Boxted, Badley and Stowmarket in Suffolk, with roots in Cottered, Herts

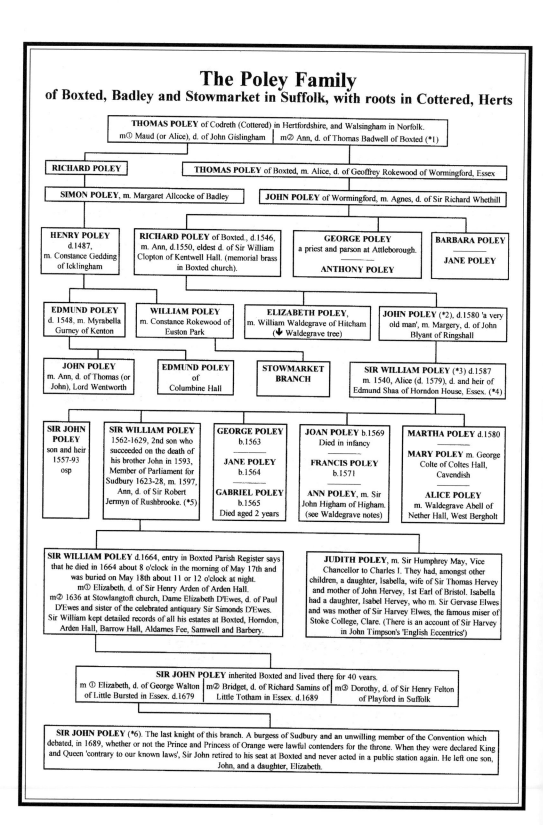

THOMAS POLEY of Codreth (Cottered) in Hertfordshire, and Walsingham in Norfolk.
m① Maud (or Alice), d. of John Gislingham | m② Ann, d. of Thomas Badwell of Boxted (*1)

RICHARD POLEY

THOMAS POLEY of Boxted, m. Alice, d. of Geoffrey Rokewood of Wormingford, Essex

SIMON POLEY, m. Margaret Allcocke of Badley

JOHN POLEY of Wormingford, m. Agnes, d. of Sir Richard Whethill

HENRY POLEY d.1487, m. Constance Gedding of Icklingham

RICHARD POLEY of Boxted., d.1546, m. Ann, d.1550, eldest d. of Sir William Clopton of Kentwell Hall. (memorial brass in Boxted church).

GEORGE POLEY a priest and parson at Attleborough.

ANTHONY POLEY

BARBARA POLEY

JANE POLEY

EDMUND POLEY d. 1548, m. Myrabella Gurney of Kenton

WILLIAM POLEY m. Constance Rokewood of Euston Park

ELIZABETH POLEY, m. William Waldegrave of Hitcham (⬇ Waldegrave tree)

JOHN POLEY (*2), d.1580 'a very old man', m. Margery, d. of John Blyant of Ringshall

JOHN POLEY m. Ann, d. of Thomas (or John), Lord Wentworth

EDMUND POLEY of Columbine Hall

STOWMARKET BRANCH

SIR WILLIAM POLEY (*3) d.1587 m. 1540, Alice (d. 1579), d. and heir of Edmund Shaa of Horndon House, Essex. (*4)

SIR JOHN POLEY son and heir 1557-93 osp

SIR WILLIAM POLEY 1562-1629, 2nd son who succeeded on the death of his brother John in 1593, Member of Parliament for Sudbury 1623-28, m. 1597, Ann, d. of Sir Robert Jermyn of Rushbrooke. (*5)

GEORGE POLEY b.1563

JANE POLEY b.1564

GABRIEL POLEY b.1565 Died aged 2 years

JOAN POLEY b.1569 Died in infancy

FRANCIS POLEY b.1571

ANN POLEY, m. Sir John Higham of Higham. (see Waldegrave notes)

MARTHA POLEY d.1580

MARY POLEY m. George Colte of Coltes Hall, Cavendish

ALICE POLEY m. Waldegrave Abell of Nether Hall, West Bergholt

SIR WILLIAM POLEY d.1664, entry in Boxted Parish Register says that he died in 1664 about 8 o'clock in the morning of May 17th and was buried on May 18th about 11 or 12 o'clock at night.
m① Elizabeth, d. of Sir Henry Arden of Arden Hall.
m② 1636 at Stowlangtoft church, Dame Elizabeth D'Ewes, d. of Paul D'Ewes and sister of the celebrated antiquary Sir Simonds D'Ewes.
Sir William kept detailed records of all his estates at Boxted, Horndon, Arden Hall, Barrow Hall, Aldames Fee, Samwell and Barbery.

JUDITH POLEY, m. Sir Humphrey May, Vice Chancellor to Charles I. They had, amongst other children, a daughter, Isabella, wife of Sir Thomas Hervey and mother of John Hervey, 1st Earl of Bristol. Isabella had a daughter, Isabel Hervey, who m. Sir Gervase Elwes and was mother of Sir Harvey Elwes, the famous miser of Stoke College, Clare. (There is an account of Sir Harvey in John Timpson's 'English Eccentrics')

SIR JOHN POLEY inherited Boxted and lived there for 40 years.
m ① Elizabeth, d. of George Walton of Little Bursted in Essex. d.1679 | m② Bridget, d. of Richard Samins of Little Totham in Essex. d.1689 | m③ Dorothy, d. of Sir Henry Felton of Playford in Suffolk

SIR JOHN POLEY (*6). The last knight of this branch. A burgess of Sudbury and an unwilling member of the Convention which debated, in 1689, whether or not the Prince and Princess of Orange were lawful contenders for the throne. When they were declared King and Queen 'contrary to our known laws', Sir John retired to his seat at Boxted and never acted in a public station again. He left one son, John, and a daughter, Elizabeth.

The Poley Family
of Boxted, Badley and Stowmarket in Suffolk, with roots in Cottered, Herts.

(*1) Ann's great-grandfather was William Harvey, whose family held the manor of Boxted and also of Ickworth in the 13th century. It appears that the male line died out and the Harveys of Thurleigh acquired Ickworth in the 15th century, by a marriage with Jane Drury.

(*2) In 1561, John, now an old man, handed over Boxted to his son William, reserving for his own use only 'the parlour at the end of the hall with the chamber within the said parlour, stabling for two horses in the stable at the end of the barn, liberty to fish in the moat, river and other waters ... and liberty to be in walks, orchards and other gardens at all times mete and convenient'.

(*3) After he inherited the estate in 1561 William built a mansion house, Boxted Hall. He died in 1587 and was buried in the church at Boxted, where an effigy remains.

(*4) Edmund Shaa's father, Sir John Shaa, was Lord Mayor of London in 1501, and his grandfather, Edmund Shaa was Lord Mayor in 1482.

(*5) Sir Robert Jermyn was grandfather to Henry, Earl of St Albans KG, and his sister, Susan Jermyn, was the wife of Sir William Hervey of Ickworth and grandmother to John Hervey, 1st Earl of Bristol.

(*6) A Thomas Poley of Boxted (possibly a brother of John) had a daughter, Elizabeth 1681-1761, who married Robert Weller 1676-1751. They had a son, George Weller, born in 1710, who took the name of Poley. The Weller Poley family still own Boxted at the present day.

The Poleys of Bedfordshire and Hertfordshire were a branch of the same family and held the manors of Clothall and Astwick. Richard Sheldon held land at Astwick from 1487 until his death in 1495. His son Richard held court at Astwick from 1497 until he died without issue some time after 1513, when it passed to his sister Prudence and her husband John Poley. In 1539 they sold Astwick and Clothall to Edmund Kympton. These manors had previously belonged to the Piggot family who were kinsmen of the Sheldons and Poleys.

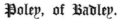

𝔓𝔬𝔩𝔢𝔶, 𝔬𝔣 𝔅𝔞𝔡𝔩𝔢𝔶.

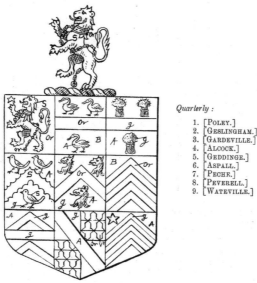

Quarterly :

1. [POLEY.]
2. [GESLINGHAM.]
3. [GARDEVILLE.]
4. [ALCOCK.]
5. [GEDDINGE.]
6. [ASPALL.]
7. [PECHE.]
8. [PEVERELL.]
9. [WATEVILLE.]

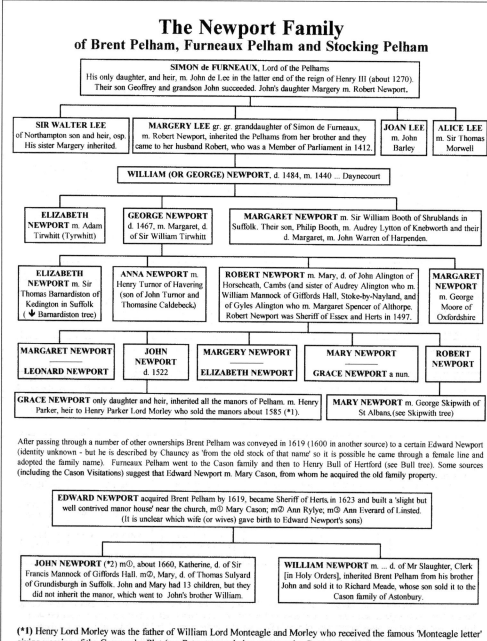

The Newport Family
of Brent Pelham, Furneaux Pelham and Stocking Pelham

SIMON de FURNEAUX, Lord of the Pelhams
His only daughter, and heir, m. John de Lee in the latter end of the reign of Henry III (about 1270).
Their son Geoffrey and grandson John succeeded. John's daughter Margery m. Robert Newport.

SIR WALTER LEE of Northampton son and heir, osp. His sister Margery inherited.

MARGERY LEE gr. gr. granddaughter of Simon de Furneaux, m. Robert Newport, inherited the Pelhams from her brother and they came to her husband Robert, who was a Member of Parliament in 1412.

JOAN LEE m. John Barley

ALICE LEE m. Sir Thomas Morwell

WILLIAM (OR GEORGE) NEWPORT, d. 1484, m. 1440 ... Daynecourt

ELIZABETH NEWPORT m. Adam Tirwhitt (Tyrwhitt)

GEORGE NEWPORT d. 1467, m. Margaret, d. of Sir William Tirwhitt

MARGARET NEWPORT m. Sir William Booth of Shrublands in Suffolk. Their son, Philip Booth, m. Audrey Lytton of Knebworth and their d. Margaret, m. John Warren of Harpenden.

ELIZABETH NEWPORT m. Sir Thomas Barnardiston of Kedington in Suffolk (↓ Barnardiston tree)

ANNA NEWPORT m. Henry Turnor of Havering (son of John Turnor and Thomasine Caldebeck.)

ROBERT NEWPORT m. Mary, d. of John Alington of Horseheath, Cambs (and sister of Audrey Alington who m. William Mannock of Giffords Hall, Stoke-by-Nayland, and of Gyles Alington who m. Margaret Spencer of Althorpe. Robert Newport was Sheriff of Essex and Herts in 1497.

MARGARET NEWPORT m. George Moore of Oxfordshire

MARGARET NEWPORT
———
LEONARD NEWPORT

JOHN NEWPORT d. 1522

MARGERY NEWPORT
———
ELIZABETH NEWPORT

MARY NEWPORT
———
GRACE NEWPORT a nun.

ROBERT NEWPORT

GRACE NEWPORT only daughter and heir, inherited all the manors of Pelham. m. Henry Parker, heir to Henry Parker Lord Morley who sold the manors about 1585 (*1).

MARY NEWPORT m. George Skipwith of St Albans, (see Skipwith tree)

After passing through a number of other ownerships Brent Pelham was conveyed in 1619 (1600 in another source) to a certain Edward Newport (identity unknown - but he is described by Chauncy as 'from the old stock of that name' so it is possible he came through a female line and adopted the family name). Furneaux Pelham went to the Cason family and then to Henry Bull of Hertford (see Bull tree). Some sources (including the Cason Visitations) suggest that Edward Newport m. Mary Cason, from whom he acquired the old family property.

EDWARD NEWPORT acquired Brent Pelham by 1619, became Sheriff of Herts in 1623 and built a 'slight but well contrived manor house' near the church, m① Mary Cason; m② Ann Rylye; m③ Ann Everard of Linsted.
(It is unclear which wife (or wives) gave birth to Edward Newport's sons)

JOHN NEWPORT (*2) m①, about 1660, Katherine, d. of Sir Francis Mannock of Giffords Hall. m②, Mary, d. of Thomas Sulyard of Grundisburgh in Suffolk. John and Mary had 13 children, but they did not inherit the manor, which went to John's brother William.

WILLIAM NEWPORT m. ... d. of Mr Slaughter, Clerk [in Holy Orders], inherited Brent Pelham from his brother John and sold it to Richard Meade, whose son sold it to the Cason family of Astonbury.

(*1) Henry Lord Morley was the father of William Lord Monteagle and Morley who received the famous 'Monteagle letter' giving warning of the Gunpowder Plot (see Petre tree and also notes on the Gunpowder Plot).

(*2) Chauncy writes about this John Newport: 'Anno 10 Car. I [1635] he manifested his loyalty to that King, in the time of the Rebellion, when his majesty was exposed to excessive Distresses, for then he engaged himself with Horse and Arms on behalf of his Majesty, and continued in the Wars until his Army was totally dissipated; during which time, his House was plundered, all his Goods and Cattel taken away, his Mother, Brothers and Sisters turned out of their House, exposed to great Want; and his Estate was sequestered, until King Charles II was restored to his Crown, then he returned to his own, and married Katharine one of the daughters of Sir Francis Mannock, of Giffords Hall, in the Parish of Stoke-Neyland, in the County of Suffolk'.

The St John Family
of Bletsoe

SIR OLIVER ST JOHN m.1425 Margaret Beauchamp of Bletsoe	After Sir Oliver's death Margaret m. John Beaufort Duke of Somerset (*1) and later Lionel Lord Welles

SIR JOHN ST JOHN m. Alice, d. of Sir Thomas Bradshaw	OLIVER ST JOHN ———— EDITH ST JOHN	MARY ST JOHN	AGNES ST JOHN m. Sir David Malpas	ELIZABETH ST JOHN m. Lord Scroop

ST. JOHN OF BLETSOE
Argent a chief gules with two molets or therein

FISHER. *Argent a cheveron between three demilions gules with three roundels argent on the cheveron*

SIR JOHN ST JOHN m. Sibell ...

ALICE ST JOHN m. Henry Parker Lord Morley ———— CATHERINE ST JOHN m. Sir Richard Edgecombe of Edgecombe in Devon	ELIZABETH ST JOHN m. Sir Thomas Rotherham of Someries Manor, Luton ———— SIBELL ST JOHN m. Sir Robert Kirkham	SIR JOHN ST JOHN eldest son and heir. m. Margaret, d. of Sir William Waldegrave of Smallbridge in Suffolk. (see Waldegrave tree)	OLIVER ST JOHN of Sharnbrook. m. Mary, d. of William Fitz Geoffrey of Thurleigh	ALEXANDER ST JOHN of Thurleigh

MARGERY ST JOHN m① Henry, son of Sir Henry Grey of Wrest Park, Earl of Kent m② Francis Piggot of Gravenhurst	MARGARET ST JOHN m. John Gostwick of Willington ———— ALICE ST JOHN ———— ANN ST JOHN	ELIZABETH ST JOHN m. Sir William Becher of Renhold	SIR OLIVER ST JOHN d.1594. m. Agnes Fisher, granddaughter of Sir Michael Fisher of Clifton and of Sir Henry Frowick	MARY ST JOHN m. John Harvey of Thurleigh (see Harvey tree)

MARTHA ST JOHN m① Richard Cheney m② John Colbrand m③ George Wingate.	MARGARET ST JOHN m. Nicholas Luke of Woodend, Beds.	ANN ST JOHN m① Robert Corbett of Salop m② Sir Rowland Lytton of Knebworth	LORD ST JOHN OF BLETSOE m. Catherine, d. of William Dormer of Wing, Bucks, and sister of Mary who m. Sir Anthony Browne of Cowdray. (see Browne tree)	OLIVER ST JOHN created Earl of Bolingbroke in 1624 ———— THOMAS ST JOHN ———— FRANCIS ST JOHN ———— MARGERY ST JOHN	AGNES ST JOHN ———— JUDITH ST JOHN m. Sir John Pelham

(*1) They had one child, Lady Margaret Beaufort, born in 1441. Her father died three years later, leaving her a wealthy heiress. She was brought up and educated at Bletsoe with her St John and Welles half-brothers and sisters. Later she went to live at Court. One of her many suitors was John de la Pole, but she finally married, in 1455, Edmund Tudor, half-brother of King Henry VI. Their only son, Henry Tudor, later became Henry VII. As mother and grandmother to Kings, Lady Margaret Beaufort became a very powerful lady in the country. Her half-brother's son, Sir John St John, later became her Chamberlain. Oliver St John, the grandson of this John, was educated at Court with Lady Margaret's grandson, Prince Henry, later Henry VIII, who spent long periods at Bletsoe Castle with his St John cousins. Oliver St John later became guardian to the two princesses Mary and Elizabeth (later Queen Mary and Queen Elizabeth) and was Chamberlain to Elizabeth when she became Queen. Lady Margaret Beaufort founded two of the Cambridge Colleges - Christ's College in 1505 and St John's College in 1508. She died in 1509.

The Skipwith Family
of St Albans

SIR WILLIAM SKIPWITH, Chief Baron of the Exchequer at the time of Edward III (1327-77)

JOHN SKIPWITH of Colthorpe

ALICE SKIPWITH m. Robert, 4th Baron Willoughby of Parham in Suffolk	**JOHN SKIPWITH** m① Johan, by whom he had 3 children	m② ... d. of Henry Godfrey

WILLIAM SKIPWITH Sheriff of Hertfordshire 1504, m. Johan Buckland	**JOHN SKIPWITH** ——— **ROBERT SKIPWITH**	**RICHARD SKIPWITH** ——— **EDWARD SKIPWITH**	**GREGORY SKIPWITH**	**MARGARET SKIPWITH** ——— **GRACE SKIPWITH**

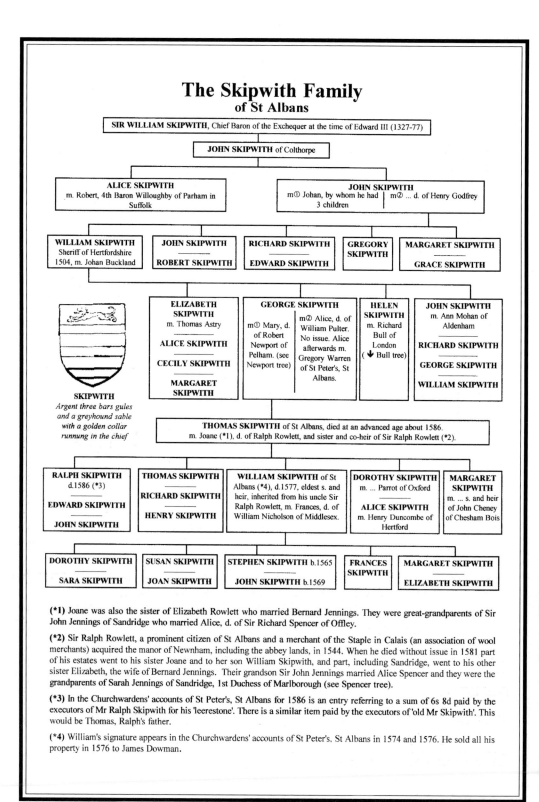

SKIPWITH
Argent three bars gules and a greyhound sable with a golden collar running in the chief

ELIZABETH SKIPWITH m. Thomas Astry ——— **ALICE SKIPWITH** ——— **CECILY SKIPWITH** ——— **MARGARET SKIPWITH**	**GEORGE SKIPWITH** m① Mary, d. of Robert Newport of Pelham. (see Newport tree)	m② Alice, d. of William Pulter. No issue. Alice afterwards m. Gregory Warren of St Peter's, St Albans.	**HELEN SKIPWITH** m. Richard Bull of London (↓ Bull tree)	**JOHN SKIPWITH** m. Ann Mohan of Aldenham ——— **RICHARD SKIPWITH** ——— **GEORGE SKIPWITH** ——— **WILLIAM SKIPWITH**

THOMAS SKIPWITH of St Albans, died at an advanced age about 1586.
m. Joane (*1), d. of Ralph Rowlett, and sister and co-heir of Sir Ralph Rowlett (*2).

RALPH SKIPWITH d.1586 (*3) ——— **EDWARD SKIPWITH** ——— **JOHN SKIPWITH**	**THOMAS SKIPWITH** ——— **RICHARD SKIPWITH** ——— **HENRY SKIPWITH**	**WILLIAM SKIPWITH** of St Albans (*4), d.1577, eldest s. and heir, inherited from his uncle Sir Ralph Rowlett, m. Frances, d. of William Nicholson of Middlesex.	**DOROTHY SKIPWITH** m. ... Parrot of Oxford ——— **ALICE SKIPWITH** m. Henry Duncombe of Hertford	**MARGARET SKIPWITH** m. ... s. and heir of John Cheney of Chesham Bois

DOROTHY SKIPWITH ——— **SARA SKIPWITH**	**SUSAN SKIPWITH** ——— **JOAN SKIPWITH**	**STEPHEN SKIPWITH** b.1565 ——— **JOHN SKIPWITH** b.1569	**FRANCES SKIPWITH**	**MARGARET SKIPWITH** ——— **ELIZABETH SKIPWITH**

(***1**) Joane was also the sister of Elizabeth Rowlett who married Bernard Jennings. They were great-grandparents of Sir John Jennings of Sandridge who married Alice, d. of Sir Richard Spencer of Offley.

(***2**) Sir Ralph Rowlett, a prominent citizen of St Albans and a merchant of the Staple in Calais (an association of wool merchants) acquired the manor of Newnham, including the abbey lands, in 1544. When he died without issue in 1581 part of his estates went to his sister Joane and to her son William Skipwith, and part, including Sandridge, went to his other sister Elizabeth, the wife of Bernard Jennings. Their grandson Sir John Jennings married Alice Spencer and they were the grandparents of Sarah Jennings of Sandridge, 1st Duchess of Marlborough (see Spencer tree).

(***3**) In the Churchwardens' accounts of St Peter's, St Albans for 1586 is an entry referring to a sum of 6s 8d paid by the executors of Mr Ralph Skipwith for his 'leerestone'. There is a similar item paid by the executors of 'old Mr Skipwith'. This would be Thomas, Ralph's father.

(***4**) William's signature appears in the Churchwardens' accounts of St Peter's, St Albans in 1574 and 1576. He sold all his property in 1576 to James Dowman.

The Spencer Family
of Offley, Herts. and Althorp, Northants.

SPENCER, Earl Spencer
Argent quartered with gules fretty or over all a bend sable with three scallops argent thereon.

SIR JOHN SPENCER of Wormleighton. m. Isabel, d. of Walter Graunt

SIR WILLIAM SPENCER of Althorp, m.1510, Susan, d. of Sir Richard Knightley of Fawsley

SIR JOHN SPENCER of Althorp m. Catherine Kitson of Hengrave Hall in Suffolk

SIR JOHN SPENCER m. Mary, d. of Sir Robert Catlin, Lord Chief Justice. Sir Robert was married to Ann, d. of Thomas Bowles of Wallington and Ann Hyde of Throcking.	SIR WILLIAM SPENCER m. Margaret, d. of Sir Francis Bowyer. Margaret's sister Elizabeth married Sir John Anderson.	SIR RICHARD SPENCER m. Helen, d. of Sir John Brocket of Brocket Hall	MARGARET SPENCER m. Sir Gyles Alington of Horseheath, Cambs (*1)	ELIZABETH SPENCER m. Sir George Cary Lord Hunsdon. (see Cary tree)

ROBERT SPENCER created Baron of Wormleighton in 1604, m. Margaret, d. of Sir Francis Willington	SIR JOHN SPENCER created Baron in 1626 m.① Mary (or Sarah), d. of Sir John Anderson and Elizabeth Bowyer, m.② ... d. of Sir Thomas Rotherham	BROCKET SPENCER created Baron in 1642, m. Susan, d. of Nicholas Cary. ——— ELIZABETH (or Ann) SPENCER, m. Sir John Boteler of Watton, Woodhall.	ALICE SPENCER m. Sir John Jennings of Sandrich (Sandridge), Knight of the Bath. They were the grandparents of Sarah, 1st Duchess of Marlborough (*2).	ELLEN SPENCER m. Sir William Culpepper of Alesford in Kent. (Kinsman of Walter Culpepper who m. Agnes Roper)

JOHN SPENCER eldest son, died in France	MARGARET SPENCER m. Sir Richard Anderson of Pendley (d.1632) who was brother of Mary who m. Sir John Spencer above. Sir Richard's mother was Elizabeth Bowyer, sister of Sir William Spencer's wife Margaret.	SIR WILLIAM SPENCER Knight of the Bath, Baron of Wormleighton, m. Lady Penelope, d. of Henry Wriothsley, Earl of Southampton	RICHARD SPENCER m. .... daughter of Edward Sandys ——— SIR EDWARD SPENCER m. ... daughter of John Goldsmith of Wilby in Suffolk

SANDYS
Or a fesse dancetty between three crosslets fitchy gules.

(*1) Sir Gyles was the brother of Audrey Alington who m. William Mannock and of Mary Alington who m. Robert Newport. Giles Alington, the son of Gyles Alington and Margaret Spencer, m. Ursula Drury of Hawstead (brass in Hawstead Church).

(*2) Sir John Jennings and Alice Spencer had a son Richard who was the father of Sarah Jennings of Sandridge 1st Duchess of Marlborough (6x great-grandmother of Sir Winston Churchill). The Jennings were related to the Bull family through the Skipwiths and the Rowletts.

The Spencer Family of Cople in Bedfordshire

THOMAS SPENCER of Cople, m. Anne, d. of Robert Bulkley of Burgate in Southampton

ROBERT SPENCER, m. Rhose, d. of ... Cockaine of Cockaine Hatley	ANNE SPENCER, m. John Fairclough of Weston, Herts.

MARGARET SPENCER, m. Thomas Cary of Chilton, Devon	NICHOLAS SPENCER m. Mary, d. of Thomas Elmes of Lylford, Northants.

ALICE SPENCER, m. Gaius, son and heir of Rowland Squire	NICHOLAS SPENCER, m. Mary, d. of Sir Edward Gostwick of Willington, Beds.	ROBERT SPENCER ------ MARY SPENCER	CHRISTIAN SPENCER ------ RHOSE SPENCER

WILLIAM SPENCER, b. 1632	NICHOLAS SPENCER, b. 1634

The Soame Family
of Little Bradley in Suffolk, and Throcking and Aspenden in Hertfordshire
(showing links with the Alington family of Horseheath in Cambridgeshire)

SIR WILLIAM ALINGTON of Horseheath, killed in the battle of Bosworth 1485 (*1), m. Elizabeth Wentworth

SIR GYLES ALINGTON m. Margaret Spencer of Althorpe (⬇ Spencer tree)

MARY ALINGTON m. Robert Newport (⬇ Newport tree)

AUDREY ALINGTON m. William Mannock of Giffords Hall (Mannock tree ⬇)

SOAME, Baronet
Gules a cheveron between three mallets or

ROBERT ALINGTON of Horseheath, Cambs

SIR GILES ALINGTON 1500-86, Lord of the Manor of Wymondley, m. Ursula Drury (*2).

THOMAS SOAME of Beetley, Norfolk, d. 16 April 1569, m.23 December 1558, Ann, d. of Thomas Knighton of Little Bradley, (widow of Richard le Hunt of Hunts Hall who died 1540 - see Hunt tree). They had 14 children.

ELIZABETH ALINGTON m. **THOMAS SOAME** of Little Bradley. Thomas lived 1543-1606. There is a brass in Little Bradley Church showing Thomas and Elizabeth with five sons and two daughters

SIR STEPHEN SOAME of Brickendon Herts and Beetley in Norfolk. 1544-1619, Lord Mayor of London 1598, Patron of St Andrew's Church, Hertford (where he would have known the Bull family), buried at Little Thurlow, Suffolk (next to Little Bradley), m. Anne (d.1622), d. of William Stone of Segenhoe in Bedfordshire. (*3)

ROBERT SOAME, osp 1589, Doctor of Divinity, Master of Peterhouse, Cambridge.

BARTHOLOMEW SOAME of London, silkman. m. Katherine, d. of Thomas Banks. She later m. Sir Thomas Barnardiston of Keddington, Suffolk. (Barnardiston tree ⬇)

SIR WILLIAM SOAME, d.1655, Sheriff of Suffolk in 1632, followed Thomas Knighton as patron of St Andrew's, Hertford, m. Bridget, d. of Benedict Barnham, Alderman of London.

SIR STEPHEN SOAME of Haydon, Essex, d.1639, m.1619, at Sotterley, Elizabeth (b.1598), d. of Thomas Plater of Sotterley

SIR THOMAS SOAME of Throcking, d.1670, Sheriff of London 1635, MP for the City of London 1640, m.1620, Joan, d. of William Freeman of Aspenden, buried at Throcking. Memorial in Throcking Church (*4).

JOHN SOAME of Burnham, Norfolk. m. Mary, d. of Thomas Perient

MERCY SOAME, m. Sir Calthorpe Parker

ANNE SOAME m. Sir John Wentworth

JANE SOAME m. Sir Nathanial Barnardiston (see Barnardiston tree)

JUDITH SOAME m. Sir Francis Anderson of Stratton and Edworth, Beds.

SIR PETER SOAME 1633-97, m. 1656, Susannah, d. of Ralph Freeman of Aspenden (who was probably the brother of Joan who married Peter's uncle Thomas. Susannah would be the sister of Elizabeth who married Robert Elwes in 1684).

JOHN SOAME osp

STEPHEN SOAME osp

ANNE SOAME m. Sir Gabriel How

JANE SOAME m. Sir John Hoskyns

MARY SOAME m. Edward Fettiplace

WILLIAM SOAME

STEPHEN SOAME

EDMUND SOAME

All died young and are buried at Throcking

SAMUEL SOAME bapt at Throcking 1636, osp.1714, buried at Little Thurlow, Suffolk.

MARY SOAME m. Abraham Clark of London

ELIZABETH SOAME m. John Garneys of Boyland Hall, Norfolk

ANNE SOAME d.1679, buried at Kelveden, Essex, m. Sir Thomas Abdy (d.1685) of Felix Hall, Essex

SIR PETER SOAME, d.1709, m. Jane, d. and heir of George Shute of Stockwell. They had one son, Peter (osp) and three daughters.

The Soame Family
of Little Bradley in Suffolk, and Throcking and Aspenden in Hertfordshire
(showing links with the Alington family of Horseheath in Cambridgeshire)

(*1) In 1427 the Alingtons had inherited the Lordship of Wymondley from the Argenteins when Elizabeth, sole heir of John Argentein, married William Alington (grandfather of this William). With the manor they also inherited the office of Cup-bearer to the King, which had been granted to the Argenteins in the 12th century. The Lords of the Manor of Wymondley are still officially Cup-bearers to the monarch. It is unlikely that the Alingtons ever lived at Wymondley, preferring their mansion house at Horseheath (see Descent of the Argenteins and Alingtons).

(*2) In St Leonard's Church Bengeo there is a chalice and patten inscribed 'An Fanshawe 1626-27'. She was the daughter of Sir Giles Alington of Horseheath 1572-1638 and the granddaughter of Sir Giles Alington and Ursula Drury. The silver was probably presented on the occasion of her marriage to Sir Thomas Fanshawe of Ware, who later married the widow of Knighton Ferrers (see Knighton tree).

(*3) Ann Stone, wife of Sir Stephen Soame, was the daughter of William Stone of Segenhoe in Bedfordshire. He was married to Massy Grey, whose family had held the manor of Segenhoe and other land in the area since the 12th century, when Rugemont Castle (situated near Brogborough) was a stronghold of the Grey family. They also held Wrest Park and the Pelhams. Sir Stephen Soame's mother, Ann Knighton of Little Bradley, had previously been married to Richard Hunt, and they had a daughter Alice Hunt (Stephen's half-sister). Alice Hunt, who first married John Daye the printer, afterwards married William Stone, who was the nephew of her half-brother Stephen's wife Ann. Their memorial brass shown on page 73 is in Little Bradley Church, Suffolk.

GREY of WREST
Barry argent and azure with three roundels gules in the chief.

The chart below may help to clarify this very involved relationship.

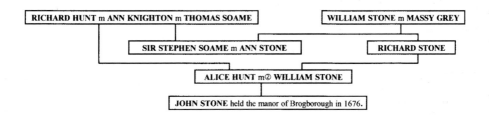

There were two other links with the Stone family. William Stone's wife Massy Grey was first cousin to Elizabeth Waldegrave of Suffolk, and Ann Stone's great-niece Dorothy married Thomas Docwra of Lilley.

(*4) In 1684 William Freeman's granddaughter Elizabeth Freeman married Robert Elwes and it was probably through this connection that Throcking passed from the Soames to the Elwes family. Their son Robert Elwes married Martha, daughter of Richard Cary, and they had a son, Cary Elwes.

The Underhill, Knighton, Soame and Daye Families

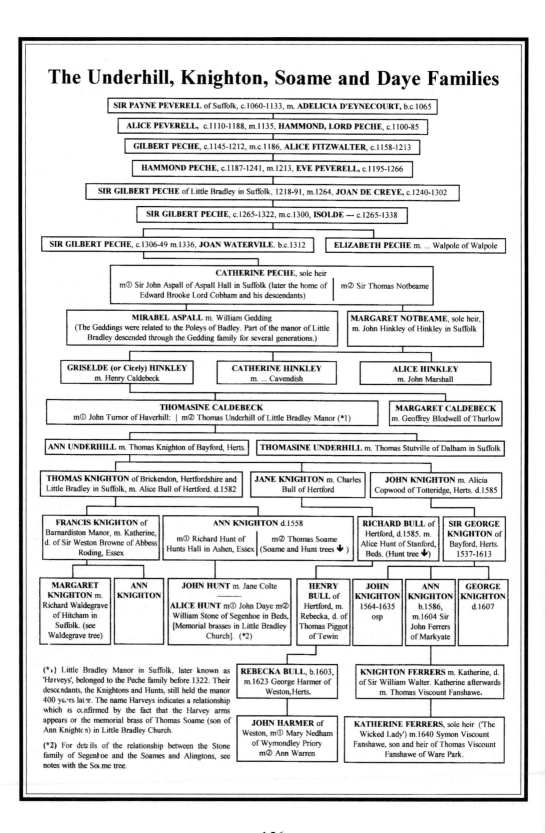

SIR PAYNE PEVERELL of Suffolk, c.1060-1133, m. **ADELICIA D'EYNECOURT**, b.c.1065

ALICE PEVERELL, c.1110-1188, m.1135, **HAMMOND, LORD PECHE**, c.1100-85

GILBERT PECHE, c.1145-1212, m.c.1186, **ALICE FITZWALTER**, c.1158-1213

HAMMOND PECHE, c.1187-1241, m.1213, **EVE PEVERELL**, c.1195-1266

SIR GILBERT PECHE of Little Bradley in Suffolk, 1218-91, m.1264, **JOAN DE CREYE**, c.1240-1302

SIR GILBERT PECHE, c.1265-1322, m.c.1300, **ISOLDE** --- c.1265-1338

SIR GILBERT PECHE, c.1306-49 m.1336, **JOAN WATERVILE**, b.c.1312 | **ELIZABETH PECHE** m. ... Walpole of Walpole

CATHERINE PECHE, sole heir
m① Sir John Aspall of Aspall Hall in Suffolk (later the home of Edward Brooke Lord Cobham and his descendants) | m② Sir Thomas Notbeame

MIRABEL ASPALL m. William Gedding
(The Geddings were related to the Poleys of Badley. Part of the manor of Little Bradley descended through the Gedding family for several generations.) | **MARGARET NOTBEAME**, sole heir, m. John Hinkley of Hinkley in Suffolk

GRISELDE (or Cicely) HINKLEY m. Henry Caldebeck | **CATHERINE HINKLEY** m. ... Cavendish | **ALICE HINKLEY** m. John Marshall

THOMASINE CALDEBECK
m① John Turnor of Haverhill: | m② Thomas Underhill of Little Bradley Manor (*1) | **MARGARET CALDEBECK** m. Geoffrey Blodwell of Thurlow

ANN UNDERHILL m. Thomas Knighton of Bayford, Herts. | **THOMASINE UNDERHILL** m. Thomas Stutville of Dalham in Suffolk

THOMAS KNIGHTON of Brickendon, Hertfordshire and Little Bradley in Suffolk, m. Alice Bull of Hertford. d.1582 | **JANE KNIGHTON** m. Charles Bull of Hertford | **JOHN KNIGHTON** m. Alicia Copwood of Totteridge, Herts. d.1585

FRANCIS KNIGHTON of Barnardiston Manor, m. Katherine, d. of Sir Weston Browne of Abbess Roding, Essex | **ANN KNIGHTON** d.1558
m① Richard Hunt of Hunts Hall in Ashen, Essex | m② Thomas Soame (Soame and Hunt trees ↓) | **RICHARD BULL** of Hertford, d.1585. m. Alice Hunt of Stanford, Beds. (Hunt tree ↓) | **SIR GEORGE KNIGHTON** of Bayford, Herts. 1537-1613

MARGARET KNIGHTON m. Richard Waldegrave of Hitcham in Suffolk. (see Waldegrave tree) | **ANN KNIGHTON** | **JOHN HUNT** m. Jane Colte
——————
ALICE HUNT m① John Daye m② William Stone of Segenhoe in Beds, [Memorial brasses in Little Bradley Church]. (*2) | **HENRY BULL** of Hertford, m. Rebecka, d. of Thomas Piggot of Tewin | **JOHN KNIGHTON** 1564-1635 osp | **ANN KNIGHTON** b.1586, m.1604 Sir John Ferrers of Markyate | **GEORGE KNIGHTON** d.1607

(*1) Little Bradley Manor in Suffolk, later known as 'Harveys', belonged to the Peche family before 1322. Their descendants, the Knightons and Hunts, still held the manor 400 years later. The name Harveys indicates a relationship which is confirmed by the fact that the Harvey arms appears or the memorial brass of Thomas Soame (son of Ann Knighton) in Little Bradley Church.

(*2) For details of the relationship between the Stone family of Segenhoe and the Soames and Alingtons, see notes with the Soame tree. | **REBECKA BULL**, b.1603, m.1623 George Harmer of Weston, Herts. | **KNIGHTON FERRERS** m. Katherine, d. of Sir William Walter. Katherine afterwards m. Thomas Viscount Fanshawe.

JOHN HARMER of Weston, m① Mary Nedham of Wymondley Priory m② Ann Warren | **KATHERINE FERRERS**, sole heir ('The Wicked Lady') m.1640 Symon Viscount Fanshawe, son and heir of Thomas Viscount Fanshawe of Ware Park.

The Underhill, Knighton, Soame and Daye Families
and the Manors of Great Bradley, Little Bradley (Overhall or Harveys) and Netherhall in Suffolk

In 1305 the manors belonged to Sir John Botetourt and his wife Matilda who was grand-daughter of William de Beauchamp Baron of Bedford. By 1322 the manor of Little Bradley (Overhall or Harveys) was held by Gilbert Peche, ancestor of the Hunts, Underhills, Knightons, Bulls and Harmers. His descendants were there for nearly 400 years. Part of the manor passed down through the Gedding family, and during the minority of Robert Gedding it was held in trust jointly by John de la Pole Duke of Suffolk (related through the Peverell family), Sir John Heveningham, and Anthony Earl Rivers (Robert's guardian). Through the marriage of Robert's daughter, Constance Gedding, the manor passed to the Poley family of Badley. Henry Poley died in 1487 and it passed to his son Edmund, grandson John, and then to his kinsman John le Hunte of Hunt Hall in Ashen. The Hunts intermarried several times with the Knightons, Soames and Stutvilles, all of whom were connected with the manor of Little Bradley. As the alternative name 'Harveys' suggests, there were several connections with the Harvey family of Ickworth. In the 16th century the Underhills, direct descendants of Sir Gilbert Peche, were at Little Bradley, and their Knighton and Hunt descendants were there until the early 18th century. The last member of the family to live there was Thomas le Hunt who died age 76 in 1703.

The history of the manor of Great Bradley also has many familiar names. In 1491 it was held by Thomas Scroop, whose mother was a member of the Botetourt family (who held both manors in the 13th and 14th centuries). This Thomas was the father of another Thomas Scroop, a noted Carthusian monk, who inherited the estate. We are told in Copinger's 'Manors of Suffolk', 'He was a native of this parish and derives from the illustrious family of Scroope in Yorkshire. ... He became Suffragan to the Bishop of Norwich, and Vicar of Lowestoft, where he died in 1491 and was buried in the chancel of that church being nearly 100 years of age'.

In the 16th century the manor was vested in Bartholomew Brokesbye who died in 1524 when the manor went to his grandson, also Bartholomew Brokesbye. In 1561 it was bought by Francis Clopton, then Robert Peyton in 1565 and Peter Osborne in 1580.

In 1764 it went to Thomas Brand of Kimpton Hoo in Hertfordshire who on 20th April 1771 married the Hon Gertrude Roper, sister of Charles Trevor Roper 18th Lord Dacre. The Ropers were descended from the ancient family of Roper in Kent, who were also ancestors of the Harmer family. Thomas Brand died on 21st February 1794 and the manor passed to his eldest son Thomas Brand 20th Lord Dacre. He married in 1819 Barbarina, daughter of Admiral Chaloner Ogle, but died without issue and the manor passed to his brother Henry Otway Brand 21st Lord Dacre. He married Pyne, the daughter of the Hon and Very Rev'd Dean Crosbie, and sister of Lord Brandon. He assumed by sign manual in 1824 the surname of Trevor, and when he died in 1853 the manor passed to his son, Thomas Crosbie William Trevor 22nd Lord Dacre. He died without issue in 1890 and was succeeded by his brother Henry Bouverie William Trevor, MP for Lewes 1852-68, for Cambridge 1868-84, and Speaker of the House of Commons 1872-84. He was a Privy Councillor and was created Viscount Hampden in 1884. He died in 1892 and his son, Henry Robert Brand 2nd Viscount Hampden and 24th Lord Dacre, inherited. He was MP for Hertfordshire, and a Captain in the Coldstream Guards. He married in 1868 (2nd marriage) Susan Henrietta, daughter of Lord George Henry Cavendish.

During the years from 1771 the manor of Great Bradley had followed the same line as the manors of Kimpton and St Pauls Walden, once again reinforcing the link between these two localities.

The manor of Netherhall (presumably downhill from the manor of Overhall or Harveys) was held by the Hunt family in the 16th century, and followed the same line as Overhall until it was acquired by the Turnor family (also related to the Hunts, Knightons, Stutvilles and Underhills).

The Waldegrave Family (A)
of Smallbridge and Bures in Suffolk, and Borley in Essex

SIR RICHARD WALDEGRAVE, of Smallbridge, Suffolk. d. 1406. m. Joan, d. of ... Silvester of Bures

SIR RICHARD WALDEGRAVE, d. 1434, m. Jane, d. and heir of Sir Thomas Mountchancy.

SIR WILLIAM WALDEGRAVE
m. Joan, d. of William Dorward of Barking, Essex

AGNES WALDEGRAVE, m. William Hunt of Hunts Hall in Ashen
(⬇ Hunt tree)

RICHARD WALDEGRAVE, d. 1440 sp, m. Alice ... d. 1479

DAUGHTER, m. John Mannock of Giffords Hall, Stoke-by-Nayland

SIR THOMAS WALDEGRAVE, m. Elizabeth, d. of Sir John Fray (She later m. Sir William Saye)

EDWARD WALDEGRAVE
d. 1561, in the Tower, at an advanced age, m. Elizabeth, d. of John Cheney of Lynde (⬇ B)

RICHARD WALDEGRAVE
———
JANE WALDEGRAVE
m. Sir Edmund Arundell. osp

ANN WALDEGRAVE
m. ... Fabion
———
KATHERINE WALDEGRAVE,
m. George Mannock of Giffords Hall, Stoke by Nayland. (⬇ Mannock tree)

SIR WILLIAM WALDEGRAVE
d. 1526, m. Margaret, d. of Sir Henry Wentworth and sister of Sir Roger Wentworth of Codham

ANTHONY WALDEGRAVE
m. Elizabeth, d. and heir of Ralph Grey of Burnt Pelham, Herts, and Wrest Park, Beds. Anthony was one of the Barons of the Exchequer. They had 2 sons, William and Thomas (who m. Elizabeth, d. of Robert Gurdon of Assington, Suffolk)

GEORGE WALDEGRAVE
of Smallbridge, d. 1528. (*1)
m. Anne, d. of Sir Robert Drury of Hawstead, Speaker of the House of Commons, who is buried in an armorial altar tomb in St Mary's, Bury St Edmunds. Anne later m. Sir Thomas Jermyn of Rushbrooke. She d. 1572. There is a memorial brass in Debden Church to Lady Anne Jermyn. The Drury family memorials are at Hawstead. (*2)

WILLIAM WALDEGRAVE
———
EDMUND WALDEGRAVE
———
MARY WALDEGRAVE
m. John, Lord Marney
———
MARGARET WALDEGRAVE
m. John Lord St John of Bletsoe, Beds. (see St John tree)
———
A DAUGHTER m. Robert Drury

JANE WALDEGRAVE
a nun in The Minories, London
———
DOROTHY WALDEGRAVE
m. Sir John Spring of Lavenham
———
BRIDGETT WALDEGRAVE
m. Sir John Findenne
———
ANN WALDEGRAVE
m. ... Barley of Hertfordshire

EDWARD WALDEGRAVE
of Lawford Hall, 1514-1584, m. Joan, d. of George Ackworth of Lawford and widow of William Bulmer. Edward and his future wife Joan were confined in the Tower during the trial of Queen Katherine Howard for witholding information. Joan d. 1590 aged 84.

GEORGE WALDEGRAVE of Hitcham, d.1551, m. Mary, d. of Richard Corbett of Assington. George lived at Witherton Manor at Hitcham, Suffolk. Mary d. 1562 (wall monument in Hitcham Church). George and Mary were cousins, their mothers were Ann and Mary Drury. (see Tyrrell tree).

ANN WALDEGRAVE
m① Henry Bures (or Bewers) of Acton
m② Sir Clement Higham (*3)
(see Poley tree)
———
PHYLLIS WALDEGRAVE
m. Thomas Higham
(brother of Sir Clement)

SIR WILLIAM WALDEGRAVE
m. Julian, d. of Sir John Rainsford.
Sir William died in Calais in 1554 and was buried there in St Marie's Church
(⬇ C)

EDWARD WALDEGRAVE
m① Elizabeth, d. of Bartholomew Averell | m② Sarah, d. of John Higham of Giffords Hall, Wickhambrook (*4).

MARGERY WALDEGRAVE
m. William Clopton of Bretton in Essex

RICHARD WALDEGRAVE,
m. Margaret Knighton of Barnardiston Manor.
(⬇ Underhill tree)

WILLIAM WALDEGRAVE
of Hitcham, Suffolk m. Elizabeth, d. of Richard Poley of Boxted. (see Poley tree)

ANN WALDEGRAVE
m. Drew, s. of Sir Drew Drury

JEMIMA WALDEGRAVE
unmarried

WILLIAM WALDEGRAVE
osp

THOMASINE WALDEGRAVE
m① William Kempe of Cavendish | m② Harsenett, Bishop of Chichester

SIR GEORGE WALDEGRAVE of Hitcham. m. May, d. of John Moore of Ipswich

ELIZABETH WALDEGRAVE
m. William Appleton of Kettlebaston

(*1) George Waldegrave was buried at Sudbury, although he requested to be buried at Bures with his father. His widow Anne m. Sir Thomas Jermyn of Rushbrooke Hall. They had 2 sons, John and Thomas. John married Mary, daughter of Lionel Tollemache of Helmingham Hall, and they had 12 children.

(*2) The Drury family memorials in Hawstead Church include a set of brasses on a chest tomb to Anne's brother, Sir William Drury, and also a memorial to Anne's sister, Ursula Drury, who married Giles Alington. The Drury mansion in London gave its name to Drury Lane. The heiress, Joan Drury, who married Thomas Harvey of Thurleigh and founded the Harvey family of Ickworth Hall, was also a member of this family.

(*3) Sir John Higham, the son of Sir Clement Higham and Ann Waldegrave, was married to Ann Poley, and their daughter Ann Higham was married to Thomas Turnor. There are brasses to Sir Clement Higham and his family in Barrow Church. (see Poley tree).

(*4) There are two manor houses known as Gifford's Hall, both originally built by the Gifford family. The Stoke-by-Nayland mansion was later the home of the Mannocks, and Wickhambrook was the home of the Higham family.

The Waldegrave Family (B)

EDWARD WALDEGRAVE, d. 1561 in the Tower, at an advanced age, m. Elizabeth, d. of John Cheney of Lynde

ELIZABETH WALDEGRAVE m. Thomas Eden, Clarke of the Star Chamber	JOHN WALDEGRAVE of Borley, Essex, d.1514, m. Laura, d. of Sir John Rochester	MARGERY WALDEGRAVE m. Robert Rye of Preston

ROBERT WALDEGRAVE ——— JOHN WALDEGRAVE ——— THOMAS WALDEGRAVE	SIR EDWARD WALDEGRAVE Lord of the Manor of Borley in Essex (*1), Chancellor of the Duchy (1553-58) and Privy Councillor to Queen Mary. m. Frances, d. of Sir Edward Nevill	MARY WALDEGRAVE m. ... Abell of Coggeshall ——— ANNE WALDEGRAVE

CHRISTOPHER (OR CHARLES) WALDEGRAVE, son and heir m. Jeromina, d. of Sir Henry Jernagen of Costessy in Norfolk	NICHOLAS WALDEGRAVE of Borley m. Katherine, d. of Weston Browne of Abbess Roding (↓ Browne tree)	MARY WALDEGRAVE m. Lord John Petre of Writtle (↓ Petre tree)

EDWARD WALDEGRAVE m. ... d. of Sir Thomas Lovell of Harlinge	FRANCIS WALDEGRAVE m. Richard, Earl of Portland, Lord Treasurer of England.	PHILIP WALDEGRAVE Lord of the Manor of Borley m① ... d. m② Margaret, d. of Richard of John Eve White of of Essex Hutton	ANN WALDEGRAVE ——— DOROTHY WALDEGRAVE ——— BARBARA WALDEGRAVE ——— JEMIMA WALDEGRAVE	CHARLES WALDEGRAVE ——— NICHOLAS WALDEGRAVE ——— MAGDALAN WALDEGRAVE m. John Whitbread of Writtle, Essex

JOHN WALDEGRAVE, b.1615	WILLIAM WALDEGRAVE	FRANCES WALDEGRAVE	MARY WALDEGRAVE

(*1) In the 1930s Borley Rectory, once the home of members of the Waldegrave family, gained the reputation of being the most haunted house in England. It was investigated by a number of eminent people, including the philosopher C E M Joad. The ghost, a nun, is claimed to have been strangled there on 17th May 1667. In 1939 the Rectory was mysteriously destroyed by fire, said to have been started by an oil lamp knocked over by an unknown hand. In 1943 the bones of a young woman were found buried 3 feet beneath the cellar floor.

The Waldegrave Family (C)

SIR WILLIAM WALDEGRAVE m. Julian, d. of Sir John Rainsford. Sir William died at Calais in 1554 and was buried there at St Marie's Church

MARGERY WALDEGRAVE m. John Wiseman of Canfield in Essex	A DAUGHTER	SIR WILLIAM WALDEGRAVE of Smallbridge, near Bures in Essex m① Elizabeth Mildmay, m② Grissel, d. of d. 1581, sister to William Lord Paget and Thomas Mildmay of widow of Sir Thomas Moulsham in Essex Rivett	MARY WALDEGRAVE m. Sir Walter Mildmay	AGNES WALDEGRAVE m. William le Hunt of Ashen (Hunt, Bull & Knighton trees ↓)

ELIZABETH WALDEGRAVE m. Sir Thomas Beckingham of Essex	SIR WILLIAM WALDEGRAVE d. 1613 m① Judith, d. of Sir m② Jennemache, d. Robert Jermyn of Sir Nicholas Bacon of Redgrave	MARY WALDEGRAVE m. Sir Thomas Clopton of Kentwell Hall	FIVE MORE SONS ——— TWO MORE DAUGHTERS

ELIZABETH WALDEGRAVE m. Sir Charles Gawdey	WILLIAM WALDEGRAVE of Smallbridge, m. Frances, d. of Thomas Athlow, Sergeant at Law	JENNEMACHE WALDEGRAVE	PHILIPPA WALDEGRAVE m. Gyles Barnardiston (see Barnardiston tree)	SIR WILLIAM CLOPTON (see Clopton tree)

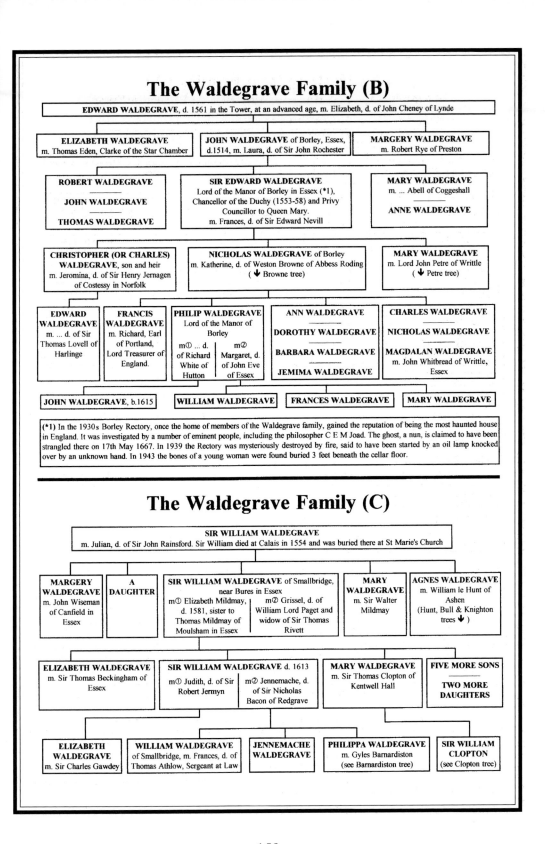

The Wingfields of Wingfield, Dennington and Letheringham

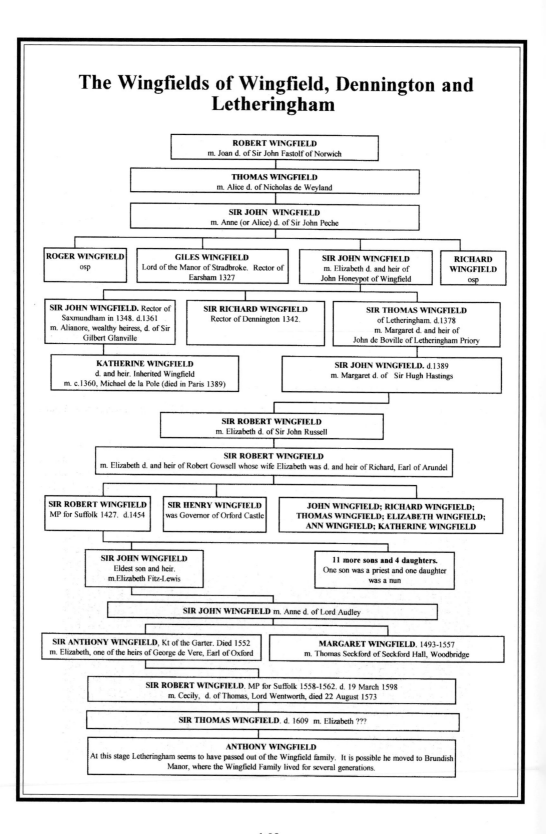

ROBERT WINGFIELD
m. Joan d. of Sir John Fastolf of Norwich

THOMAS WINGFIELD
m. Alice d. of Nicholas de Weyland

SIR JOHN WINGFIELD
m. Anne (or Alice) d. of Sir John Peche

ROGER WINGFIELD
osp

GILES WINGFIELD
Lord of the Manor of Stradbroke. Rector of Earsham 1327

SIR JOHN WINGFIELD
m. Elizabeth d. and heir of John Honeypot of Wingfield

RICHARD WINGFIELD
osp

SIR JOHN WINGFIELD. Rector of Saxmundham in 1348. d.1361 m. Alianore, wealthy heiress, d. of Sir Gilbert Glanville

SIR RICHARD WINGFIELD
Rector of Dennington 1342.

SIR THOMAS WINGFIELD
of Letheringham. d.1378 m. Margaret d. and heir of John de Boville of Letheringham Priory

KATHERINE WINGFIELD
d. and heir. Inherited Wingfield m. c.1360, Michael de la Pole (died in Paris 1389)

SIR JOHN WINGFIELD. d.1389
m. Margaret d. of Sir Hugh Hastings

SIR ROBERT WINGFIELD
m. Elizabeth d. of Sir John Russell

SIR ROBERT WINGFIELD
m. Elizabeth d. and heir of Robert Gowsell whose wife Elizabeth was d. and heir of Richard, Earl of Arundel

SIR ROBERT WINGFIELD
MP for Suffolk 1427. d.1454

SIR HENRY WINGFIELD
was Governor of Orford Castle

JOHN WINGFIELD; RICHARD WINGFIELD; THOMAS WINGFIELD; ELIZABETH WINGFIELD; ANN WINGFIELD; KATHERINE WINGFIELD

SIR JOHN WINGFIELD
Eldest son and heir.
m.Elizabeth Fitz-Lewis

11 more sons and 4 daughters.
One son was a priest and one daughter was a nun

SIR JOHN WINGFIELD m. Anne d. of Lord Audley

SIR ANTHONY WINGFIELD, Kt of the Garter. Died 1552 m. Elizabeth, one of the heirs of George de Vere, Earl of Oxford

MARGARET WINGFIELD. 1493-1557
m. Thomas Seckford of Seckford Hall, Woodbridge

SIR ROBERT WINGFIELD. MP for Suffolk 1558-1562. d. 19 March 1598 m. Cecily, d. of Thomas, Lord Wentworth, died 22 August 1573

SIR THOMAS WINGFIELD. d. 1609 m. Elizabeth ???

ANTHONY WINGFIELD
At this stage Letheringham seems to have passed out of the Wingfield family. It is possible he moved to Brundish Manor, where the Wingfield Family lived for several generations.

The Wingfields of Wingfield, Dennington and Letheringham

When John Wingfield died in 1361 leaving no male heir the family name died out in their home village. But there were already other branches of the Wingfield family living in various parts of Suffolk.

John had two brothers, Sir Richard who was Rector of Dennungton in 1342, and Sir Thomas, who married Margaret, daughter and heir of John de Boville of Letheringham Priory. The manor belonged to the Augustinian monks (the Black Canons) and included properties in Glevering and Easton, a few miles to the west of Wickham Market.

Letheringham Hall was the seat of the Bovilles and Wingfields from the 14th century to the time of the Dissolution. At this stage the Wingfield family seems to have moved to Letheringham Lodge, which was thought to have been built originally as an annexe to provide living quarters for some of the monks.

Some time in the early 17th century the Lodge was extended and a second bridge was built across the moat, suggesting perhaps that the extension was to provide a Dower House for Lady Elizabeth Wingfield, the widow of Sir Thomas who died in 1609. The initials EW and the date 1610 seem to support this theory.

Letheringham Lodge remains, a beautiful moated house with features of historical importance.

It is recorded that in the 17th century there were Wingfields living at Brundish Manor, about 4 miles from the village of Wingfield.

Eric Sandon suggests that Brundish Manor was never a manor house, but was probably built for a gentleman farmer, and was part of the manorial property of Brundish Hall. Copinger tells us that the manor passed from the Malets, who were tenants-in-chief at the time of the Domesday Survey, to the Willoughbys, who were later at Parham Hall, and then into the ownership of Anthony Wingfield. Anthony is the last recorded member of the Wingfield family to live at Letheringham Lodge, so it seems likely that he may have moved to Brundish.

Brundish Manor

The Tyrell Family
of Heron Hall at East Horndon in Essex and Gipping Hall near Stowmarket, Suffolk

SIR JOHN TYRELL of Heron Hall, Essex, m. Ann Coggeshall (d. 1422)

SIR WILLIAM TYRELL, m. Eleanor, d. of Sir Robert Darcy (and sister of Sir Robert, Margaret and John below)

SIR THOMAS TYRELL

WILLIAM TYRELL of Heron Hall, m. Margaret, d. of Sir Robert Darcy of Maldon (see Darcy tree). It is probable that the so-called Abbot's Tomb in Stowmarket Church, with effigies (formerly in brass) of a lady in mitre head-dress, with 5 sons and 8 daughters, is for this Margaret.

ANN TYRELL m. John Darcy

ELIZABETH TYRELL m. Sir Robert, s. of Sir Robert Darcy

TYRELL
Argent two cheverons azure and a border engrailed gules

SIR JAMES TYRELL of Gipping Hall, d.1502, Master of the Horse to Richard III. Stated by some authorities to have been responsible for the murder of the Princes in the Tower. Beheaded for treason in May 1502, accused of communicating with the de la Poles. m. Ann, d. of Sir John Arundell of Lanherne, Cornwall.

JOHN TYRELL whose d. Alice m. George Brooke (⬇ Brooke tree)

SIR THOMAS TYRELL Knighted in 1487. A friend of the Browne family of Abbess Roding.

DOROTHY TYRELL m. John Boteler of Hatfield, Woodhall.

7 MORE DAUGH-TERS
————
2 MORE SONS

SIR THOMAS TYRELL of Gipping, d.1551. Attainted of treason with his father and imprisoned in 1502, pardoned 1504, estates restored 1507, Knighted 1513, Master of the Horse 1520.

m① Margaret, d. of Christopher, Lord Willoughby of Parham | m② Joan

JAMES TYRELL of Columbine Hall near Stowmarket, m. Anne, d. of Sir John Hotoft of Columbine Hall

ANNE TYRELL m. Sir Richard Wentworth

JOHN TYRELL betrothed as a child to Anne, 4-year-old d. of William Browne of Abbess Roding (Lord Mayor of London, who died 1514). John and Anne were married before 1521 - when Anne would have been 12 years old. John died without a male heir in 1540 and Anne m.1542, Sir William Petre of Ingatestone Hall.

SIR JOHN TYRELL of Gipping, d. 1574. Attended Mary Tudor at Kenninghall July 1553, knighted Oct 1553, m. Elizabeth, d. of Sir John Mundy (Lord Mayor of London 1522)

ANN TYRELL d.1576 and buried at Cotton 14 May 1576 m.1529 Sir John Clere of Ormesby in Norfolk. (In Sir Thomas Tyrell's will there are scathing remarks about his son-in-law)

ANNE TYRELL m.1548

CATHERINE TYRELL m.1552 Richard, s. of Sir John Baker (Privy Councillor).

JOHN TYRELL osp 1590
m① 1556 Ann, (d.1558), d. of Sir John Sulyard of Wetherden, Suffolk | m② 1565 Mary, d. of Sir William Drury of Hawstead, Suffolk. Mary was the widow of Sir Richard Corbett of Assington. Their d. Mary m. her cousin George Waldegrave (*1). (see Waldegrave tree)

THOMAS TYRELL d.1606, inherited Gipping and Wetherden from his brother, m. Mary, d. of John Gray of Gosfield. Effigy in Stowmarket church erected by his sister Margaret.

EDMUND TYRELL m.1571, Prudence, d. of Martin Frense of Dickleburgh, Norfolk

MARGARET TYRELL (*2) m. twice, her 2nd husband was Edward English

OTHER ISSUE: Charles Tyrell, George Tyrell, James Tyrell, Vincent Tyrell, Anne Tyrell, Joan Tyrell, Alice Tyrell.

(*1) Below is a chart showing the Drury/Corbett/Waldegrave/Alington relationship:

SIR ROBERT DRURY of Hawstead, Speaker of the House of Commons, buried in an armorial altar tomb in St Mary's Chucrh, Bury St Edmunds, married Ann Calthorpe of Norfolk

SIR WILLIAM DRURY, d.1557, member of Queen Mary's Privy Council, m② Elizabeth Sotehill

ANN DRURY, m. George Waldegrave of Smallbridge

URSULA DRURY, d.1552, m. Giles, s. of Sir Gyles Alington and Margaret Spencer

MARY DRURY, m① Sir Richard Corbett, m② John Tyrell

MARY CORBETT m. **GEORGE WALDEGRAVE**

In Hawstead Church in Suffolk there is a brass to Sir William Drury (d.1557) on a chest tomb on the south side of the nave. There is also a brass in the floor of the chancel to his sister Ursula (Alington) who d.1522. Sir William Drury appears in the Mannock tree and in the note on the Spencer tree.

(*2) There is an effigy of Margaret in Stowmarket Church showing her kneeling, facing her brother Thomas and his wife, Mary, with their 6 sons and 4 daughters. Margaret herself had no children. She left £100 to provide an annuity for the relief of the poor of Stowmarket.

Historical Notes and Tables

Lists of Members of Parliament, Sheriffs and Lord Mayors have been compiled from a number of independent sources which have differing spellings of names and places and follow their own individual styles of punctuation and presentation. Wherever possible the records here retain the form and content of the original.

Names from this section are not included in the indexes

A Descent from Egbert of Wessex
(Page 1)

Egbert of Wessex c.784-838
= **Raedburgh of Carolingians** c.788-840

Ethelwulf of Wessex b.c.806 d.13 Jan 857 Stambridge, Rochford, Essex
= 830 - **Osburgh of Wessex** b.c.810 d.c,853, Kent

Alfred the Great of England b.c.848, Wantage d.26 Oct 901, Winchester
= 868, Winchester - **Ethelwida of England** b.c.852 d.5 Dec 905, Winchester

Edward I of England b.c.871 d.c.924, Farringdon, Berkshire
= 919 - **Eadgifu Edgiva** b.c.896 d.961, Canterbury

Edmund I (the Magnificent) of England b.c.922 d.26 May 946, Bucklechurch
= 940 - **Elgivia of England** b.c.912 d.28 Oct 951, France

Edgar the Peaceable of England b.c.943 d.8 Jul 975, Winchester
= **Aethelflaeda the Fair** b.c.945 d.1000, Wherwell Abbey, Longparish, Hampshire

Ethelred the Unready of England b.c.968 d.23 Apr 1016, London
= 1002, Winchester - **Emma of Normandy** b.c.982, Normandy

Ingelric of England b.c.1006, St Martin le Grand d.c.1060
= **Aelis Adele** b.c.1009 d.8 Jan1079

Ingelica Maude of England b.c.1032, St Martins le Grand d.2 Nov 1083, Caen, France
= **Ranulph Peverell** b.c.1030, Normandy d.1072, Hatfield

Sir Payne Peverell b.c.1060, Bourn, Cambridgeshire d.1133, Bourn
= **Adelicia D'Eynecourt** b.c.1065, Bourn

Alice Peverell b.c.1110, Bourn d.c.1188, Hampshire
= 1135, Great Thurlow, Suffolk - **Hammond Lord Pecche** b.c.1100, Clopton, Suffolk
d.c.1185, Hampshire

Gilbert Pecche b.c.1145, Clopton d.1212, Gt. Bealings, Woodbridge
= c.1186, Cheveley, Cambs - **Alice Fitzwalter** b.1158, Clopton d.c.1213

Hammond Peche b.c.1187, Cheveley d.1241, Barnwell, Isle of Ely, Cambs
= 1 Jan 1213, Gt. Thurlow - **Eve Peverell** b.c.1195, Barnwell d.1266

Sir Gilbert Peche b.1218, Little Bradley, Suffolk d.1291, West Cliffe, Dover
= 1264 - **Joan de Creye** b.1240, Corby, Lincs d.1302

Sir Gilbert Peche b.c.1265, Gt Thurlow d.1322, Gloucestershire
= c.1300, Gt Thurlow - **Isolde ???** c.1265-1338

A Descent from Egbert of Wessex
(Page 2)

Sir Gilbert Peche b.c.1306, Bitchfield, Lincs d.1349, Suffolk
= Mar 1336, Gt Thurlow - **Joan Waterville** b.c.1312, Gt Thurlow

Catherine Peche b.c.1339, Gt Thurlow
= **Sir Thomas Notbeame** b.1370, Hampton in Arden, Warwickshire

Margaret Notbeame b.1414, Hampton in Arden
= c.1437 **John Hinkley** b.c.1410, Lenham, Kent d.1483, Lenham

Griselda (Cecily) Hinkley b.c.1438
= **Henry Caldebeck** b.c.1412, Plecheden Hall, Essex

Thomasine Caldebeck b.c.1450, Plecheden Hall, Essex
= 12 Jul 1464, Little Bradley - **Thomas Underhill** b.c.1442, Little Bradley Manor d.c.1509

Ann Underhill b.c.1470, Little Bradley d.c.1506, Bayford, Hertfordshire
= c.1490, Little Bradley - **Thomas Knighton** b.c.1470, Bayford d.7 Apr 1544, Bayford

Jane Knighton b.c.1494, Bayford d.c.1539
= c.1510, Hertfordshire - **Charles Bull** b.c.1495, Herts d.27 Jun 1532, Herts

Richard Bull b.c.1511, St Albans d.14 Sep 1585, Hertford
= 1560, Hertfordshire - **Alice Hunt** b.c.1532, Stanford, Bedfordshire d. 17 Mar1586

Henry Bull b.1 Jan 1565, St Andrew, Hertford d.1637
= 1596 - **Rebecka Piggot** b.1577, Tewin Water d.1637

Rebecka Bull 1603-1685
= 1623, St Andrew, Hertford - **George Harmer** 1593-1655

John Harmer 1628-1711 = 2 Aug 1698 - **Ann Warren** b.1676

John Harmer 1701-1787 = 1733, Therfield - **Mary Ralphs** 1703-1789

John Harmer 1752-1817 = 1776, Sandon, Herts - **Sarah Fisher** 1752-1821

George Harmer b.1783 = 1806 - **Elizabeth Goldsmith**

William Harmer 1813-1870 = 1839 - **Mary Harmer** 1817-1905

William Harmer 1849-1907
= 1883, St Marylebone, London - **Mary Hare** b.1856 d. Jun 1955, Wingfield, Suffolk

Thomas Hare Harmer b.24 Jan 1891, Tonwell, Herts d.31 Dec 1973, Gt Finborough,
Suffolk = 24 Nov 1923, Watton, Herts - **Mercy Wilson Galbraith** b.5 Jan 1895, Bath
d. 29 Aug1986, Bedford

Evelyn Dorothy Harmer b.26 Oct 1926, Wingfield, Suffolk
= 2 Aug 1952, Gt Finborough - **John Fisher Wright** b.8 May 1930, Stowmarket, Suffolk

Family connections with
The Gunpowder Plot

The 'network' included many families who in the 16th and 17th centuries remained faithful to the old religion, Roman Catholicism, and several were suspected of having connections with the Gunpowder Plot. Most closely involved were: the Brownes of Sussex, the Mordaunts, Petres, Ropers, Brookes, Throckmortons, and Lord Monteagle and Morley. The story of the Browne family is told in Chapter 4.

The Mordaunt Family of Turvey Abbey
One of the conspirators, Robert Keyes, was closely connected with the Mordaunt family. Robert's wife Christiana was governess to the Mordaunt children, and Lord Mordaunt was Robert's patron and friend. Because of this involvement Lord Mordaunt was imprisoned in the Tower, tried in front of the Star Chamber, and fined £10,000. The mother of Robert Keyes was a member of the Tyrwhitt family of Lincolnshire. Robert's cousin, Elizabeth Tyrwhitt, was married to another of the conspirators, Ambrose Rookwood of Coldham Hall in Suffolk.

The Petre Family
Robert Wintour, another of the conspirators, was married to Gertrude Talbot, a member of a well-known recusant family at Grafton Manor near Bromsgrove. Her mother was Katherine Petre, daughter of Sir William Petre of Ingatestone Hall in Essex (see Chapter 2). The Petres were neighbours and patrons of William Byrd, who wrote a Mass to mark the occasion when John Petre, William's son, was created 1st Baron of Writtle in July 1603. William Byrd had a Catholic wife, and was probably himself a Catholic at heart, but as Court Musician it would have been unwise to publicise the fact. He once said of Ingatestone Hall, 'It is a house truly most friendly to me and mine'. Here many of his Masses were sung. They were invariably written for small numbers since they could only be used secretly in private houses and chapels.

The Roper Family
Eliza Vaux (formerly Eliza Roper of Eltham in Kent) was one of the most courageous women at this time, when the Catholic families were suffering great hardship and persecution. She was the sister of Alice Roper who was married to George Hyde of Throcking, and sister-in-law of Sir Thomas More's daughter Margaret. Eliza was the widow of George Vaux, who died in 1594 when Eliza was only about 30 years old, leaving her with six young children as the sole head of a large Catholic house, Harrowden Hall, near Wellingborough. Eliza was the daughter of Sir John Roper, Clerk of the Common Pleas. Because of his position it was important to show absolute loyalty to the king, and his daughter's recusancy and possible involvement in the Plot (she was imprisoned for a short time in the Tower) caused problems in the family. Eliza was a highly-educated woman

with many talents, but devoted her life to her children and also to the rebuilding of Harrowden Hall to include ingenious hiding places for the many priests who found refuge there. She was known with respect and affection (even by non-Catholics) as 'Eliza Vaux, the Dowager of Harrowden'. Ann Vaux, sister-in-law of Eliza, remained unmarried so that she could devote all her energy to the Catholic cause, and played a vital part in the circumstances surrounding the Gunpowder Plot. From 1590 onwards she protected and managed the affairs of Father Henry Garnet, Superior of the Jesuits.

The Brooke Family (including Lord Cobham)
In 1603 when King James failed to give the Catholics the tolerance which had been promised, discontented priests and laymen began to plot against him. The laymen included Henry Lord Cobham and his brother George, and also Sir Walter Raleigh. One plan was to imprison the king and demand concessions, and a second plan included an attempt to put Arbella Stuart (1st cousin of the king) on the throne. As a result of his involvement in these plots George Brooke was executed, but Lord Cobham and Raleigh were released on payment of heavy fines. Lord Cobham's titles were forfeited, but they were restored to his heir some years later. Robert Lord Salisbury, who was responsible for ordering these punishments, was married to Elizabeth Brooke, the sister of Lord Cobham and George Brooke.

The Throckmorton Family of Coughton Court in Warwickshire
This was another leading Catholic family. Ann Vaux had a Throckmorton grandmother and a Tresham stepmother, and Robert Catesby and his cousin Francis Tresham of Rushton Hall in Northamptonshire both had Throckmorton grandmothers. Sir Thomas Tresham, the father of Francis, had been fined frequently and spent many years in prison, and his cousin Thomas Throckmorton had been executed in 1584 for taking part in a plot to free Mary Queen of Scots.

Lord Monteagle and Morley
William Parker Lord Monteagle and Morley was married to Elizabeth Tresham, daugher of Sir Thomas Tresham and first cousin to Robert Catesby. On 26th October 1605 Lord Monteagle received an anonymous letter warning him not to attend Parliament on 5th November. Because of this letter, known as 'The Monteagle Letter', the Plot was discovered and disaster averted. This 'dark and doubtful letter' is preserved in the Public Record Office. Lord Monteagle's daughter Catherine was married to John Petre, the grandson of Sir William Petre of Ingatestone Hall.

Members of Parliament for Suffolk 1423 - 1510

1423-24	Sir Henry Ingles	1453-54	Sir Philip Wentworth
1427	Gilbert Debenham, the elder	1455-56	William Jenney
1431	John Harleston	1459	William Tyrell
	Sir Thomas Tuddenham		Sir Philip Wentworth
1432	Gilbert Debenham, the elder	1463-65	Sir John Howard
1435	Sir Thomas Brewes	1467-68	Sir Thomas Brewes
1437	Gilbert Debenham, the elder		Sir John Howard
1439-40	John Harleston	1470-71	William Jenney
	Sir Miles Stapleton	1472-75	Sir William Brandon
1442	Gilbert Debenham, the elder		Sir Robert Chamberlain
	John Harleston	1478	John Broughton
1445-46	John Timperley, the first		Sir John Wingfield
	Sir Thomas Brewes	1483	Sir Robert Chamberlain
1447	William Tyrell	1484	Gilbert Debenham, the younger
	Sir Philip Wentworth	1484	Sir Henry Wentworth
1449	Gilbert Debenham, the elder	1487	Simon Wiseman
	Sir Philip Wentworth	1489-90	Sir Robert Broughton
1449-50	Thomas Cornwallis		Sir William Carew
	Sir John Howard	1491-98	Sir Robert Drury
1450-51	Sir Roger Chamberlain		Simon Wiseman
	Sir Edmund Mulsho	1495-97	Sir Robert Drury
1453-54	Gilbert Debenham, the elder	1504-10	Sir Robert Drury

Members of Parliament for Dunwich 1421 - 1492

1421-31	Robert Codon	1455-56	Thomas Pears
1437	Reynold Rous		John Strange
1439-40	Reynold Rous	1459	John Micklefield
1442	Robert Codon		Sir John Sulyard
	Reynold Rous	1463-65	John Strange
1447	John Gyne	1467	John Strange
	Thomas Pears	1467-68	John Allen
	John Pears	1472-73	William Styward (Stewart)
1449-50	John Gyne		William Rabett (Rabbes)
	Richard Scutting	1478	Robert Brewes
1450-51	Robert Codon		Edmund Jenney
	William Jenney	1483-90	Edmund Jenney
1453-54	Thomas Pears	1491-92	Nicholas Jenney
	Richard Scutting		William Pears

Sheriffs of Suffolk 1234-1901

(From 1234-1666 selected names with family connections)

HENRY III - 1216
1234 Thomas de Hemmegrave
EDWARD II - 1307
1320 Edmund de Hengrave
HENRY V - 1413
1417 Andrew Botiler
HENRY VI - 1422
1426 John Tyrell
1428 Henry Drewery
1445 William Tyrell the Elder
1450 John Jermyn
1451 John Clopton
1454 John Wyngfeld
1455 John Clopton
EDWARD IV - 1461
1471 John Wyngfeld
1482 John Wyngfeld
EDW.V   RICH.III - 1483
1483 Ralph Willoughby
1485 John Paston
HENRY VII - 1485
1486 Edmund Bedyngfeld
1492 John Wyngfeld
1499 William Boleyn
HENRY VIII - 1509
1520 Humphrey Wyngfeld
1530 Thomas Jermyn
1536 William Drury
1538 William Paston
1541 Thomas Jermyn
1544 William Drury
EDWARD VI - 1547
1550 William Walgrave
PHIL and MARY - 1553
1555 John Sulyard
1558 Ambrose Jermyn
ELIZABETH I - 1558
1560 Robert Wyngfeld
1565 William Paston
1568 William Waldegrave
1589 William Waldegrave
JAMES I - 1603
1623 Nathaniel Barnardiston
CHARLES II - 1647 - Usurpation
1650 William Harvey

CHARLES II - 1660 - Restoration
1666 Samuel Barnardiston Esq
1667 Geoffrey Howland Esq
1668 John Clarke Esq
1669 Thomas or John Blackeby Esq
1669 Robert Dycer, Bart.
1670 John Clarke Esq
1671 John Risby Esq
1672 William Gibbs Esq
1672 William Soame Esq
1673 William Sherington of London Esq
1674 William Springe Bart.
1675 John Warner of Sudbury Esq
1676 John Acton of Bramford Esq
1677 William Gibbs of Stoke Esq
1677 Willoughby D'Ewes Bart.
1678 John Rous Bart.
1679 Robert Broke or Brookes, Bart.
1680 John Acton Esq
1681 Thomas Bedingfield Esq
1682 Thomas Waldegrave Esq
1683 Jacob Garrard or Garret Esq
1684 Robert King Esq
JAMES II - 1685
1685 Geoffrey Nightingale Esq
1686 John Castleton Knt.
1687 Samuel Clarke Esq
1688 Edmund Sheppard Esq
WILLIAM and MARY - 1689
1689 Roger Kerrington Esq
1690 Joseph Brand Knt.
1691 George Goodday Esq
1692 John Hammond Esq
1693 William Cooke Esq
1694 Daniel Browning Esq
1695 Richard Brokenham Esq
1696 John Pack Esq
1697 John Cornwallis Esq
1698 Thomas Aldrich Esq
1699 Samuel Warner Esq
1700 Henry Cooper Esq
1701 John Scrivener Esq
ANNE - 1702
1702 John Corance Esq
1703 Richard Philips Esq

1704	Thomas Kerridge Esq
1705	Leicester Martin Esq
1706	Thomas Macro Esq
1707	William Lynch Esq
1708	James Barker of Thorndon Esq
1709	Stephen Bacon Esq
1710	Thomas Blosse Esq
1711	Francis Coleman Esq
1712	John Smyth of Roulton Esq
1713	John Ewer of Chediston Esq
1714	Jonathan Miles Esq

GEORGE I - 1714

1715	Joseph Chaplin Esq
1716	John Inwood Esq
1717	Edward Clarke of East Bergholt
1718	Nicholas Jacob of Armeringhall
1719	Bartholomew Young of Bradfield
1720	Edward Crisp of Bury St Edmunds
1721	Jasper Cullum Bart.
1722	John Bogges of Finborrow Magna
1723	George Coppinger Esq
1724	Hustings Wilkinson of Linstead Parva
1725	Thomas Driver of Earls Stoneham
1726	Francis Barker of Sypton Esq
1727	John Playters Bart.

GEORGE II - 1727

1728	Tobias Blosse of Belstead Esq
1729	Thomas Allin Bart.
1730	Nathaniel Acton Esq
1731	George Dashwood of Havenham
1732	Alexander Bence of Thorrington
1734	John Eldred of Saxham Esq
1734	John Reynolds of Felcham Esq
1735	John Corrance of Rougham Esq
1736	John Cooper of Sturnfield Esq
1737	Reginald Rabett of Bramfield Esq
1738	William Barker of Ringshall Bart.
1739	Millisent Edgarr of Ipswich Esq
1740	Edmund Jenny of Bredfield Esq
1741	Samuel Lucas of Harwich Esq
1742	Baron Prettyman of Bacton Esq
1743	John Barker of Sproughton Bart.
1744	Robert Leman of Westhow Esq
1745	Charles Scrivener of Sibton Esq
1746	Philip Coleman of Ipswich Esq
1747	Robert Edgar of Ipswich Esq
1748	Lamb Baery of Sileham Esq

1749	Thomas White of Taffingstone Esq
1750	Robert Oneby Esq
1751	George Gooday of Fornham Esq
1752	William Saunton Esq
1753	Robert Sparrow of Kettleborough
1754	William Jennens of Acton Esq
1755	Cooke Freston of Mendham Esq
1756	John Canham of Milden Esq
1757	Henry Moore of Melford Esq
1758	Robert May of Sutton Esq
1759	John Rous Bart.
1760	Thomas Thorowgood of Kersey

GEORGE III - 1760

1761	Thomas Moseley of Ousden Esq
1762	Shadrich Brice of Clare Esq
1763	Ezekiel Sparke of Walsham le Willows
1764	John Blois of Yoxford Bart.
1765	George Golding of Thorington Esq
1766	Gabriel Trusson of Kilsale Esq
1767	William Chapman of Lowdham Hall
1768	Osborne Fuller of Carlton Hall Esq
1769	Hutchinson Mure of Grt Saxham
1770	Eleazer Davy of Ubbeston Hall
1771	John Freston Scrivener of Sibton
1772	Nathaniel Acton of Bramford Esq
1773	Thomas Maynard of Wrentham
1774	Edmund Tyrell of Gipping Hall
1775	Richard Moore of Melford Esq
1776	John Frere of Bacton Esq
1777	Robert Sparrow of Worlingham
1778	Reginald Rabet of Bramfield Esq
1779	John Sheppard of Campsey Ash
1780	Samuel Rush of Benhall Esq
1781	Charles Kent of Fornham Esq
1782	William Middleton of Crowfield
1783	Robert Trotman of Ipswich Esq
1784	John Wenyeve of Brettenham Esq
1785	Thomas Gooch of Benacre Esq
1786	James Sewell of Strutton Esq
1787	John Medows Theobald of Henley
1788	Thomas Charles Bunberry of Barton
1789	Nathaniel Lee Acton of Livermere
1790	Miles Barne of Sotterly Esq
1791	William Rowley of Stoke Bart.
1792	Alexander Adair of Flixton Esq

1793 George Doughty of Leiston Esq
1794 Charles Purvis of Barham Esq
1795 Jacob Whitbread of Loudham Esq
1796 John Clayton of Sibton Esq
1797 Chaloner Arcedeckne of Glemham
1798 John Sheppard of Campsey Ash
1799 George Rush of Benhall Esq
1800 William Beaumarice Rush of
Roydon Esq (Knighted 19 June)
1801 Charles Streynsham Collinson of
Sproughton Esq
1802 Thomas Cocksedge of Bury Saint
Edmunds Esq
1803 harry Parker of Melford Bart.
1804 Robert Pocklington of Chelsworth
Knt
1805 George Nassau of Trimley St
Martin's
1806 William Michael Le Hemp of Bury
St Edmunds Esq
1807 Thomas Mills of Great Saxham
1808 John Vernon of Nacton Esq
1809 John Dresser of Blyford Esq
1810 Joshua Grigby of Drinkstone Esq
1811 Roger Pettiward of Finborough
1812 Richard Moore of Melford Esq
1813 Henry Spencer Waddington of
Cavenham Esq
1814 Edward Holland of Benhall Esq
1815 Charles Tyrell of Gipping Esq
1816 Charles Blois of Cockfield Hall,
Bart.
1817 Robert Harland of Nacton, Bart.
1818 Charles Berners of Woolverstone
1819 Andrew Arcedeckne of Glemham
1820 George Thomas of Woodbridge
GEORGE IV - 1820
1821 Philip Bennet of Rougham Hall
1822 Ambrose Harbord Steward of
Stoke Park Esq
1823 Henry Usborne of Branches Park
1824 John Fitzgerald of Bredfield Esq
1825 Henry Edward Bunbury of Great
Barton, Bart.
1826 John Payne Elwes of Stoke next
Clare
1827 John Francis Leathes of
Harringfleet

1828 Hart Logan of Kentwell Hall Esq
1829 John Ruggles-Brise of Clare Esq
1830 John Wilson Sheppard of Campsey
Ashe Esq
WILLIAM IV - 1830
1831 John Read of Primrose Hill
Holbrook
1832 Joseph Burch Smyth of Stoke Hall,
Ipswich Esq
1833 Sir Thomas Sherlock Gooch, Bart.
of Benacre
1834 John Garden Esq of Redisham
1835 Robert Sayer Esq of Sifton Park
1836 Edward Blys Esq of Brandon
1837 Sir Hyde Parker, Bart.of Long
Melford
VICTORIA - 1837
1838 Thomas Hallifax Esq the elder of
Chadacre Hall
1839 Arthur John Brooke Esq of
Horningsheath
1840 George St Vincent Wilson Esq of
Redgrave
1841 Sir Joshua Ricketts Rowley, Bart
of Tendring Hall
1842 Edward Bridgman Esq of Coney
Weston
1843 William Long Esq of
Saxmundham
1844 Sir Philip Broke, Bart. of Nacton
1845 Henry Wilson Esq of Stowlangtoft
1846 Sir Robert Shafto Adair, Bart of
Flixton
1847 Henry James Oakes Esq of
Nowton Court
1848 Charles Andrew Lord Huntingfield
of Haveningham Hall
1849 Thomas James Ireland Esq of
Owsden Hall
1850 Sir Thomas Gage of Hengrave Hall
1851 Frederick Barne Esq
1852 James H L Anstruther Esq
1853 John Lord Henniker
1854 Windsor Parker Esq
1855 John Josselyn Esq
1856 Andrew Arcedeckne Esq
1857 John George Weller Poley Esq
1858 Peter Robert Burrell Esq

1859	John George Sheppard Esq	1881	Robert Emlyn Lofft Esq
1860	Thomas Thornhill Esq	1882	Edward Philippe Mackenzie Esq
1861	Edward Robert Starkie Bence Esq	1883	John George Weller Poley Esq
1862	Sir John Ralph Blois	1884	Walter Thomas Brown Esq
1863	John William Brooke Esq	1885	Sir Alfred Sherlock Gooch, Bart.
1864	Sir G N Brooke Middleton, Bart.	1886	H B Mackworth Praed Esq
1865	John Page Reade Esq	1887	William Edmund Image Esq
1866	William Gilstrap Esq	1888	Gery Milner-Gibson Cullum Esq
1867	Robert John Pettiward	1889	John Paley Esq
1868	Sir Charles J Fox Bunbury, Bart.	1890	John Paley Esq
1869	Francis Capper Brooke Esq	1891	Arthur Heywood Esq
1870	The Rt Hon Lord Rendlesham	1892	F St John Newdegate Barne Esq
1871	Thomas Richard Mills Esq	1893	Ferdinand John Eyre Esq
1872	Henry A Starkie Bence Esq	1894	William Naunton Waller Esq
1873	Fuller Maitland Wilson Esq	1895	Charles Hugh Berners Esq
1874	Thomas Barbot Beale Esq	1896	Sir Savile Brinton Crossley, Bart.
1875	Sir Robert Affleck, Bart.	1897	Edward Walter Greene Esq
1876	Harry Spencer Waddington Esq	1898	Thomas Henry Tacon Esq
1877	George Holt Wilson Esq	1899	Edwin James Johnstone Esq
1878	Sir Francis R S L Gooch, Bart.	1900	Roger Kerrison Esq
1879	William Beetson Long Esq	1901	John Dupuis Cobbold Esq
1880	George Henry Pocklington Esq		

Sheriffs of Hertfordshire and Essex
1333 - 1566

1333 Adam Bloy for the first half year, and William Hand for the last half year
1334 John de Cogeshale, continued six years
1340 William Atemore
1341 Richard de Monte Caniso for the first half year and Henry Garnet for the last half year
1342 Henry Garnet
1343 John de Cogeshale, continued four years
1347 John de Cogeshale for the first half year, and Peter de Boxted for the last half year
1348 William Bret for the first half year, and Humphrey de Walden for the last half year
1349 Peter de Boxted
1350 Thomas Lacy
1351 John de Cogeshale, continued for three years
1354 Hugh Fitz Simon
1355 William de Enefield
1356 Thoams de Chabham, continued two years
1358 Roger de Louth, continued two years
1360 Hugh Blount
1361 William de Lyre
1362 Guy de Boys
1363 Thomas Futling
1364 John Jernoun
1365 Thomas de Helpeston
1366 John Oliver of Sandon
1367 John Oliver for the first half year, and John Shardelow for the last half year
1368 John Henxteworth
1369 John Henxteworth from the Feast of St Michael, 44th Edw.III until the 22nd of January following Roger Keterich from the 22nd of Jan. to the Feast of St Michael

1370 Thomas de Bassingbourn
1371 William Baud of Little Hadham
1372 John de Bampton
1373 John Filiol
1374 Edward Fitz Symond of Hatfield
1375 John Battaile
1376 Robert Fitz William
RICH. II
1377 Robert Goldington of Hunsdon
1378 John Fitz Symonds
1379 Edward Bensted
1380 John Sewale
1381 Walter Godmaston
1382 Geoffrey de Dersham
1383 Thomas Battaile
1384 John Walton
1385 Geoffrey Brockhole
1386 John Rygewin, continued 2 years
1388 Henry English
1389 Walter Attelee
1390 Geoffrey Michale
1391 Sir William Cogeshale, Kt.
1392 Adam Frances
1393 Thomas Cogeshale
1394 Thomas Sampkin
1395 William Bateman, cont. 3 years
1398 Robert Turke
HEN. IV.
1399 Henry Bensted
1400 John Howard
1401 William Marney
1402 Helming Leget
1403 Sir Thomas Swinbourn, Kt.
1404 William Cogeshale
1405 Gerard Braybrook
1406 Helming Leget, continued two years
1408 William Loveney
1409 John Walden
1410 Thomas Aston
1411 Sir William Cogeshale, Kt.
HEN. V.
1412 Philip Englefeld
1413 John Tyrell

1414 Sir John Howard, Kt.
1415 Sir Thomas Barre, Kt.
1416 Lewis Johan
1417 Reginald Malyns
1418 Sir John Howard, Kt.
1419 Robert Darcy of Danbury, in Essex
1420 Lewis Johan, continued for two years

HEN. VI.
1422 John Tyrell
1423 Sir Maurice Brewyn of South Ockington, Kt.
1424 John Barley of Albury
1425 John Doreward of Bocking
1426 Conand Aske
1427 Thomas Tyrell of Heron
1428 John Hotoft of Knebworth
1429 Nicholas Rickhull
1430 Henry Lanfley of Rickling
1431 Sir Nic. Thorley, Kt.
1432 John Durward
1433 Robert Whytingham of Pendley
1434 Geoffrey Rockyll
1435 Sir Maurice Brewyn, Kt.
1436 Edward Tyrell
1437 Richard Alrede
1438 Robert Whytingham
1439 Richard Witherton
1440 Thomas Tyrell
1441 Ralph Asteley
1442 Nicholas Morley of Hellingbury
1443 John Hende
1444 Thomas Tyrell of Heron
1445 Thomas Pigot
1446 Thomas Baud of Hadham-hall
1447 John Hende the younger
1448 George Langham
1449 Geoffrey Rockhill
1450 Philip Boteler of Watton
1451 Thomas Barrington
1452 John Godmanston
1453 Sir Thomas Cobham, Kt.
1454 Humphry Bohun
1455 Ralph Bothe, Esq.
1456 John Hende the younger
1457 Lewis John, Esq.
1458 Robert Darcy of Danbury, Esq.
1459 Thomas Tyrell of Heron

EDW. IV.
1460 Thomas Juce
1461 Thomas Langley, Esq. continued two years
1463 Sir John Clay, Kt.
1464 Roger Ree, Esq. of Bardolphs in Watton.
1465 Laurence Raynesgord, Kt.
1466 Henry Barlee, Esq.
1467 William Pyrton, Kt.
1468 Walter Writtle, Esq. of Astlyns in H. Ongar
1469 Ralph Baud, Esq. of Hadham-hall
1470 Walter Writtle, Esq.
1471 Roger Kee, Kt.
1472 Alured Cornburgh, Esq.
1473 John Sturgeon, Esq. of Hitchin
1474 Richard Hance, Esq. of Danbury
1475 Henry Langley, Esq.
1476 William Grene, Esq.
1477 Alured Cornburgh, Esq.
1478 John Wode, Esq.
1479 John Sturgeon, Esq. of Hitchin
1480 Thomas Tyrell, Esq. of Heron
1481 John Fortescue, Esq. of Rivenhall

EDW.V. And RIC.III.
1482 William Saye, Kt. of the Bath, of Broxbourne.
1483 John Sturgeon, Esq.
1484 Robert Percy, Kt.

HEN.VII.
1485 John Fortescue, Kt.
1486 Henry Marney, Esq.
1487 William Pyrton, Kt.
1488 Henry Teye, Esq. of Old-holt in Messing
1489 John Boteler, Esq.
1490 Rob. Turberville Esq. of St. Stephens
1491 John Bardfield, Esq. of Margareting
1492 Henry Marney, Esq. afterwards Ld. Marney
1493 Richard Fitz-Lewis, Kt.
1494 Robert Plomer, Esq.
1495 William Pulter, Esq. of Hitchin
1496 Robert Newport, Esq. of Furneaux Pelham

1497	Tho. Peryent, Esq. of Digswell	1536	Thomas Peryent the Elder, Esq of Digenswell
1498	John Verney, Kt. of Penley	1537	Sir Henry Parker, Kt.
1499	Roger Wentworth, Kt. of Wethersfield	1538	Sir John Raynsford, Kt.
1500	Henry Teye, Kt.	1539	John Smyth, Esq
1501	William Pyrton, Esq.	1540	Sir Philip Boteler, Kt. of Watton
1502	Humfrey Tyrell, Esq. of Heron	1541	Sir John Mordant, Kt.
1503	William Skypwith, Esq. of St Albans for 2 years	1542	Ralph Rowlett, Esq of St Albans
1505	Roger Darcy, Esq.	1543	John Bowles of Wallington, 1st half year, John Sewster, Esq 2nd half year
1506	John Brocket, Esq. of Bishops Hatfield, for 2 years	1544	John Wentworth, Esq
1507	Humfrey Tyrell, Esq. of Heron	1545	Anthony Cook, Esq

HEN.VIII.

		1546	Robert Lytton, Esq of Knebworth
1510	John Leventhorpe, Esq of Shingle Hall	1547	John Coningsby, Esq of North-Mims

EDW. VI.

1511	William Lytton, Esq of Knebworth	1547	Edward Brocket, Esq of Hatfield
1512	Anthony Darcy, Esq of Danbury	1548	John Cock, Esq of Brokesborne
1513	Edward Tyrell, Esq of Heron	1549	Sir John Gates, Kt. of Cheshunt
1514	John Seyntclere, Esq	1550	Sir George Norton, Kt.
1515	William Fitz Williams, Esq	1551	Sir Henry Tyrell, Kt. of Heron
1516	Sir John Veere, Kt.	1552	Sir Thomas Pope, Kt. Of Tittenhanger
1517	Thomas Bonham, Esq		
1518	Sir Thomas Tyrell, Kt. of Heron		

MARY.

1519	Sir John Cutts, Kt.	1553	Sir John Wentworth, Kt.

PHIL. and MARY.

1520	Sir John Veere, Kt.	1534	Edward Brocket, Esq of Hatfield
1521	Thomas Bonham, Esq	1555	William Harris, Esq
1522	Sir Thomas Tey, Kt.	1556	Sir John Boteler, Kt. of Watton
1523	John Christmass, Esq	1557	Sir Thomas Pope, Kt. Of Tittenhanger
1524	Henry Barley, Esq	1558	Thomas Mildmay, Esq
1525	Sir John Veere, Kt.		

ELIZ.

1526	Thomas Leventhorpe, Esq of Shingle-hall	1559	Ralph Rowlett, Esq of St Albans
1527	Thomas Bonham, Esq	1560	Edward Capell, Esq of Hadham
1528	Edward Tyrell, Esq of Heron	1561	Sir Thomas Goldyng, Kt.
1529	Sir Gyles Capell, Kt. of Hadham	1562	Thomas Barrington, Esq
1530	John Bollys, Esq of Wallington	1563	Henry Fortescue, Esq
1531	John Brocket, Esq of Hatfield	1564	William Aloffe, Esq
1532	John Smyth, Esq	1565	Robert Chester, Esq of Royston
1533	Sir Philip Boteler, Kt. of Watton	1566	John Brocket, Esq of Hatfield
1534	Sir Brian Took, Kt. of Hatfield		
1535	Sir William West, Kt.		

From 1566 Essex elected their own Sheriffs

Sheriffs of Essex from 1566
1567-1760 from Morant's "History of Essex"
1761-1893 from "The Essex Review"

ELIZ. (An. Reg. 9)

1567 Geo. Tuke Esq; of Layer-Marney
1568 Thos. Lucas Esq; of St. John's Colchester
1569 Tho. Golding Kt.
1570 James Altham Esq; of Mark-hall in Latton
1571 Edw. Barret Esq; of Belhouse in Aveley
1572 Thomas Mildmay Kt. of Moulsham
1573 Arthur Harris Esq; of Cricklea
1574 Edmund Pyrton Esq
1575 John Petre Kt. of Writtle and Ingatestone
1576 Winstan Browne Esq; of S.Weald and W.Roding
1577 Gabriel Poyntz Esq; of North Okingdon
1578 Edm. Hodleston Esq; of Newport-pond
1579 Henry Capel Esq; of Rayne
1580 Thomas Barington Kt. and Thos. Darcy Esq of Tolleshunt Darcy
1581 John Wentworth Esq; of Gosfield
1582 Thomas Teye Esq
1583 Tho. Lucas Kt.
1584 Henry Apleton Esq; of South
1585 Brian Darcy Esq; of S. Osith
1586 Arthur Harris Esq
1587 Robert Wroth Esq; of Loughton
1588 Edm. Hodleston Kt.
1589 Gabriel Poyntz Esq
1590 Ralph Wiseman Esq; of Rivenhall
1591 Richard Warren Esq; of Claybury
1592 John Wentworth Esq
1593 Humfrey Mildmay Esq; of Danbury
1594 William Ayloffe Esq; of Gr. Brackstead
1595 Edward Sulyard Esq; of Runwell
1596 Geo. Hervey Esq; of Merks near Romford

1597 Thomas Mildmay Esq; of Moulsham
1598 William Harris Esq; of Cricksea
1599 Jerom Weston Esq; of Roxwell
1600 Tho. Mede Esq; of Wendon Lofts
1601 Henry Smith Esq; of Cressing Temple
1602 Richard Franke Esq; of Malden Abbey

JAMES I.

1603 Henry Maynard Kt. of Little Easton
1604 Tho. Rawlyns Esq
1605 John Sammes Kt. of Little Totham
1606 Gamaliel Capel Kt. of Abbots Roding
1607 Henry Maxey Kt. of Gr. Saling
1608 Roger Apleton Esq
1609 Thomas Mildmay Kt.
1610 John Deane Kt. of Gr. Maplested
1611 Thomas Wiseman Kt.
1612 Henry Leigh Kt.
1613 Sir Robert Wroth Kt. He died: In his room Edw. Elrington Esq; of Theydon Boys
1614 Harbottle Grimston Kt. and Bart of Bradfield
1615 William Smyth Esq; of Theydon Mount
1616 Thomas Lucas Esq
1617 Paul Bayning Bart. of Little Bentley
1618 Thomas Bendyshe Bart. of Steeple Bumstead
1619 William Smyth Knt.
1620 William Pert Esq; of Mountneys-ing
1621 Stephen Soame Kt. of Haydon
1622 Thomas Gournay Kt.
1623 Charles Pratt Esq
1624 Edward Boteler Esq

CHARLES I.

1625 Arthur Harris Kt.
1626 Hugh Everard Esq of Gr. Waltham

1627	Thomas Nightingale Esq of Newport-pond	1658	Thomas Wiseman Knt. of Rivenhall
1628	Henry Mildmay Esq of Woodham Walter	1659	William Wiseman Bart.

CHARLES II - The Restoration

1629	Ed. Alleyn Bart. of Hatfield Peverell	1660	Robert Abdy Kt. and Bart. of Stapleford
1630	Thomas Bendyshe Bart.	1661	Sir Thomas Wiseman Bart. and William Wiseman Bart.
1631	John Mede Kt. or William Martin Kt.	1662	Martin Lumley Bart. of Gr. Bardfield
1632	Henry Smith Esq	1663	Tho. Snyth Bart. of Theydon Mount
1633	Richard Staltonstall Knt. of S. Okingdon	1664	William Luckyn Bart. of Messing
1634	Cranmer Harris Knt.	1665	Heneage Featherston Bart. of Stanford le Hope
1635	Humfrey Mildmay Kt. of Danbury	1666	Stephen Soame Esq of Heydon
1636	John Lucas Esq	1667	John Birch Esq of Geddying-hall
1637	William Luckyn Bart. of Little Waltham	1668	John James Kt. of Creshall
1638	William Wiseman Bart. of Gr. Canfield	1669	Thomas Gerrard Knt. of East-Ham
1639	Richard Luckyn Esq of Chicknall-Smeley	1670	Edward Lewen Esq
1640		1671	Thomas Turner Esq of Quendon
1641	Robert Smyth Esq of Upton	1672	John Howland Esq
1642	Benj. Ayloffe Bart.	1673	Thomas Chamber Kt.
1643	Timo. Middleton Esq of Stansted Montfichet	1674	Stephen White Kt.
1644	Richard Everard Bart.	1675	Mark Guyon Esq of Great Coggeshall
1645	Richard Harlackenden Esq of Earl's Colne	1676	John Morecroft Esq of Shenfield
1646	John Pyot Esq of Low Leyton	1677	Francis Osbaldeston of Little Ilford. He dyed 22 Apr. 1678. Will. Dyer Esq the rest of the year.
1647	Hanameel Chibburne Esq of Messing. He dyed. In his room Robert Bourne Esq of Bobbingworth	1678	William Palmer Esq of Stratford, or Lambourn

CHARLES II - The Usurpation

1648	George Pyke Esq of Bathon-end	1679	Richard Barrett Esq of Belhouse
1649	Samuel Tryon Bart. of Halstead	1680	Edward Smyth Bart. of Hill-Hall
1650	John Trafford Esq of Low Leyton	1681	Thomas Dawney Esq of Doddinghurst
1651	Thomas Abdy Bart. of Kelvedon	1682	William Glascock Kt. of Aldham
1652	Thomas Cambell Esq of Clay-hall	1683	William Hicks Kt. and Bart. of Low Leyton
1653	William Marten Kt. according to others Cuthbert Martyn Esq of Nettleswell	1684	Joseph Smart Esq of Theydon-Boys

JAMES II

1654	John Barrington Kt. and Bart.	1685	Cane James Bart. of Creshall
1655	John Sparrow Esq of Gr. Maplestead	1686	William Peck Esq of Little Samford
1656		1687	Thomas Manby Kt. of Southweald
1657	Thomas Middleton Esq of Stansted	1688	Benjamin Disborow Esq of Downham

WILLIAM and MARY

1689 Josias Child Bart. of Wanstead
1690 John La Mott Honeywood Esq of Marks-hall
1691 John Cookes Esq of Low Layton
1692 George Ford Esq
1693 Timothy Felton Esq of Ovington
1694 John Lockey Esq of Albury-hatch
1695 John Littell Esq of Ballington
1696 Edw. Bullock Esq of Falbourne, or Charles Tyrell Bart. of Herongate
1697 Edmund Godwin Esq
1698 Samuel Moyer Esq of Pitsey
1699 Samuel Wake, alias Jone Esq of Waltham Abbey
1700 George Pochin Esq of Fyfield
1701 Edward Luther Esq; John Luther Esq; of Stapleford Tany or Kelvedon-hatch

ANNE

1702 Peter Whitcombe Esq of Brackstead
1703 Edward Bullock Esq of Falkbourn
1704 Thomas Webster Esq of Copped-hall
1705 William Peck Esq
1706 Dacre-Lennard Barrett Esq of Belhouse
1707 John Olmius Esq of Braintree
1708 Daniel Wray Esq or Kt.
1709 Thomas Millington Esq of Gosfield
      Justus Beck Esq
1710 Martyn Lumley Bart. of Gr. Bardfield
1711 Samuel Smith Esq of South-Weald
1712 Fisher Tench Esq of Low Layton
1713 Carew Hervey, alias Mildmay, Esq of Marks
1714 Henry Featherstone Bart. of Stanford le Hope

GEORGE I

1714 Henry Featherstone part of 1 Geo. I/
1715 William Blackbourne Esq of Dagenham
1716 William Cole Esq of Magdalen Laver
1717 David Gansel Esq of Low-Layton
1718 Robert Dennet Esq of Waltham-Stow
1719 William Lockey Esq of Alborough-hatch
1720 Hugh Raymond Esq of Saling
1721 Timothy Brand Esq of Frierning
1722 Richard Chamberlayne Esq of Hatfield-Regis
1723 Josiah Kinsman Esq of Horndon on the Hill
1724 James Braine Esq of Matching
1725 John Turner Esq of Widdington
1726 Edward Peatson Esq of Upton
1727 Philip Hall Kt. of Upton

GEORGE II

1728 Willioam Ashurst Esq of Hedingham Castle
1729 Catlin Thorogood Esq of Lambourn
1730 John How Esq of Stondon Marci
1731 William Peck Esq of Little Samford
1732 Samuel Feake Esq of Shering
1733 William Harvey Esq of Chigwell
1734 Champion Bramsill Esq of Upminster
1735 Thomas Ambrose Esq of Shenfield
1736 William Dawtrey Esq of Doddinghurst
1737 Herbert Trist Esq of Cranham
1738 Hugh Smith Esq of Southweald
1739 Thomas Bowes Esq of Upton
1740 Thomas Drury Bart. of Gr. Ilford
1741 James Hannot Esq of Woodford-bridge
1742 Osmond Beauvoir Esq of Downham
1743 Edward Stephenson Esq of Gr. Bardfield
1744 Thomas Ashhurst Esq of Hedingham-castle
1745 Peter Du Cane Esq of Gr. Coggeshall
1746 John Olmius Esq of Newhall
1747 Nicholas Corsellis Esq of Wivenhou
1748 Bailey Heath Esq of Stansted

1749 John Fishpool Esq of Billerica
1750 John Tyrell Bart. of Herongate
1751 Peter le Fevre Esq of Walthamstow
1752 Edmund Alleyn Bart. of Hatfield Peverell
1753 William Hunt Esq of Woodford
1754 Richard Benion Esq of Geddying-hall
1755 Richard Chiswell Esq of Depden
1756 Edward Emmett Esq of Alboroug-Hatch
1757 Humfrey Bellamy Esq of Walthamstow
1758 John Henniker Esq of Dunmow
1759 Jasper Kinsman Esq of Stifford
1760 Thomas Towers Esq of South-weald

GEORGE III

1761 Charles Smith Bart. of Theyden
1762 Richard Newman Esq of West-ham
1763 William Sheldon of Walthamstow
1764 John Wilkes of Wendon Loughts
1765 Sir William Mildmay Bart.
1766 Joseph Keeling Esq of Fingringhou
1767 Thomas Fytch Esq of Danbury
1768 Richard-Lomas Clay of Loughton
1769 Daniel Matthews of Felix Hall Kelvedon
1770 John Tyrrel of Boreham
1771 Charles Raymond of Ilford Ward
1772 Samuel Bosanquet of Walthamstow
1773 John Archer of Coopersall
1774 H Lovibond Collins of Boreham
1775 John Pardoe of Low Leyton
1776 Richard Muilman Trench Chiswell of Debden Hall
1777 Henry Sperling of Dynes Hall, Great Maplestead
1778 William Lushington of Latton
1779 William Godfrey of Woodford
1780 Henry Hinde Pelly of Upton
1781 Richard Wyatt of Hornchurch
1782 William Dalby of Walthamstow
1783 John Godsalve Crosse of Baddow
1784 Richard Preston of Woodford
1785 George Bowles of Wanstead

1786 John Joliffe Tufnell of Langleys, Great Waltham
1787 John Judd of Chelmsford
1788 Thomas Theophilus Cock of Messing
1789 Thomas Fowell Buxton of Earls Colne
1790 T. Nottage of Bocking
1791 Donald Cameron of Great Ilford
1792 Zachariah Button of Stifford
1793 Staines Chamberlayne of Hatfield Broad Oak
1794 James Hatch of Claybury
1795 John Hanson of Great Bromley Hall
1796 Jackson Barwise of Marshalls Romford
1797 William Manby of Stratford
1798 John Perry of Moor Hall, Harlow
1799 Capel Cure of Blake Hall, Ongar
1800 George Lee of Great Ilford
1801 John Archer Houldon of Hallingbury Place
1802 Robert Raikes of Great Ilford
1803 Stephen Frier Gilluffi of Shenfield
1804 William Palmer of Nazing
1805 James Read of Warleys, Waltham Abbey
1806 James Urmston of Chigwell
1807 William Matthew Raikes of Walthamstow
1808 John Coggan of Wanstead
1809 J. Rutherford Abdy of Albyns, Stapleford Abbots
1810 John Rigg of Walthamstow
1811 Charles Smith of Suttons, Romford
1812 Sir Robert Wigram, Bart., of Walthamstow
1813 R. J. Brassey of Great Ilford
1814 R. Wilson of Woodhouse
1815 Luke William Walford of Little Bardfield
1816 Nicholas Pearce of Loughton
1817 John Hall of Woodford
1818 J. T. Daubuz of Leyton
1819 John Wilkes of Wendon Loughts
1820 Sir Thomas Neave, Bart., of Dagnam Park

GEORGE IV

1821 Robert Westley Hall, junr., of Great Ilford
1822 Sir George Henry Smith, Bart., of Berechurch Hall
1823 John Joliffe Tufnell of Langleys, Great Waltham
1824 N. Garland of Michaelstowe Hall, Ramsey
1825 Peter Ducane of Braxted Park
1826 Frederic Nassau of St. Osyth
1827 Sir John Tyrrel, Bart., of Boreham
1828 Sir Charles J. Smith, Bart., of Suttons, Romford
1829 Brice Pearse of Monkhams, Woodford
1830 Capel Cure of Blake Hall, Ongar

WILLIAM IV

1831 William Davis of Leyton
1832 John T Selwin of Down Hall, Hatfield Broad Oak
1833 R. B. Wolfe of Woodhall, Arksden
1834 John Round of Danbury
1835 George W. Gent of Moyns, Steeple Bumpsted
1836 William Whitaker Maitland of Loughton Hall
1837 Jonathan Bullock of Faulkbourn Hall

VICTORIA

1838 William Cotton of Wallwood, Leyton
1839 John Fletcher Mills of Lexden Park
1840 Christopher T. Tower of Weald Hall
1841 John Archer Houldon of Great Hallingbury Place
1842 J. F. Fortescue of Writtle Lodge
1843 H. J. Conyers of Copped Hall
1844 Staines Brocket Brocket of Spains Hall, Willingale, Spain
1845 George Round of Colchester
1846 John Clarmont Whiteman of The Grove, Theydon Garnon
1847 William Coxhead Marsh of Park Hall, Theydon Garnon
1848 Beale Blackwell Colvin of Monkhams Hall, Waltham Abbey

1849 Only Savill-Only of Stisted Hall
1850 Thomas B. Western of Felix Hall, Kelvedon
1851 William P. Honeywood of Marks Hall
1852 Sir Charles Cunliffe Smith of Suttons, Romford
1853 John Gurdon-Rebow of Wivenhoe Prk
1854 Thomas White of Wethersfield
1855 John Watlington Perry-Watlington of Moor Hall, Harlow
1856 Robert Hills of Colne Park, Colne Engaine
1857 John Francis Wright of Kelvedon Hatch
1858 Osgood Hanbury of Holfield Grange, Coggeshall
1859 Champion Russell of Upminster
1860 George Henry Errington of Lexden Park
1861 George Alan Lowndes of Barrington Hall, Hatfield Broad Oak
1862 Joseph Samuel Lescher of Boyles Court, Brentwood
1863 George Palmer of Nazing Park
1864 Edgar Disney of The Hyde, Ingatestone
1865 Sir Thomas Barrett-Lennard, Bart., of Belhus, Aveley
1866 Arthur Pryor of Hylands, Widford
1867 Richard Baker Wingfield-Baker of Orsett Hall
1868 William Charles Smith of Shortgrove, Saffron Walden
1869 John Wright of Hatfield Peverell
1870 John Joliffe Tufnell of Langleys, Great Waltham
1871 Robert Gosling of Hassobury, Farnham
1872 Thomas Kemble of Runwell Hall
1873 Robert John Bagshaw of Dovercourt
1874 Thomas George Graham White of Wethersfield
1875 Sir Thomas Neville Abdy of Albyns, Stapleford Abbots

1876 Christopher John Hume Tower of South Weald Hall

1877 John Robert Vaizey of Attwoods Halstead

1878 Philip John Budworth of Greensted Hall, Ongar

1879 Edward Ind of Combe Lodge, Great Warley

1880 Andrew Johnston of Woodford

1881 Thomas Jenner Spitty of Billericay

1882 Hector John Gurdon-Rebow of Wivenhoe Park

1883 John Oxley Parker of Woodham Mortimer

1884 Sir William Neville Abdy of Albyns, Stapleford Abbots

1885 Joseph Francis Lescher of Hutton

1886 Henry Ford Barclay of Monkhams, Woodford

1887 John Lionel Tufnell-Tyrrel of Boreham House

1888 Edward North Buxton of Knighton, Woodford

1889 Sir William Bowyer-Smith, Bart., of Hill Hall, Theydon Mount

1890 Richard Beale Calvin of Monkhams, Waltham Abbey

1891 Thomas Courtenay Theydon Warner of Higham, Woodford

1892 William Swayne Chisenhale-Marsh of Gaynes Park, Epping

1893 Arthur Janion Edwards of Beech Hill Park, Waltham Abbey

Lord Mayors of the City of London 1271 - 1781

1271 - 1272	Walter Hervey		1354	Thomas Leggy
1273	Henry le Walleis		1355	Simon Frauncis
1274 - 1280	Gregory de Rokesley		1356	Henry Picard
1281 - 1283	Henry le Walleis		1357	John de Stodeye
1284	Gregory de Rokesley		1358	John Lovekyn
1285 - 1289	Ralph de Sandwich		1359	Simon Dolseley
1289	John le Breton		1360	John Wroth
1289 - 1292	Ralph de Sandwich		1361	John Pecche
1293 - 1298	John le Breton		1362	Stephen Cavendisshe
1298	Henry le Walleis		1363	John Nott
1299 - 1300	Elia Russell		1364 - 1365	Adam de Bury
1301 - 1307	John le Blund		1366	John Lovekyn
1308	Nicholas de Farndone		1367	James Andreu
1309	Thomas Romeyn		1368	Simon de Mordone
1310	Richer de Refham		1369	John de Chichester
1311 - 1312	John de Gisors		1370 - 1371	John Bernes
1313	Nicholas de Farndone		1372	John Pyel
1314	John de Gisors		1373	Adam de Bury
1315	Stephen de Abyndon		1374	William Walworth
1316 - 1318	John de Wengrave		1375	John Warde
1319	Hamo de Chigwell		1376	Adam Stable
1320	Nicholas de Farndone		1377	Nicholas Brembre
1321	Robert de Kendale		1378	John Philipot
1321 - 1322	Hamo de Chigwell		1379	John Hadle
1323	Nicholas de Farndone		1380	William Walworth
1323 - 1325	Hamo de Chigwell		1381 - 1382	John de Northampton
1326	Richard de Betoyne		1383 - 1385	Sir Nicholas Brembre
1327	Hamo de Chigwell		1386 - 1387	Nicholas Exton
1328	John de Grantham		1388	Sir Nicholas Twyford
1329	Simon Swanlond		1389	William Venour
1330 - 1331	John de Pulteney		1390	Adam Bamme
1332	John de Prestone		1391	John Heende
1333	John de Pulteney		1392	Sir Edward Dalyngrigge
1334 - 1335	Reginald de Conduit		1392	Sir Baldwin Radynton
1336	John de Pulteney		1392	William Staundon
1337 - 1338	Henry Darci		1393	John Hadle
1339 - 1340	Andrew Aubrey		1394	John Fresshe
1341	John de Oxenford		1395	William More
1342	Simon Frauncis		1396	Adam Bamme
1343 - 1344	John Hamond		1397	Richard Whytyngdone
1345	Richard le Lacer		1398	Drugo Barentyn
1346	Geoffrey de Wichingham		1399	Thomas Knolles
1347	Thomas Leggy		1400	John Frounceys
1348	John Lovekyn		1401	John Shadworth
1349	Walter Turke		1402	John Walcote
1350	Richard de Kislingbury		1403	William Askham
1351	Andrew Aubrey		1404	John Heende
1352 - 1353	Adam Frounceys		1405	John Wodecok

1406	Richard Whytyngdone	1454	Stephen Forster
1407	William Staundon	1455	William Marowe
1408	Drugo Barentyn	1456	Thomas Canynges
1409	Richard Merlawe	1457	Geoffrey Boleyn
1410	Thomas Knolles	1458	Thomas Scott
1411	Robert Chichele	1459	William Hulyn
1412	William Walderne	1460	Richard Lee
1413	William Crowmere	1461	Hugh Wiche
1414	Thomas Fauconer	1462	Thomas Cooke
1415	Nicholas Wotton	1463	Mathew Philip
1416	Henry Barton	1464	Ralph Josselyn
1417	Richard Merlawe	1465	Ralph Verney
1418	William Sevenoke	1466	John Yonge
1419	Richard Whytyngdone	1467	Thomas Oulegrave
1420	William Cauntbrigge	1468	William Taillour
1421	Robert Chichele	1469	Richard Lee
1422	William Walderne	1470	John Stockton
1423	William Crowmere	1471	William Edward
1424	John Michell	1472	Sir William Hampton
1425	John Coventre	1473	John Tate
1426	John Reynwell	1474	Robert Drope
1427	John Gedney	1475	Robert Bassett
1428	Henry Barton	1476	Sir Ralph Josselyn
1429	William Estfeld	1477	Humphrey Hayford
1430	Nicholas Wotton	1478	Richard Gardyner
1431	John Welles	1479	Sir Bartholomew James
1432	John Perneys	1480	John Browne
1433	John Brokle	1481	William Haryot
1434	Robert Otele	1482	Edmund Shaa
1435	Henry Frowyk	1483	Robert Billesdon
1436	John Michell	1484	Thomas Hill
1437	William Estfeld	1485	Sir William Stokker
1438	Stephen Broun	1486	Henry Colet
1439	Robert Large	1487	William Home
1440	John Paddesle	1488	Robert Tate
1441	Robert Clopton	1489	William White
1442	John Hatherle	1490	John Mathews
1443	Thomas Catworth	1491	Hugh Clopton
1444	Henry Frowyk	1492	William Martin
1445	Simon Eyre	1493	Ralp Astry
1446	John Olney	1494	Richard Chawry
1447	John Gedney	1495	Sir Henry Colet
1448	Stephen Broun	1496	John Tate
1449	Thomas Chalton	1497	William Purchase
1450	Nicholas Wyfold	1498	Sir John Percyvale
1451	William Gregory	1499	Nicholas Ailwyn
1452	Geoffrey Feldynge	1500	William Remyngton
1453	John Norman	1501	Sir John Shaa

1502	Bartholomew Rede	1548	Henry Amcotts
1503	Sir William Capel	1549	Sir Rowland Hill
1504	John Wynger	1550	Andrew Judde
1505	Thomas Kneseworth	1551	Richard Dobbis
1506	Sir Richard Haddon	1552	George Barne
1507	William Browne	1553	Thomas Whyte
1508	Sir Lawrence Aylmer	1554	John Lyon
1508	Stephen Jenyns	1555	William Garrade
1509	Thomas Bradbury	1556	Thomas Offley
1510	Sir William Capel	1557	Thomas Curres
1511	Roger Achleley	1558	Thomas Leigh
1512	William Chopynger	1559	William Hewet
1513	Sir Richard Haddon	1560	Sir William Chester
1514	William Browne (died)	1561	William Harpur
1514	Sir John Tate	1562	Thomas Lodge
1515	William Boteler	1563	John Whyte
1516	John Rest	1564	Richard Malorye
1517	Thomas Exmewe	1565	Richard Champyon
1518	Thomas Mirfyn	1566	Christopher Draper
1519	James Yarford	1567	Roger Martyn
1520	John Brugge	1568	Thomas Rowe
1521	John Milborne	1569	Alexander Avenon
1522	John Mundy	1570	Rowland Heyward
1523	Thomas Baldry	1571	William Allen
1524	William Bayley	1572	Lionel Duckett
1525	John Aleyn	1573	John Ryvers
1526	Sir Thomas Semer	1574	James Hawes
1527	James Spencer	1575	Ambrose Nicholas
1528	John Rudstone	1576	John Langley
1529	Ralph Dodmer	1577	Thomas Ramsay
1530	Thomas Pargeter	1578	Richard Pype
1531	Nicholas Lambarde	1579	Nicholas Woodroffe
1532	Stephen Pecocke	1580	John Branche
1533	Christopher Ascue	1581	James Harvye
1534	Sir John Champneys	1582	Thomas Blanke
1535	Sir John Aleyn	1583	Edward Osborne
1536	Ralph Warren	1584	Thomas Pullyson
1537	Sir Ralph Gresham	1585	Wolstan Dixie
1538	William Forman	1586	George Barne
1539	Sir William Hollyes	1587	George Bonde
1540	William Roche	1588	Martin Calthorp
1541	Michael Dormer	1589	Richard Martin
1542	John Cores	1589	John Harte
1543	William Bowyer	1590	John Allot
1544	Sir Ralph Warren	1591	Sir Rowland Heyward
1545	Sir Martin Bowes	1592	William Rowe
1546	Henry Huberthorn	1593	Cuthbert Buckell
1547	Sir John Gresham	1594	John Spencer

1595	Stephen Slanye	1643	Sir John Wollaston
1596	Thomas Skinner	1644	Thomas Atkyn
1597	Richard Saltonstall	1645	Thomas Adams
1598	Stephen Soame	1646	Sir John Gayer
1599	Nicholas Mosley	1647	John Warner
1600	William Ryder	1648	Abraham Reynardson
1601	John Garrarde	1649	Thomas Foot
1602	Robert Lee	1650	Thomas Andrewes
1603	Sir Thomas Bennett	1651	John Kendricke
1604	Sir Thomas Lowe	1652	John Fowke
1605	Sir Leonard Halliday	1653	Thomas Vyner
1606	Sir John Watts	1654	Christopher Pack
1607	Sir Henry Rowe	1655	John Dethick
1608	Sir Humphrey Weld	1656	Robert Tichborne
1609	Sir Thomas Cambell	1657	Richard Chiverton
1610	Sir William Craven	1658	Sir John Ireton
1611	Sir James Pemberton	1659	Thomas Alleyn
1612	Sir John Swynnerton	1660	Sir Richard Browne, Bt.
1613	Sir Thomas Middleton	1661	Sir John Frederick
1614	Sir Thomas Hayes	1662	Sir John Robinson, Bt
1615	Sir John Jolles	1663	Sir Anthony Bateman
1616	John Leman	1664	Sir John Lawrence
1617	George Bolles	1665	Sir Thomas Bludworth
1618	Sir Sebastian Harvey	1666	Sir William Bolton
1619	Sir William Cokayne	1667	Sir William Peake
1620	Sir Frances Jones	1668	Sir William Turner
1621	Edward Barkham	1669	Sir Samuel Starling
1622	Peter Probie	1670	Sir Richard Ford
1623	Martin Lumley	1671	Sir George Waterman
1624	John Gore	1672	Sir Robert Hanson
1625	Allan Cotton	1673	Sir William Hooker
1626	Cuthbert Hacket	1674	Sir Robert Vyner, Bt
1627	Hugh Hammersley	1675	Sir Joseph Sheldon
1628	Richard Deane	1676	Sir Thomas Davies
1629	James Cambell	1677	Sir Francis Chaplin
1630	Sir Robert Ducye, Bt	1678	Sir James Edwards
1631	George Whitmore	1679	Sir Robert Clayton
1632	Nicholas Rainton	1680	Sir Patience Ward
1633	Ralph Freeman	1681	Sir John Moore
1634	Thomas Moulson	1682	Sir William Prichard
1635	Christopher Clitherow	1683	Sir Henry Tulse
1636	Edward Bromfield	1684	Sir James Smyth
1637	Richard Ven	1685	Sir Robert Geffery
1638	Sir Morris Abbot	1686	Sir John Peake
1639	Henry Garraway	1687	Sir John Shorter
1640	Edmund Wright	1688	Sir John Chapman
1641	Richard Gurney	1689 - 1690	Thomas Pilkington
1642	Isaac Penington	1691	Sir Thomas Stampe

1692	Sir John Fleet	1738	Micajah Perry
1693	Sir William Ashurst	1739	Sir John Salter
1694	Sir Thomas Lane	1740	Humphrey Parsons
1695	Sir John Houblon	1741	Daniel Lambert
1696	Sir Edward Clarke	1742	George Heathcote
1697	Sir Humphrey Edwin	1743	Robert Westley
1698	Sir Francis Child	1744	Henry Marshall
1699	Sir Richard Levett	1745	Richard Hoare
1700	Sir Thomas Abney	1746	William Benn
1701	Sir William Gore	1747	Sir Robert Ladbroke
1702	Sir Samuel Dashwood	1748	Sir William Calvert
1703	Sir John Parsons	1749	Sir Samuel Pennant
1704	Sir Owen Buckingham	1750	Francis Cockayne
1705	Sir Thomas Rawlinson	1751	Thomas Winterbottom
1706	Sir Robert Bedingfield	1752	Crisp Gascoyne
1707	Sir William Withers	1753	Edward Ironside
1708	Sir Charles Duncombe	1754	Stephen T Janssen
1709	Sir Samuel Garrard, Bt	1755	Slingsby Bethell
1710	Sir Gilbert Heathcote	1756	Marshe Dickinson
1711	Sir Robert Beachcroft	1757	Sir Charles Asgill
1712	Sir Richard Hoare	1758	Sir Richard Glyn
1713	Sir Samuel Stanier	1759	Sir Thomas Chitty
1714	Sir William Humfreys	1760	Sir Mathew Blakiston
1715	Sir Charles Peers	1761	Sir Samuel Fludyer, Bt
1716	Sir James Bateman	1762	William Beckford
1717	Sir William Lewett	1763	William Bridgen
1718	Sir John Ward	1764	Sir William Stephenson
1719	Sir George Thorold, Bt.	1765	George Nelson
1720	Sir John Fryer, Bt	1766	Sir Robert Kite
1721	Sir William Stewart	1767	Thomas Harley
1722	Sir Gerard Conyers	1768	Samuel Turner
1723	Sir Peter Delme	1769	William Beckford
1724	Sir George Merttins	1770	Barlow Trecothick
1725	Sir Francis Forbes	1770	Brass Crosby
1726	Sir John Eyles, Bt	1771	William Nash
1727	Sir Edward Becher	1772	James Townsend
1728	Sir Robert Baylis	1773	Frederick Bull
1729	Sir Robert Brocas	1774	John Wilkes
1730	Humphrey Parsons	1775	John Sawbridge
1731	Francis Child	1776	Sir Thomas Hallifax
1732	John Barber	1777	Sir James Esdaile
1733	Sir William Billers	1778	Samuel Plumbe
1734	Sir Edward Bellamy	1779	Brackley Kennett
1735	Sir John Williams	1780	Sir Watkin Lewes
1736	Sir John Thompson	1781	William Plomer
1737	Sir John Barnard		

Index of People

Ackworth 83.
Aldwell. Rev'd S.W.H. 7, 11.
Alfred the Great 2, 67.
Alington 75, 76, 94, 104.
Argentein 59, 75.
Arundell 51, 82.
Ashfield 28.
Ashton 117.
Aspall 25, 67, 68.
Asprucci 63.
Audley. Lord 25.
Bacon 88.
Badwell 41.
Baker 17.
Barley. Abbess 14.
Barnardiston 60, 87, 88, 103, 104, 105, 106, 107.
Baskerville 22.
Bath. Earl of 111, 114.
Beauchamp 67.
Bedford. Duke of 10.
Bess of Hardwick 26, 115.
Black Prince 2.
Bocking 61.
Boleyn 13, 52.
Bond 119.
Botetout 67.
Bourchier 111, 112, 114.
Bowes 29.
Brackenbury 51.
Braybrooke 25.
Bristol. Earl/Marquess Ch.7.
Britten 32.
Brograve 36.
Brooke Ch.3, 34, 35, 67, 68.
Browne Ch.4, 14, 17, 21, 22, 27, 35, 56, 71, 82, 89, 94, 95, 97.
Buckingham. Duke of 109.
Bull 68, 70, 71, 72, 76, 80.
Bures. Lord 81, 83.

Burke 42, 43.
Burley 91.
Burns 72.
Byrd 19, 20, 38.
Caldebeck 67, 68, 69.
Capability Brown 63.
Capell 34, 36, 37, 39, 86.
Carr 61.
Cary. (Lord Hunsdon) 13, 28, 43, 51.
Catesby 37.
Catherine of Braganza 61.
Cavendish. Lady 26, 28, 115.
Cecil 16, 17, 20, 21, 27, 38, 72.
Chamberleyn 91, 92.
Chance 11.
Charles I 45, 61, 96.
Charles II 61.
Chastelyn 99.
Chaucer 5, 9.
Chevallier Ch.3.
Churchyard 115.
Clare 25, 32, 52.
Clifton Brown 69.
Clopton Ch.11, 43, 87, 93, 115.
Cobham. Lord Ch.3.
Colte 75.
Comyns 99.
Constable 92.
Copinger 80.
Corbett 53, 83.
Cornwallis 113, 114.
Cromwell 13, 15, 34.
Dacre 35, 95.
Darcy 37, 49, 61, 101, 108, 115, 116.
Davers (Jermyn) 62.
Daye 68, 69, 71, 72, 74, 77.
de la Pole Ch.1, 25, 42, 45, 67.
de Vere 29, 34, 36, 37.
Denny 95.
Denton 108.
Despotine 107.

Donnington 109.
Dormer 38.
Dorwood 81.
Downing 55.
Drury 13, 53, 59, 60, 82, 83, 101, 115.
Dudley 72.
D'Ewes 41, 42, 45, 87, 102, 104, 105, 106, 107, 108.
Eden 88, 95.
Edward I 1, 3.
Edward III 2, 3, 80.
Edward IV 9, 45, 50, 79, 112.
Edward V 50.
Elwes 64.
Ely. Bishop of 45.
Emperor Charles V 60.
English 55.
Everton 28.
Fairclough 60.
Fastolf 2, 29.
Felton 62.
Fielding 117.
Fitch 95.
Foxe 72.
Francis 101.
Fray 81.
Frith 72.
Gage Ch.12, 61, 95,
Gardiner 43, 51.
Gates 103.
Gedding 25, 42, 43.
George IV 75.
Gibbs 54.
Gifford 91, 92, 93.
Gipps 46.
Gislingham 42, 43.
Glanville 2.
Gloucester. Duke of 65.
Grey 27, 65, 77, 82.
Guicciardini 61.
Guild 32.
Gurney 42, 43.
Harleston 101.
Harmer 11, 26, 59, 60, 66, 68.

Index of People

Index of People

Index of Places

Index of Places

Index of Places

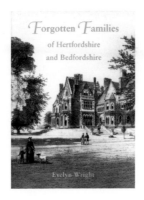

FORGOTTEN FAMILIES

of Hertfordshire and Bedfordshire

Evelyn Wright

This book tells the story of families once famous but whose fame is now mainly forgotten. They all lived in Hertfordshire and Bedfordshire in the 16th and 17th centuries, and include the Bechers of Renhold (of Becher's Brook fame), the Mordaunts of Turvey Abbey, Lady Cathcart of Tewin, the Bull family of Hertford, the Nodes family of Stevenage, the Docuras of Lilley and the Wicked Lady of Markyate Cell. All the families were related to each other, forming an intricate network over two counties: Hertfordshire and Bedfordshire. The author is one of their 20th century descendants. The book includes pedigrees showing the relationship between various families, and illustrations of many of the manor houses and mansions in which they lived.

The
Book
Castle

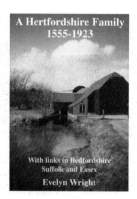

A HERTFORDSHIRE FAMILY

1555 - 1923

Evelyn Wright

This book traces the history of the Harmer family of Weston through ten generations from the reign of Mary I down to the early years of the present century. Following some of the maternal lines we travel back even further, to William Chichele, brother of a 15th century Archbishop of Canterbury, the de la Poles, Dukes of Suffolk and Hugh de Beauchamp of Bedford Castle.

As the story unfolds we see glimpses of both the political and social history of the period. The description of Catherine Tyrell's wedding feast in 1552, the inventory of John Harmer's house at Baldock in 1613, and the menus for Mrs Becher's dinner guests at Howbury Hall in 1709, all give us an insight into the domestic life of our ancestors in the 16th, 17th and 18th centuries.

The Docwra notes record cases tried in the 16th century Manor Courts, including 'buying up poultry before the market bell be rung', and 'taking a stranger to dwell without the consent of the Churchwardens'. We meet Rebecka Harmer who took her son John to court for not paying her 'thirds', and Lady Cathcart of Tewin who, after her 4th marriage, declared 'If I survive I will have five'.

The main story is woven together to form a continuous narrative, but in addition there are over 50 biographical pedigrees, showing a network of family relationships in Hertfordshire, Bedfordshire, Suffolk and Essex.

The Book Castle

JOURNEYS INTO BEDFORDSHIRE
JOURNEYS INTO BUCKINGHAMSHIRE
JOURNEYS INTO HERTFORDSHIRE

Anthony Mackay

These three books of ink drawings reveal an intriguing historic heritage and capture the spirit of England's rural heartland, ranging widely over cottages and stately homes, over bridges, churches and mills, over sandy woods, chalk downs and watery river valleys.

Every corner of Bedfordshire, Buckinghamshire and Hertfordshire has been explored in the search for material, and, although the choice of subjects is essentially a personal one, the resulting collection represents a unique record of the environment today.

The notes and maps, which accompany the drawings, lend depth to the books, and will assist others on their own journeys around the counties.

Anthony Mackay's pen-and-ink drawings are of outstanding quality. An architectural graduate, he is equally at home depicting landscapes and buildings. The medium he uses is better able to show both depth and detail than any photograph.

PLAIN MR WHITBREAD

Seven Centuries of a Bedfordshire Family

Sam Whitbread

The Whitbread family have been a part of Bedfordshire life since at least the 13th Century (and probably earlier). From small beginnings as peasant farmers, through appointments as local officials to the founder of the Brewery, one of the most notable success stories of the Industrial Revolution, and his son, the radical Whig politician and follower of Fox, the Whitbreads have gradually made their presence felt, first locally and later nationally. Six Whitbreads sat in the House of Commons for a total of 128 years, while at the same time building roads, bridges and hospitals, improving cottages and the local churches, and serving as magistrates, High Sheriffs and Lord-Lieutenants of the County.

The book's title is taken from the fact that at least two members of the family were offered peerages but preferred to "remain plain Mr Whitbread".

The author originally conceived the book as a simplified family history for his children and grandchildren but it will also appeal to those interested in the local history of Bedfordshire.

The narrative ends with the death of the author's father in 1985, but the author has added a "postscript" outlining the first seventy years of his own life.

The
Book
Castle

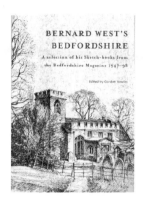

BERNARD WEST'S BEDFORDSHIRE

Edited by Gordon Vowles

This book is made up of a selection of Bernard West's Sketch-book of drawings and comment which appeared in the Bedfordshire Magazine over a fifty year period from 1947. The sketches are of village and townscapes or of individual buildings or features spread throughout the whole of the County of Bedfordshire. Each sketch is accompanied by a lively commentary which displays Bernard West's wide-ranging knowledge of the County, its history and its buildings, and his keen interest, as a professional architect, in good design and the preservation of both the natural and the man-made environments. The volume is a tribute to a gifted artist and an ardent campaigner.

It is a book which should have a wide appeal, but especially to those who have an interest in Bedfordshire's past and its continued preservation.

LEAFING THROUGH LITERATURE

Writers' Lives in Hertfordshire and Bedfordshire

David Carroll

The neighbouring counties of Hertfordshire and Bedfordshire have had close links, over the years, with some of the world's greatest writers. John Bunyan, of course, spent all his life in and around Bedford, and George Bernard Shaw lived for nearly half a century at Ayot St. Lawrence.

George Orwell, Beatrix Potter, Arnold Bennett and Charles Dickens are just some of the many famous names to be found in this lively and informative book. But there are some less familiar ones too: George Gascoigne of Cardington, for example and Edward Young at Welwyn. However, from Sir Thomas More in the sixteenth century to Graham Greene who died in 1991, they all have one thing in common: a connection, at some stage in their lives, with Hertfordshire or Bedfordshire.